Ella McMahon

The Secret of Sanctity

According to St. Francis de Sales and Father Crasset

Ella McMahon

The Secret of Sanctity
According to St. Francis de Sales and Father Crasset

ISBN/EAN: 9783743388710

Manufactured in Europe, USA, Canada, Australia, Japa

Cover: Foto ©ninafisch / pixelio.de

Manufactured and distributed by brebook publishing software (www.brebook.com)

Ella McMahon

The Secret of Sanctity

THE SECRET OF SANCTITY

ACCORDING TO

ST. FRANCIS DE SALES
AND
FATHER CRASSET, S.J.

Translated from the French

By Ella McMahon

New York, Cincinnati, Chicago
BENZIGER BROTHERS

PRINTERS TO THE | PUBLISHERS OF
HOLY APOSTOLIC SEE | BENZIGER'S MAGAZINE

PREFACE.

Our great happiness as Christians is to possess, in this world, through grace and love, Him Who deigns to be our beatitude for all eternity; and our greatest misfortune, after sin, is not to know or to recognize this secret of eternal charity. God would have us holy even as He is holy; He would have us live His very life. It is for this end that He has given us His divine Son, and with Him the infinite riches of His heart; that is, His merits, His sacraments, His Church. Sanctity consists in believing and receiving these divine communications, of which Jesus Christ is the source, the instrument, and the end; consequently, it also consists in uniting ourselves with Him by loving Him, and in modelling ourselves upon Him by imitating Him; it can and ought to pervade every life, the busiest as well as the simplest.

"I believe," says Father de Caussade, "that if souls seriously aspiring to perfection understood this, and knew how direct is their path, they would be spared much difficulty. I say the same of souls living in the world, and of souls consecrated to God. If the first knew the means of merit afforded them by their ever-recurring daily duties and the ordinary actions of their state of life; if the second could persuade themselves that the foundation of sanctity lies in those very things which they consider unimportant and even foreign to them; if both could understand that the crosses sent by Providence which they constantly find in their state of life lead them to the highest perfection by a surer and shorter path than do extraordinary states or extraordinary works; and that the true philosopher's stone is submission to the order of God, which changes into pure gold all their occupations, all their weariness, all their sufferings,—how happy they would be! What consolation and what courage they would gather from this thought, that to acquire the friendship of God and all the glory of heaven they have but to do what they are doing, suffer what they are suffering, and that what they lose and count as naught would suffice to obtain for them eminent sanctity!

"O my God, that I might be the missionary of Thy holy will, and teach the whole world that there is nothing so easy, so simple, so within the reach of all, as sanctity! Would that I could make them understand that just as the good and bad thief had the same to do and suffer to obtain their salvation, so two souls, one worldly and the other wholly interior and spiritual, have nothing more to do one than the other; that he who sanctifies himself acquires eternal happiness by doing in submission to the will of God what he who is lost does through caprice; and that the latter is lost by suffering unwillingly and impatiently what he who is saved endures with resignation. The difference, therefore, is only in the heart. O dear souls who read this, let me repeat to you: Sanctity will cost you no more; do what you are doing; suffer what you are suffering: it is only your heart that need be changed. By the heart we mean the will. This change, then, consists in willing what comes to us by the order of God. Yes, holiness of heart is a simple *fiat*, a simple disposition of conformity to the will of God. And what is easier? For who could not love so adorable and merciful a will? Let us love it, then, and through this love alone all within us will become divine." ("Abandonment to Divine Providence.")

But what will enable us to realize this ideal of a Christian and holy life? Prayer, or rather a spirit of confidence and faith which must pervade all our relations with God. I mean by this that disposition of the soul in which it recognizes that God loves it, that He cares for it, and that He desires in all things only the greater good of His little creature.

He who possesses the secret of this blessed science has the secret of a good life, of true strength, and of perfect happiness. "He lives well who prays well," says St. Augustine.

Prayer, thus understood, should not be either a rare or a difficult exercise; for God is our Father, He is our end, He is the indulgent, merciful, untiring Benefactor of our exile; His relations with us are ever present and always infinitely kind. How is it possible that a means by which we correspond to all that He is, and to all that He does for us, should be a difficult exercise? Important and necessary, yes, but difficult, no. I should even say that the more necessary prayer is the more frequent and easy it should be. Providence, in fact, has ordained that the more necessary a thing is the more attainable it is. See, for example, air, water, bread, the sustenance of corporal life. Water, the matter of the sacrament which communicates spiritual life; bread and wine, the matter of the sacrament which sustains and increases this life of grace. All these elements, being necessary, are very easily procured. But is not God still more within our reach? "There is nothing," says St. Bernard, "of which God is so prodigal as of Himself." Therefore, prayer which gives Him to us, prayer which makes us live in Him, with Him, and by Him, should not be difficult, but easy. We must be convinced of this, and bring to the exercise of this duty the good-will which makes God's gifts bear fruit in us. It is to aid this good-will that we purpose to collect the safest rules given by the saints for performing well this double *prayer of the heart and of acts.*

We have taken these rules first from the doctor of piety, St. Francis de Sales, by reproducing some of the most beautiful passages of his "Introduction to a Devout Life" and his immortal "Treatise on the Love of God." Then, as he himself was formed by the Fathers of the Society of Jesus, whom he was always pleased to call his masters, we have taken from one of these Fathers, most commendable for his doctrine and piety (and who, moreover, loved to quote St. Francis de Sales in his writings), practical rules for making the life of a Christian a continual prayer, and prayer, properly speaking, an apprenticeship to the life of heaven.

In this way we have given in an abridgment, carefully preserving the sense and expressions of the writer, Father Crasset's beautiful and profound *Considérations Chrétienne* on the sanctification of our actions, and the various ways of prayer from his *Méthode d'Oraison* and his *Dévotion du Calvaire*.

We have deemed it useful also to add to these teachings certain analogous passages from the writings of Fathers Gonnelieu, Lallemant, and Faber, which, taken together, complete the principles on union with God, and on what our life should be by means of this much-to-be-desired union, and of mortification, a necessary condition thereof.

Finally, as son of St. Sulpice, we could not forget M. Olier, whom St. Francis de Sales blessed in his infancy, foretelling his piety and his mission in the Church. Therefore we have taken much pleasure in terminating our humble work of copyist with some of the most beautiful passages from his *Journée Chrétienne* upon the life of Jesus and Mary.

We have divided the collection into three parts; the first includes that which relates to the sanctification of our actions; the various intentions with which we should be animated in order to receive the sacraments profitably, to purify our hearts, and to walk constantly in the presence of God. Father Crasset's *Considérations Chrétiennes* form the foundation of these teachings; the passages not from him will be indicated.

The second part includes that which relates to the interior life. The first chapter indicates briefly the sources of our imperfections and their remedies. Then come certain ideas and rules of mortification, of prayer, and the spiritual life, from treatises written on these subjects by Fathers Faber, Crasset, and Lallemant.

The subject of the third part is *union with God through contemplation*. It will include a treatise on this subject by Father Crasset, and the doctrine of St. Francis de Sales on contemplation. A letter of the saint's on the marks of true recollection will complete these teachings, and another extract from the works of St. Chantal will show us the heart of the saint in the exercise of this continual union with God.

And, as all these different ways are of Jesus and lead to Jesus, we are finally led to contemplating Jesus Himself on His beautiful throne of grace, His virginal Mother the glorious and most fruitful manifestation of His life.

May this divine Saviour, through the intercession of His immaculate Mother, deign to bless us and to grant us all the spirit of prayer and love, that we may thus begin here below for the glory of His Father that blessed reign of God which is without end! *Adveniat regnum tuum.*

CONTENTS.

	PAGE
Preface,	3

PART FIRST.—SANCTIFICATION OF OUR ACTIONS.

		PAGE
Chapter	I.—Of the Regulation of our Actions,	15
	I.—Advantage of a Rule,	15
	II.—Rule of Life,	18
Chapter	II.—The First Actions of the Day,	24
	The First-fruits of our Actions,	24
Chapter	III.—Mental and Vocal Prayer,	28
	I.—Mental Prayer,	28
	II.—Vocal Prayer,	31
Chapter	IV.—Short Method of Prayer according to the Spirit of St. Francis de Sales, and Preliminary Advice on Prayer by Mgr. Camus, Bishop of Belley,	34
Chapter	V.—On the Presence of God,	36
Chapter	VI.—Advice on Prayer,	39
Chapter	VII.—St. Francis de Sales' Rules for Meditation,	44
Chapter	VIII.—The Holy Sacrifice of the Mass,	48
Chapter	IX.—The two Examens,	56
	Particular Examen,	56
	General Examen,	61
Chapter	X.—Of Confession and Direction,	64
Chapter	XI.—Holy Communion,	71
Chapter	XII.—The Occupations of the Day,	80
Chapter	XIII.—Of a State of Life,	86
Chapter	XIV.—Of the Exercise of One's Charge,	91
Chapter	XV.—Of Visits and Conversation,	94
Chapter	XVI.—Silence,	101
Chapter	XVII.—Visits to the Blessed Sacrament,	103
Chapter	XVIII.—Spiritual Recollection,	106

	PAGE
Chapter XIX.—Of Aspirations, Ejaculatory Prayers, and Good Thoughts,	110
Chapter XX.—St. Francis de Sales' Manner of Performing his Actions,	117

PART SECOND.—THE INTERIOR LIFE.

First Treatise.—The Sources of our Imperfections and their Remedies,	121
Second Treatise.—Mortification,	129
I.—True Idea of Mortification,	129
II.—Necessity of Mortification,	130
III.—Reply to Various Objections,	133
IV.—Benefits and Advantages of Mortification,	137
V.—Discretion in the Use of Mortification,	146
VI.—Dangers to be Avoided,	149
Third Treatise.—Prayer,	153
Chapter I.—The Excellence and Necessity of Mental Prayer,	153
Chapter II.—Dispositions for Prayer,	157
Chapter III.—Various Kinds of Prayer,	160
Chapter IV.—Meditation,	164
Chapter V.—Distractions,	174
Chapter VI.—Causes of Distractions and Aridity,	176
Chapter VII.—We must never be troubled because of Distractions and Aridity,	182
Chapter VIII.—Remedies for Distractions,	189
Chapter IX.—First Means of Devotion,	191
Chapter X.—Second Means of Devotion,	194
Chapter XI.—Third Means of Devotion,	196
Chapter XII.—Fourth Means of Devotion,	199
Chapter XIII.—Fifth Means of Devotion,	200
Chapter XIV.—Sixth Means of Devotion,	202
Chapter XV.—Seventh Means of Devotion,	204
Chapter XVI.—Last Means of Devotion,	205
Fourth Treatise.—The Devotion of Calvary,	211
First Instruction.—How Important it is to Meditate on the Passion of Our Lord Jesus Christ,	211
Second Instruction.—A New Manner of Meditating on the Passion,	213
Third Instruction.—What they should do who cannot Meditate on the Passion,	218

	PAGE
Fourth Instruction.—What they should do who have ceased to be able to Meditate on the Passion,	221
Fifth Instruction.—In what Manner Perfect Souls may Meditate on the Passion,	226
Fifth Treatise.—The Interior Life,	230
Chapter I. Article I.—In what Interior Life consists,	230
Article II.—How we ought to imitate the Interior Life of God,	232
Article III.—How it is that we make so Little Progress in the Interior Life,	234
Chapter II.—Of the Motives that lead us to the Interior Life,	235
Article I.—We make No Progress in the Ways of Perfection unless we give ourselves to the Interior Life,	235
Article II.—Without Prayer we cannot acquit ourselves of the Duties of our Vocation, nor gather Fruit from our Ministrations,	238
Article III.—Peace is not found except in the Interior Life, and our Dissatisfactions spring only from our not being Interior Men,	242
Chapter III.—The Occupations of the Interior Life,	243
Article I.—Of Watchfulness over our Interior,	243
Article II.—How Important it is that we should join the Interior with our Exterior Occupations,	248
Article III.—We ought not to engage in Exterior Occupations of our own Accord,	252
Chapter IV.—Advice for the Interior Life,	253
Article I.—We ought to cultivate the Will more than the Understanding,	253
Article II.—The Path of Faith is a Safer Way to Perfection than that of Sensible Graces,	254
Article III.—The Best Mode of Practising the Virtues,	254
Sixth Treatise.—Means of Acquiring Perfection,	256

PART THIRD.—UNION WITH GOD BY CONTEMPLATION.

	PAGE
Chapter I.—Union of the Soul with a God through Contemplation,	269
Chapter II.—The Doctrine of St. Francis de Sales in regard to Contemplation,	281
Divine Love seeks Solitude and Silence,	281
Difference between Meditation and Contemplation,	283
The Knowledge of God is less necessary to us than Love,	283
How Contemplation reduces all this to simple Unity,	284
The Various Means which lead to Contemplation,	285
Love collects the Powers of the Soul,	286
Recollection is frequently produced and increased by a Gentle, Reverent Fear,	287
Of the Repose of a Soul recollected in God,	288
Of the Manner in which the Soul enjoys Repose in God in the Prayer of Quiet,	291
Of the Different Degrees of the Prayer of Quiet, and the Means which should be employed to preserve the Holy Repose of the Soul,	292
Self-denial is the Safest Means of establishing ourselves in the Presence of God,	296
Perfect Submission to the Will of God keeps the Soul in continual Prayer,	297
Chapter III.—Letter of St. Francis de Sales to St. Jane Frances de Chantal,	298
Chapter IV.—The Continual Prayer of St. Francis de Sales,	303
Chapter V.—The Life of Jesus in Mary,	307

PART FIRST.

SANCTIFICATION OF OUR ACTIONS.

There is no moment when God is not present with us under the appearance of some obligation or some duty.

All that is effected within us, about us, and through us involves and hides His divine action: it is veritably present, though in an invisible manner; therefore we do not discern it, and only recognize its workings when it has ceased to act. Could we pierce the veil which obscures it, and were we vigilant and attentive, God would unceasingly reveal Himself to us, and we could recognize His action in all that befell us. At every event we should exclaim, *Dominus est!* It is the Lord! And we should feel each circumstance of our life an especial gift from Him. (" Abandonment to Divine Providence.")

Just as Our Lord is in His sacrament of love by His real presence, so is He in each of our actions by His real will. . . . Jesus, only, in our minds to enlighten them; Jesus, only, in our hearts to possess them; Jesus, only, in our lives to sanctify them. (Father de Ravignan.)

Oh, that men would abandon themselves to God! . . . There are so few who understand what God would make of them if they permitted Him to do as He wills. (St. Ignatius.)

CHAPTER I.

OF THE REGULATION OF OUR ACTIONS.

I. ADVANTAGES OF A RULE.

Of the Blessing of a Life marked by Order.—Order and virtue are almost synonymous terms. Order is the guide of virtue, and virtue is the guide of order. Whatever good you do, if you do it not in order, you do it not well. Reason requires sometimes that we depart from the order we have prescribed; only to follow, however, a more perfect order required by necessity, charity, infirmity, or obedience. Inclination is the guide of beasts; reason of man; the Gospel of Christians; the rule of religious; order of all creatures. Which will you choose? It is order which makes paradise, and disorder which makes hell. If your life is marked by order, you will be happy; if your life is one of disorder, you will be miserable. Who may live in peace, making war against God? And who makes war against Him if not he who disturbs His order?

Were you at peace when your life was one of disorder? Is not a soldier who leaves his post punished at once by his captain? All that disturbs order disturbs peace, and he who is not at peace with God will never be at peace with himself. Seek the cause of your troubles.

Order assigns each thing its place; it preserves to all creatures their rank, their office, their employment; and this it is which constitutes their repose. If you keep order, it will keep you; if you disturb order, it will disturb you; if you destroy order, it will destroy you.

Contemplate the universe and you will see that it is order which constitutes the beauty, the perfection, the peace, and the happiness of all creatures. What is an army without order but a troop of victims led to death? What is a kingdom without order but a horde of brigands living by murder and rapine? What is religion without order but a body without a soul, all the parts of which are divided and detached? What is man without order but a chaos of passion waging mortal warfare and creating absolute confusion?

If the Church is an army, it is order which places it in battle-array; if the Church is a ship, order is its pilot and guide; if the Church is a body, it is order which constitutes its life; if the Church is a kingdom, by order is it governed. The same may be said of religion.

Order is the creator, so to speak, of the world; this it is which preserves and repairs it. From order do we proceed, by order are we maintained, through order do we live. All that God does is marked by order, and all that bears not this mark of order is not of God. Order leads us to God. We cannot go to a contrary by its contrary. God is order by essence; never will disorder lead us to God.

Reflection.—Is your state one of order? Is order your rule? Are your actions regulated? Do you do each thing in its appointed time? Are you not guided by inclination or caprice? Is your will sufficiently upright to serve you as a rule or guide? If so, your sanctity equals that of God; for He alone can take His will as His guide and rule. Now what is more ill-regulated than yours? What merit would you have in doing only as you please? You serve God only by your actions, and if your actions are not marked by order how can they be pleasing to God?

Practice.—Prescribe a certain order for your day and let nothing disturb it short of a command of a superior to forego or interrupt it. Regulate the time for your meals, for your work, and for your recreation. Order is the law of heaven; begin therefore here on earth a life which you will continue throughout eternity, a life which will be more pleasing to God, more convenient for those about you, and more profitable for your salvation. God dwells in order and peace; the Evil One in trouble and discord. Which of these two do you wish to follow? Which would you resemble?

False Maxims Destroyed.—There is no doubt that one must abandon a prescribed order to follow the inspiration of the Holy Spirit; but how do you know that your impulse is a movement of grace and not of nature; of the Spirit of God and not of the spirit of evil? The Holy Spirit is a spirit of order that inspires in souls submission and dependence. He withdraws men from the servitude of their passions, but not from the obedience they owe to the law. When rules are not binding, He would have us follow them without being bound thereby; when they are of precept, He would have us observe them without dispensing ourselves therefrom. The unction of divine grace does not make us reject the yoke of God's law, but helps us to bear it.

Happy he who abandons himself to the guidance of God and does nothing but by His orders, who constantly studies His will, who holds himself ever ready at the least sign to go forward, to pause, to watch, or to rest.

II. RULE OF LIFE.

I. Have a fixed hour for rising; from seven to eight hours' sleep are usually sufficient. Beware of beginning your day by sacrificing to sloth hours every moment of which may avail you for eternity.

Let your first thought be of God; let it refer as much as possible to the subject of your meditation, and let it be accompanied with the resolution to combat the fault which is the subject of your particular examen.

II. Give as much time as possible each day to prayer; determine this time according to your occupation, your attraction, and the advice of your director. Let your heart take much more part in this holy exercise than your mind; and let the mysteries of the life and passion of your Saviour be the usual subject.

III. Do not voluntarily deprive yourself, even for a day, of the inestimable happiness of assisting at the holy sacrifice of the Mass. Unite yourself to Our Lord by means of spiritual communion; offer yourself with Him to God His Father, and ask with perfect confidence, through the merits of His sacrifice, the graces of which you stand in need. Do not fail to pray thus and to offer all your actions of the day in union with the merits of Jesus Christ, for the conversion of infidels, heretics, and sinners, for the progress of the just, and the triumph of our holy mother, the Church.

IV. Give a certain time each day to the reading of a good book according to the advice of your director. Read it in the presence of God, Who speaks to you Himself. Reflect upon what you read; relish it; ask God to give you the grace to carry out the good desires with which He inspires you by means of this reading. Reading made in this way is a sort of easy meditation, and when we are deprived of a sermon may take its place.

V. Say your rosary every day, either alone or with others, and as you recite it accustom yourself to meditate affectionately on the mysteries of Our Saviour and of His holy Mother. This is the easiest and frequently the most fruitful of all meditations.

VI. Make a daily visit, if possible, to the Blessed Sacrament; go to Our Lord with the simplicity of a child; confide to His heart your joys, your sorrows, your temptations, and your faults.

VII. The life of a Christian should be a continual exercise of penance. Mortify yourself in common and ordinary things; nothing is more necessary in order to establish in your soul the empire of grace and destroy that of nature. Here are a few practices to this end: Resist your inclination to do something which is useless. Keep careful guard over your eyes. Refrain from raillery. Withhold a clever word likely to wound, or intended merely to satisfy self-love. Do not seek what merely flatters sensuality. Regulate innocent pleasures. Refrain sometimes, through a spirit of penance, even from permitted pleasures. Moderate that excessive tenderness we all have for ourselves. Detach your mind from pleasurable sentiments. Speak little and with moderation. Be courteous and kind to persons for whom you feel an antipathy. Be silent under affliction, and bear your cross with resignation.

VIII. Devote yourself to your labor as well as to the fulfilment of all your duties energetically and with a pure intention to please God and make yourself useful to your neighbor. Do not forget that the most indifferent actions acquire, through a fervent intention, inappreciable merit for eternity. Raise your heart to God from time to time by means of fervent ejaculations, that it may not be narrowed and absorbed by earthly occupations.

IX. Let no meal pass without offering a slight mortification to your Saviour, Who accepted the bitter draught on the cross for love of you. These little sacrifices will avail you many graces, and will preserve you from the dangers of sensuality.

X. Go to bed as far as possible at a fixed hour, and before doing so carefully make your particular examen as well as a general examination of the day. Let there be, if possible, family prayer, that your petitions thus united may be more efficacious before God, and more advantageous to your children and to your servants.

XI. Go to confession at least every fortnight; prepare yourself for it in the morning during your meditation and the holy sacrifice of the Mass. Give more care to exciting yourself to sincere contrition for your faults than to enumerating them with great accuracy.

XII. Receive Communion as frequently as your director permits; bring to this great action all the devotion and care of which you are capable; and remember that the disposition God asks of you is not sensible fervor, which is not always in your power, but profound humility and a sincere desire to be united with Him.

XIII. In your relations with the members of your family and those about you be full of consideration, kindness, and devotion; endeavor to make piety loved through you. Avoid with the greatest care that spirit of criticism, those little jealousies, petty weaknesses, and caprices which many vainly seek to reconcile with true piety.

XIV. When you go out into the world avoid with equal care unseemly levity and repellant austerity, and while the politeness of the old school seems to be disappearing more and more, endeavor to revive it in your social intercourse by that delicate courtesy, thoughtful consideration, and simple, modest bearing which are the natural outcome of humility and Christian charity.

XV. Be inflexible in regard to dangerous books

and plays. Let even innocent pleasures be moderate. Banish evil pleasures. The day you yield in this point you will take the first step in a downward course from which there is no redemption.

XVI. If God has placed you in a position to give yourself to good works, let them be your pleasantest recreation. Remember that in helping the poor and the afflicted you are helping Jesus Christ Himself, and that they, in thus affording you the means of meriting the gratitude of your God and the indulgence of your Judge, confer a greater benefit upon you than you can bestow upon them. Regulate your expenses, moderate your attachment to the things of this world, and remember that you will be judged by a God Who for love of you bore poverty, humility, and suffering. If your crucified Saviour wills to give you a small share of His sufferings, do not forget that the cross is the only incontestable mark of real love and the strongest bond by which your soul may be united with God. This conviction will give you strength to overcome the repugnance of nature and to bless God in the midst of the most cruel trials.

XVII. Select a day each month to prepare yourself for death, and on that day perform each duty as faithfully as if it were to be the last of your life. Go to confession and receive Communion as viaticum. Examine what might trouble you at such an hour: unjust possessions, doubts, restitutions unmade, unreconciled quarrels, etc. Repeat the acts made by the dying: acts of resignation, acts accepting the time, the place, the manner of the death God wishes you to die; acts of thanksgiving, of lively faith, of hope, of confidence, of sincere sorrow, of love of God, etc. Invoke Jesus crucified; implore the Blessed Virgin, your angel guardian, your patron saint, to plead for you, and when you lie down to rest regard your bed as your tomb.

XVIII. Faithful devotion to the Sacred Heart of Jesus and His blessed Mother is regarded as a certain means of salvation. Zealously embrace it. Unite yourself with confraternities established in their honor; practices enjoined by these associations are not onerous, do not oblige under pain of sin, and are enriched with numerous indulgences. Nourish also in your soul sincere devotion to St. Joseph, the spouse of Our Lady, to the holy angels, and the saint whose name you received in Baptism. Finally pray frequently for the dying and for the souls in purgatory.

CHAPTER II.

THE FIRST ACTIONS OF THE DAY.

THE FIRST-FRUITS OF OUR ACTIONS.

THE beginning in everything is very important. The first-fruits of our thoughts, of our affections, of our works, are tributes due to God. The manner in which we spend our day depends very much upon the beginning; this is why the Evil One makes every effort to destroy the tree at the root and to rob God of this first homage due only to Him. Therefore when you get up in the morning your first thought, your first word, your first action, should be given to God. Do you do this?

Rising.—When we are in bed and inclined to sleep is not the time for deliberating whether we should get up or not. If you parley with nature it will inevitably triumph over you. It will tell you it is cold, that you are indisposed, that you have spent a bad night, that if you are not made ill by early rising, then you will fall asleep during prayer; that one prays better and grace acts more efficaciously when the body is well cared for; that rest is necessary if we would labor well, and that it is better to take too much than too little. Is it not with such arguments that nature persuades you to keep your pillow, and to resist the inspiration to overcome yourself and rise promptly?

Determine the previous evening the hour for rising, and when the hour comes let nothing, short of serious indisposition, prevent you from being faithful to your determination.

Begin your day with this slight act of mortification; remember that if you refuse God this little sacrifice it will enable the Evil One to rejoice at your expense; while, if you are generous, this act of fidelity will bring you many graces from Heaven and preserve you from many faults into which you are liable to fall during the day.

Believe me, you will lose nothing by making this little sacrifice of your rest to God; you have to do with a Master Who is magnificent in His rewards, and Who will not fail to let you reap at another time the sweet fruits of your patience.

Of too Great Care of One's Health.—There are some people so tender of their bodies that they imagine themselves prostrated by the least indisposition, and obliged to abandon their exercises of piety. They are constantly occupied with their ailments; speak of them to every one; leave no remedy untried; consult innumerable physicians; in short, it would seem as though their life was one of the columns of nature with the destruction of which the world must come to an end. They consult Hippocrates and Galen as the gods of health; and never consult Jesus Christ, the sole Author and Preserver of our life.

Remedies and Recourse to God.—I am far from blaming reasonable care of one's health or the consulting of physicians when the illness is serious; but unless you are obliged to keep your bed I would not advise you to do so. Do not yield to every little indisposition; keep about as long as you can. God desires to be the physician of your body as well as of your soul. How many saints have found their ailments increase with remedies and diminish when they took none. Happy is he who makes his body a continual victim and who can truly say with St. Paul, "I die daily."

I have dwelt upon this excessive care of health, because St. Thomas says that the temptation of the most spiritual persons is to be too much occupied with their health, as well as with the necessities of the body, under pretext of seeking the glory of God. Moreover, all the vigor of the soul depends upon morning prayer; for this reason the Evil One creates a thousand hindrances, chiefly little ailments, to make you lose it or to make it fruitless.

All the success of our meditation depends upon this first action—that is, upon rising promptly and fervently. Alas! what can one do who has lost the graces given in prayer? They descended from heaven while you slept; then it was that you should have gathered this heavenly manna; the time for collecting it is past; there is none left for you, and then, how may you venture to present yourself before God to receive His gifts and to enjoy the delight of His company when you have begun your day by an act of infidelity—sleeping while others were at prayer?

The First Thoughts, Words, and Actions.—What is

your first thought on awakening? What is your first word? What is your first action? Your first thought should be raised to God. Your first word should be addressed to God. Your first action should be for God, the seed as it were of all the others. Observe great neatness in your attire. Repeat certain prayers, if you like, while dressing.

Remember to observe modesty at all times. If you do not pray occupy yourself, at least, with some good thought while you are dressing; or, better still, consider the subject of your meditation, and conceive a great desire to make it well.

Morning Prayer.—As soon as you are dressed render God the respect and homage due Him; adore Him as the Author and Preserver of your being. Thank Him for the grace He has bestowed upon you. Offer Him the actions of the day. Ask Him to bless you; to strengthen you to combat resolutely your great enemy, which is the sin to which you are most subject. Forecast the occasions of this sin.

Recommend yourself to your good angel and to your holy protectors. Then repeat some vocal prayers. The end depends on the beginning. You will end the day well if you begin it well. See how far you are wanting in this respect, and resolve to amend.

CHAPTER III.

MENTAL AND VOCAL PRAYER.

I. MENTAL PRAYER.

We Must Never Neglect our Morning Prayers.—As prayer is the food of the soul, the Evil One, who cannot take well a defended garrison, endeavors to weaken it by famine—by cutting off all supplies and means of assistance. Therefore he will create pressing business and notable inconveniences to make you abandon meditation, or to persuade you at least to defer it. The morning is the most fitting time; if you obey his suggestion, you will find no time to make it later, and you will be deprived of the graces destined for you that day. Are you faithful to render this duty to God? Do you never fail in it?

Would you be willing to spend a day without eating? What has your soul done that you should treat it more cruelly and harshly than you treat your body? "Blessed be God," says David, "Who hath not turned away my prayer, nor His mercy from me" (Ps. lxv. 20). Mercy and prayer are two inseparable things; one is the tree and the other is the fruit; one is the source and the other is the stream. If you abandon prayer, God will withdraw His mercy. What! Do you think you can live without food, fight without arms, fly without wings, labor without strength? Whence do you derive all this if not from prayer?

What blessing can you expect from God the day that you fail to pray to Him? But one infidelity of this kind is sufficient to ruin your fortune and prevent you from entering the nuptial hall, where the Bridegroom awaits you.

Method of Prayer.—Our prayer should be simple, faithful, humble, respectful, free from negligence as well as excessive constraint. This science is acquired less by study than by experience. Innocent souls should go to God, in a simple childlike manner, as little ones run to the arms of their nurse. They whose minds are filled with the false maxims of the world must be rid of them by means of discourse and reasoning founded on the truths of the Gospel. But they who are convinced of the maxims of our religion should give themselves more to affections than to considerations.

They should ask, desire, call, seek, and sigh incessantly, until they have found the source of living waters, and the spirit tells them: "Thou hast labored enough; it is now time to rest."

Preparation.—Read in the evening before going to bed the subject of your meditation, read it again in the morning, if necessary, when you get up. Enter into the sanctuary of grace with profound humility, a pure intention, an ardent and sincere desire to honor God and do His will. Occupy yourself with God without being occupied with yourself. Seek Him, like David, in the simplicity of your heart, uprightly, and without any mixture of self-satisfaction. Peace of heart, indifference of will, interior satisfaction of soul, whatever our state, whether of consolation or aridity, of light or darkness, are marks that we are seeking God purely, and that our prayer is excellent.

How do you converse with God? Do you find it difficult to converse with Him?

Do you not yield to weariness and vexation when you find no satisfaction in prayer? Are you tempted to abandon it entirely? Why do you not read and learn from books on prayer what you should do? You do much if you love much, and you love much if you suffer with patience the wandering of your mind, the instability of your imagination, bodily discomforts, the temptations of the Evil One, the murmurs of your passions, the vexation and weariness of nature.

Causes of Distractions.—Are you favored with consolations? Be not attached to them. Are you frequently distracted? Learn the cause. Is it not because you reflect so little during the day? Is it not because your heart is deeply attached to something? Or is it lack of preparation, or that you refuse God what He asks? Or may it not be that God wishes to try your patience and make you recognize your weakness?

Causes of Aridity.—You are deprived of consolation; perhaps it is because you desire it too passionately; or you do not endeavor to mortify yourself; or you are unfaithful to the inspiration of God; or you lack a cross; or you are proud and negligent. It may also be that God wishes to purify your soul and detach it from the senses; that He wishes to awaken your love, to excite your desire, to test your fidelity. It may also be that He desires to make you merit some signal grace which He intends to bestow upon you. Finally it may be that He desires to make you pass from meditation to affection, and from affection to union. Whatever it may be, understand well that dryness is as necessary to the earth as rain, night as day, winter as summer; that only in heaven will consolation be without alloy; that you will not merit it there if you always enjoy it here below; that a prayer of patience is incomparably better than a prayer of delight; and provided you are faithful in this state, and do not abandon meditation, God will visit you when you least expect it and lead you through this frightful desert to the promised land, where you will be fed with an abundance of milk and honey.

II. VOCAL PRAYER.

There are two kinds of vocal prayer; one of precept, like the breviary for bishops, priests, and religious, and the other is optional and of devotion. Prayers of obligation are preferable to those which are only of devotion, and should be recited in their proper time with attention and devotion. The others may be recited or omitted at any time; but if we say them it should be with the requisite devotion.

Illusions of Certain Contemplatives in Regard to Vocal Prayer.—We must beware of despising vocal prayer; for besides being frequently of obligation, it is holy and approved by the Church. The Son of God gave us an example and prescribed the form of this prayer. What! Are only the imperfect to recite the Lord's Prayer? Are we not to honor God with the mind, the body, the tongue, and the heart?

Superstitious Devotees.—Let your prayer be regulated by your director. Generally speaking, it is better to pray with the heart than with the tongue, and to say the Lords' Prayer with attention than to recite innumerable prayers carelessly.

Choice of various Vocal Prayers.—Among vocal prayers, give preference to the one which Our Lord composed and taught us, through the respect due its Author, or because of the things it contains, or because it is fitted to ask for all our needs. Next to this come the Psalms of David and the Angelic Salutation. Generally speaking, love and recite with devotion the prayers used by the Church, but do not undertake to say them all. I should like to persuade you never to let a day pass without saying your rosary.

Take some time also for reciting the Litany of the Name of Jesus and of the Blessed Virgin.

Intentions in Reciting Office.—Whatever your prayers, whether of obligation or devotion, you should never begin them until you have collected your thoughts and placed yourself in the presence of God. Consider yourself as the organ of the Holy Spirit, Who prays by your lips just as the wind plays upon the pipes of the organ when it is in proper condition. Give Him the whole disposition of your heart. Pause from time to time, principally between each psalm, and recall your mind if it has wandered. Ponder and appreciate the meaning of the words you utter; there are none which have not a divine taste and heavenly savor.

Some recite their office in all the stations where Our Lord suffered: Matins and Lauds in the cenacle and in the Garden of Olives; Prime at the house of Annas and Caiphas; Tierce in the palace of Herod; Sext in the pretorium of Pilate; None on Calvary; Vespers and Complin at the sepulchre. Others follow the attraction of grace and their present disposition. All this is good when it can be done without trouble or scruple.

Ejaculatory Prayers.—It would be well if every breath could be a loving sigh, and every moment be filled with the thought of God. If this cannot be, form a habit of recollecting yourself from time to time; the more frequently the better. Let the striking of the hour be a signal for recalling the presence of God. Accustom yourself to the easy and frequent use of ejaculatory prayers. We need but to love in order to pray and to sigh for God. These outpourings of the heart proceed from the Holy Spirit; they are a language of love readily understood by this God of love. We naturally think of what we love; hence we cannot say we love God if we rarely or never think of Him.

CHAPTER IV.

SHORT METHOD OF PRAYER ACCORDING TO THE SPIRIT OF ST. FRANCIS DE SALES, AND PRELIMINARY ADVICE ON PRAYER BY MGR. CAMUS, BISHOP OF BELLEY.

Preparation.—1. Presence of God. 2. Act of contrition. 3. Invocation of the Holy Spirit, and union with Jesus Christ.

If this preparation occupies all the time that you should give to prayer, thank God; it is the best prayer you could make; and if the same thing happens every day, continue to thank God, and do not be troubled because you have not followed a single point of the meditation. Your heart has been occupied with God and your miseries—that is the essential.

Body of the Meditation.—1. Considerations. 2. Affections. 3. Return upon yourself—that is, reflections upon the past, examination of the present, resolutions for the future.

There are some persons who, without any need of a book, have a special attraction for meditating upon the perfection of God, the mysteries of Jesus Christ or the Blessed Virgin, etc. We may follow this attraction after having asked the advice of an enlightened director.

If you have no special attraction, use a book for meditation; read a few lines, and make acts of virtue, of examination, of resolution.

When your heart begins to weary of a special thought, read further a few lines, and make similar acts upon a new thought. If one act suffices to occupy your heart, be satisfied therewith, and avoid troubling yourself to make others.

If it happen that you are filled with distractions, and find it impossible to be recollected, humble yourself before God. Keep your book always in your hand, and pause a moment after each thought that you read.

Make devout ejaculations; and read again until you find something which touches and occupies your heart.

Conclusion.—1. Thanksgiving. 2. Offering to God. 3. Prayer to Our Lord and to the Blessed Virgin. 4. Choice of a good thought.

CHAPTER V.

ON THE PRESENCE OF GOD.[1]

Now to assist you to place yourself in the presence of God, I shall set before you four principal means. The first consists in a lively and attentive apprehension of His presence in all things and in every place; for there is not a place in the world in which He is not truly present; so that, as birds, wherever they fly, always meet with the air, we, wherever we go, or wherever we are, shall always find God present.

Every one acknowledges this truth; but few consider it with a lively attention. Blind men, who see not their prince, though present among them, behave themselves, nevertheless, with respect, when they are told of his presence; but the fact is, because they see him not, they easily forget that he is present, and having forgotten it, they still more easily lose their respect for him. Alas, Philothea! we do not see God, Who is present with us; and though faith assures us of His presence, yet, not beholding Him with our eyes, we too often forget Him, and behave ourselves as though He were at a distance from us; for although we well know

[1] "Introduction to a Devout Life," Part II.

that He is present in all things, yet, not reflecting on it, we act as if we knew it not. Therefore, before prayer, we must always excite in our souls a lively apprehension of the presence of God, such as David conceived when he exclaimed: "If I ascend up into heaven, O my God, Thou art there; if I descend into hell, Thou art there!" (Ps. cxxxviii.) And we may also say in the words of Jacob, who, having seen the sacred ladder, exclaimed: "O how terrible is this place! Indeed the Lord is in this place, and I knew it not" (Gen. xxviii. 16); that is, he did not reflect on His presence, for he could not but know that God was present everywhere. When, therefore, you come to prayer, you must say with your whole heart, "O my heart, be attentive, for God is truly here."

The second means to place yourself in the sacred presence is to reflect that God is not only in the place in which you are, but that He is, in a most particular manner, in your heart; nay, in the very centre of your spirit, which He enlivens and animates by His divine presence, being there as the heart of your heart, and the spirit of your spirit; for as the soul, being diffused through the whole body, is present in every part thereof, and yet resides in a special manner in the heart, so likewise God is present in all things, yet He resides in a more particular manner in our spirit; for which reason David calls Him the God of his heart (Ps. lxxii.). And St. Paul says, that it is in God "we live and move and are" (Acts xvii.). In consideration, therefore, of this truth, excite in your heart a profound reverence toward God, so intimately present there.

A third means is to consider Our Saviour in His humanity, looking down from heaven on all mankind, but especially on Christians, who are His children, and more particularly on such as are at prayer, whose actions and behavior He minutely observes. This is by no means a flight of the imagination, but a most certain truth; for, although we see Him not yet, it is true that He beholds us from above. It was thus that St. Stephen saw Him at the time of his martyrdom. So that we may truly say with the spouse: "Behold! he standeth behind our wall, looking through the windows, looking through the lattices" (Cant. ii.).

A fourth method consists in making use of the imagination, by representing to ourselves Our Saviour in His sacred humanity, as if He were near us, as we sometimes imagine a friend to be present, saying, methinks I see Him, or something of the kind. But when you are before the Blessed Sacrament, this presence is real and not imaginary, since we must consider the species and appearance of bread only as a tapestry, behind which Our Lord, being really present, observes us, though we cannot actually see Him.

CHAPTER VI.

ADVICE ON PRAYER.[1]

Distractions.—As soon as you recognize that you are distracted, promptly return to God. Say, "O my God! all to Thee, all for Thee, all before Thee."

Then do not reflect upon your distractions, do not examine them, or let yourself be troubled about them.

You may also remain sometime before God, overwhelmed with confusion at sight of your want of respect in His presence.

Aridity.—The more wearied and overwhelmed you feel, the more you must endeavor to remain with courage and submission in God's presence; remain on your knees if possible, your hands joined, your eyes humbly cast down, your mind and heart submissive to the pain you endure. Sacrifice yourself generously and unreservedly to the rigors of divine justice; do not yield to weariness. Let yourself be crucified by all the wanderings of your mind and by all the vexations of your heart. Be convinced that, in your present state, God only asks you to suffer with patience, humility, and resignation before Him.

[1] P. de Gonnelieu. S.J.

We do not profit by meditation for various reasons.

Obstacles to Meditation.—1st. We are not sufficiently penetrated with the truths upon which we meditate.

2d. Our affections are not sufficiently ardent.

3d. Our resolutions are vague and perfunctory.

4th. We do not dwell sufficiently on each affection, and we form them very lightly.

5th. We yield too easily to weariness and to the trouble we experience in prayer or meditation; we believe our meditation useless when we imagine we have done nothing in it; though it is very certain that to endure our miseries humbly before God is to make a good meditation.

Means of Profiting by Prayer.—1st. Our mind must be free and our heart detached.

2d. We must frequently recollect ourselves during the day in the presence of God.

3d. We must mortify our senses and our humor on all occasions.

4th. We must separate ourselves somewhat from society, as well as from worldly discourse; we must love solitude.

5th. Finally, we must prepare ourselves for it carefully; preserve during it great respect for God, Who is present, and we must avoid letting our mind be distracted immediately afterward.

Affective Prayer.—If you find it difficult to reflect upon your subject, occupy yourself with affections, after you have made an act of faith in the truth which has impressed you most; but after you have formed an affection conformable to your subject, or to the inspiration God gives you, remain a moment in silence before God to let it penetrate your soul. Never pass on to a second affection until your heart is filled and satisfied with the first, for when we hurriedly multiply affections they make no impression upon the *will*.

Prayer of Recollection.—I. If the mere presence of God, Whom you behold within you, occupies you, keeps you recollected, fills you with a holy and respectful silence which diffuses a great calm in your heart, do not disturb this efficacious work of God by thoughts or affections likely to withdraw you from this attitude full of the respect due Him. This great God deigns to make you feel His presence by a sweet and intimate recollection. Content yourself with acquiescing in all that He does in you; abandon yourself completely into His hands without placing any obstacle to what He asks of you. "Thou art all, my God, and I am nothing." These words will be sufficient for you while this sacred silence lasts, and then, when it has passed, return to your subject.

II. Accustom yourself, according to the counsel of Jesus Christ Himself, to use but few words when you pray. That is, let your mind be satisfied with simply contemplating the truths upon which you meditate without wearying itself with long discourses, particularly if the simple view of some truths makes more impression upon your heart than discoursive reasoning, and you have had some practice in meditating upon these truths.

III. Do not permit your will to give itself very much even to affections; let it turn them insensibly into lively and ardent aspirations of the heart toward God. If the Holy Spirit send you any sensible grace, receive it with humility, without reflecting upon it too much; fix your heart upon the Author of such graces rather than upon the graces themselves.

IV. Act when God does not act, but be silent when He speaks. Do not be of those souls who remain in pure mental idleness, nor of those who talk incessantly, never pausing to hear God's voice. This idleness is not the prayer of quiet, which keeps the soul elevated above all the movements of inclination and self-love, which sustains it, reconciles it, which occupies it, which penetrates it with holy respect for God, which animates all its actions with the spirit of grace, which makes it relish and possess the sovereign good in a very real and veritable manner.

Contemplation.—I. Contemplation is an extraordinary state to which only God can raise the soul, and to which every one is not called; which few persons attain, because there are few who have sufficient courage and fidelity to die to themselves and to seek only God.

II. Here are the effects which contemplation produces in a soul truly favored with this gift. 1st. It keeps it raised above itself, and intimately united to God by faith, love, and abandonment. 2d. It creates in the depth of the soul a holy respect, a humble fear, a pure and courageous love for God present there. 3d. It causes the soul to speak little and do much; to consent, to cling, and abandon itself to all that God effects in it, and in this way it truly acts. But as God acts more than the soul, and it does not reflect upon what passes in it, for this reason, says St. Francis de Sales, it can not remember having done anything, or it believes it has done nothing.

III. This infused prayer detaches the soul from creatures and from itself, leads it to renounce itself and to practise all the Christian virtues; it makes it love retreat, silence, and recollection; it gives it strength to overcome itself, to mortify its passions, and to repress the sallies of its humor; makes it attentive to the movements of grace, in order to follow them, and to those of nature, in order to overcome them. In a word, this prayer is an excellent means for attaining great sanctity by the faithful practice of all the virtues, all the duties, and all the maxims of Christianity.

CHAPTER VII.

ST. FRANCIS DE SALES' RULES FOR MEDITATION.[1]

As the body needs sleep to rest and refresh its weary members, in the same way it is necessary that the soul have some time to rest, and sleep in the chaste arms of its heavenly spouse, in order to renew the strength and vigor of its spiritual powers. That is why I would fix a certain time every day for this sacred sleep, in order that my soul, after the example of the beloved disciple, might sleep in all confidence on the loving breast and in the very heart of Our Saviour, so full of love, so worthy of being loved, and Whose infinite love is the object of all our affections.

Now, just as the operations of the body in temporal sleep never extend beyond itself, so, for a similar reason, I would retain all the faculties of my soul within itself, and I would that they performed no other functions than those which concern them, and are proper to them, humbly obeying the thought of the prophet: "Rise ye after you have sitten, you that eat the bread of sorrow." That is, you who choose to eat the bread of sorrow, either through contrition for

---

[1] Works of St. Francis de Sales.

your faults or through the compassion you feel for those of others, do not rise and plunge into the exterior occupations of this world, full of misery and pain, unless you have first been thoroughly refreshed by the contemplation of eternal things.

I would contemplate the infinite wisdom of the almighty and incomprehensible goodness of my God ; I would occupy myself particularly in contemplating how these beautiful attributes shine forth in the sacred mysteries of the life and death and of the passion of Our Lord Jesus Christ, in the very eminent sanctity of Our Lady, and in the perfections of the faithful servants of God, whom I must endeavor to imitate.

Then passing from the empyreal heaven, I would admire the glory of paradise, the eternal happiness of the angelic spirits and of the souls of the blessed. I would contemplate the power, goodness, and wisdom of the Holy Trinity in the rewards with which it rejoices—the company of the saints for all eternity.

Finally, I would sleep and I would rest in the love of the one only goodness of my God, which is infinite ; I would relish it if I could, not in its effects, but in itself; I would drink of this water of life, not from vessels offered by creatures, but at its very source ; I would taste how good is this adorable Majesty in Himself and for Himself. Let me add that as He is goodness itself, all goodness, eternal, inexhaustible, incomprehensible goodness, I should say : " O Lord, Thou only art good by essence and by nature. Thou only art necessarily good, and the goodness of all creatures, whether natural or supernatural, is but a participation of Thy loving goodness."

I would begin by recalling all the benefits God had bestowed upon me; the good thoughts and pious sentiments with which He had inspired me in the past; all the graces He had granted me, particularly the grace of certain maladies and indispositions which, by enfeebling my body, were profitable to my soul; and I would, therefore, resolve never more to offend God Who had been so good to me.

With this picture of God's goodness I would contrast the vanity of all human greatness, of the riches and the pleasures of this world, their short duration, their uncertainty, their end; I would despise them, I would hold them in horror, and I would say, "Avaunt, deceitful pleasures with which the Evil One tempts and ruins souls! I will have none of you; I have nothing in common with you." Then I would consider the hideousness and malice of sin, which degrades man; which is unworthy of an upright heart; which, far from giving true and solid contentment, gives only remorse and bitterness; which finally displeases God—a consideration more than sufficient of itself to make us forever detest sin.

With these reflections I would unite all that my conscience tells me of the excellence of virtue, which is so beautiful, so noble, so worthy of an upright, honest heart, which sanctifies man, makes him an angel and almost a God, which makes him taste on earth the pleasures of paradise, and renders him an object of complaisance to his Creator. In order to excite in myself still greater horror of vice and love of virtue, I would admire the beauty of reason, that light sent from heaven to guide our steps. Alas! all our wanderings are due to the fact that we close our eyes to this light. But I would consider particularly death, the judgment of God, purgatory, hell, saying to myself, "What, then, will all the present things avail me?" After that I would raise my mind to the contemplation of the perfections of God, which I would study first in the life and death of Jesus Christ, in Mary and in all the saints. I would softly repose in the love of the divine goodness; I would taste it in itself; I would drink of this water of life at its very source, and I would say: "Thou only, O Lord, art good by essence; goodness itself—eternal, inexhaustible, incomprehensible goodness."

CHAPTER VIII.

THE HOLY SACRIFICE OF THE MASS.

What the Holy Sacrifice of the Mass is.—There is no worship on earth which renders as much honor to God as the sacrifice of the Mass. Hence, we should consider this action as the most important of our life, and accomplish it as perfectly as possible.

If the priest appreciated his position and the greatness of his ministry, he would never approach the altar but in a spirit of holy fear, and he would never leave it except with a feeling of ineffable gratitude.

Dignity of the Priest.—The priest at the altar is the mediator between God and man. He is God's anointed; chosen by the Church to treat with God in the name of all creatures, to offer Him their homage, to adore His infinite grandeur, to thank Him for His benefits, to appease His justice, and to obtain pardon for sinners; finally to ask for the corporal and spiritual succor necessary to all men.

The priest should be not only the sacrificer, but also the victim, because he represents the Church, which in this holy action annihilates herself before her Sovereign, and is immolated in the victim substituted for her.

Manner of Hearing Mass.—The faithful should assist at Mass with respect, attention, and devotion, and regard the priest as the very Son of God Who is about to offer Himself to the Father for them, and to give His life to save them from the eternal death they have merited. As Our Saviour died and was immolated for them, they also should die for Him. It is desirable that all who assist at the holy Sacrifice be in a state of grace; but those who have had the misfortune to offend God should not believe that they are thereby prohibited from assisting at the holy Sacrifice; on the contrary, if they ask pardon for their faults, they will obtain the necessary grace of conversion. The holy Council of Trent declares that "this sacrifice is truly propitiatory, and that if we draw near to God with a sincere heart and upright faith, with fear and reverence, contrite and penitent, we shall obtain, by means of it, mercy, and we shall find grace and the assistance we need. For God, appeased by this offering, grants pardon and the gift of repentance, and pardons the offences and even very grave sins of those for whom it is offered."

There are many beautiful ways of hearing Mass well. Make use of those which you find most devotional. Go to the church, like the shepherds, to seek the infant Jesus; or, like the Blessed Virgin, to Calvary to assist at the death of our divine Saviour, in order to offer Him as a sacrifice for the salvation of the world; or, like the three apostles on Mount Tabor, to behold Him transfigured.

At the beginning of the Mass present yourself before God as a criminal imploring mercy; make with a contrite heart a confession of your sins, repeating the *Confiteor* with the priest.

At the *Gloria in Excelsis* enter into the sentiments of the angels when they chanted this divine canticle, and into those of the apostles who completed it. Praise, adore, and bless God with the priest; desire that His name be known and sanctified, and that His kingdom extend throughout the world.

During the *Epistle* and *Gospel*, if you understand the words, listen with attention; if not, beg God to give the light of faith to infidels and the grace of conversion to heretics.

At the *Creed* renew your profession of faith; affirm your faith in one God in three Persons—the Father, your Creator; the Son, your Redeemer; the Holy Spirit, your Sanctifier.

At the *Offertory* place your body, your soul, your mind, your heart, your possessions, your hopes, your family, your friends, and all your desires upon the paten of the priest. Present them all to God to be immolated to Him with the body of His only Son in a perfect holocaust and odor of sweetness. Beg God to change and transform you as completely as the bread and wine are changed and transformed into His body and blood.

At the *Preface* raise your heart to heaven and prepare yourself for sacrifice. Praise and thank God with the Church; repeat with profound respect the canticle of the angel: "Holy, holy Lord God of armies." "Heaven and earth are full of Thy glory." "Blessed is He Who cometh in the name of the Lord, and Who is to come in the name of the Lord Which saved us."

After the *Sanctus*, until the consecration, meditate upon the Passion: divide it into seven parts or stations for the seven days of the week, as will be shown later on.

At the *Elevation* of the body and blood of Our Lord do not remain cold and unmoved, but adore your Lord with body and mind, bowing profoundly and accompanying this inclination with deepest respect.

Between the elevation of the body and the blood of Our Lord remain in profound silence with interior and exterior modesty, fully persuaded that it is the moment when the Victim is immolated, when the blood, in virtue of the sacramental words, is separated from the body, though one and the other remain truly united under each species; that heaven opens, the angels descend with their Lord, and that God floods with graces the hearts prepared to receive them—graces of sanctity for the just, graces of repentance for sinners.

Finally, it is in this sacred moment that we obtain from God all that we ask through the death and the sufferings of His Son.

After the Elevation offer God the adorable Victim for the four ends of the holy sacrifice. This is the special object of the Mass.

For the glory of God, by making acts of *faith* in Him as your First Principle and your Last End;

your Father, your King, your Redeemer, your Creator, your Strength, your Peace, your All.

Of *hope*, that He will pardon you all your sins, that He will give you paradise after having granted you here below temporal and spiritual favors.

Of *charity*, giving yourself to Him and sacrificing yourself to Him, to all His designs, however contrary they may be to your inclinations; annihilating yourself with your Saviour and offering yourself to live and die for His glory.

You will thank God for all the favors He has lavished upon you, not only upon you, but upon all His saints, and you will offer the body and blood of Jesus Christ to supply for your lack of gratitude.

Offer the holy Victim as a sacrifice of propitiation for the sins of all men, and for your own in particular. It is the only reparation which can appease the divine justice.

Finally, ask all the graces necessary to you and to your neighbor; to stimulate your fervor ask each request through one of the wounds of our divine Saviour.

Contemplate Him on the cross, and ask through His thorn-crowned Head grace for the Church, for our holy Father the Pope, and for all Superiors.

Ask through the wound of the right hand grace for your family, friends, and benefactors.

Through the wound of the left hand pray for the enemies of the Church and your own, repeating with Our Lord upon the cross: "Father, forgive them, for they know not what they do."

Through the wound of the right foot pray for

your subordinates, your domestics, and all those dependent upon you.

Through the wound of the left foot pray for the souls in purgatory, particularly those whom you may have offended or scandalized, for the souls dearest to the Blessed Virgin, for the souls of your relatives, and for all who stand in need of prayers.

Enter into the Heart of Jesus pierced for love of you; give Him your own heart, and beg Him to fill it with His grace and His Spirit.

This prayer may continue until the *Agnus Dei*, when you should prepare yourself for spiritual communion. Ask pardon for your sins, receive the Sacred Host in spirit from the hands of the angels, and make your thanksgiving conversing with Our Lord as if you had received Him sacramentally.

After the last *Collects* receive the priest's blessing as that of God. Listen with devotion to the last gospel, particularly to the words *Verbum caro factum est*, "The Word was made flesh." If you have received Communion, persuade yourself that this incarnation is renewed, that the Word is made flesh in you and desires to dwell in you.

After the Mass adore and thank Our Lord; return home penetrated with the grandeur of this mystery, and recite on the way the *Te Deum Laudamus*.

HOW WE SHOULD MEDITATE UPON THE PASSION DURING THE HOLY SACRIFICE OF THE MASS.

The sacrifice of the Mass is the same as that of the cross. Jesus Christ instituted it to recall His Passion; hence we must never fail to honor it by meditating on His sufferings.

Monday.—Consider the Son of God in the Garden of Olives, where He was bathed in a sweat of blood and water; then at the house of Annas and Caiphas, where He was buffeted and offered every ignominy. Ask God through the merits of Jesus Christ to give you the grace to overcome your passions and to bear injuries with patience.

Tuesday.—Consider your divine Saviour despised by Herod, treated as a fool, compared by Pilate to a thief and murderer. Love your abjection, and do not be offended at the elevation of your neighbor.

Wednesday.—Represent to yourself Our Saviour scourged and crowned with thorns. Avenge upon your body the wounds it inflicted upon your Saviour, and upon your pride the painful ignominy with which it crowned Him. Remember that one must wear the crown of gold after the crown of thorns, or the crown of thorns after the crown of gold.

Thursday.—Follow Jesus bearing His cross; bear yours after Him: if you bear it well, you will help Him to carry His. Place yourself in spirit upon the altar as upon Calvary, there to be fastened and sacrificed the rest of your days as a victim.

Friday.—Listen to Our Saviour's seven words upon the cross; repeat them with Him. After recommending to God your soul, your body, your passions, your life, all that is dearest to you in this world, die spiritually with Him, and live henceforth as one dead, with no care or desire for earthly things.

Saturday.—Enter into the tomb of Jesus, and bury yourself in spirit there with Him. Persuade yourself that the world is dead to you, and you to the world. Descend into Limbo with the holy soul of Our Saviour to rescue a suffering soul from purgatory. Enter also into the heart of His blessed Mother to participate in her sorrows.

Sunday.—Consider the glorious wounds of your risen Saviour; enter by Communion into His heart, and establish your dwelling there forever.

CHAPTER IX.

THE TWO EXAMENS.

PARTICULAR EXAMEN.[1]

I. There is usually in all men a vice or evil inclination which we may call predominant and which is the cause and the root of all their faults.

"And even though we recognize several of these inclinations or faults in ourselves, it will nevertheless be well to choose one in particular and to attack it with all our strength. After extirpating it we should apply ourselves in the same manner to conquering the others one by one.

"This is the end of particular examen.

"This examen is most useful particularly in acquiring purity of heart, as Cassien teaches (*Conférences*), and St. Bernard also in several parts of his works." (*Directoire*, Chapter XIII.)

II. Is this particular examen difficult?

Taken in itself or *objectively* it is not more difficult than meditation or any other exercise of piety. Any difficulty it could offer, therefore, would be only *subjective;* that is, it would arise only from our personal dispositions: for example, from our incon-

---

[1] P. Roothaan, S.J.

stancy, our frivolity, or levity of mind. We must acknowledge, however, that particular examen is something very serious. For it supposes in the first place, in one who wishes to make it profitably, a certain knowledge of himself. We often make our particular examen on exterior faults. It is, in fact, with these that we should begin, particularly when these faults are notable and a cause of disedification to our neighbor; but this is only a preparation for a more serious examen. There is no effect without cause. These exterior faults are streams; we must go to their source; we must search for it in the depth of our soul, and never desist until we have found it and can say, *the evil is there.* To insure more success in this search it is well to know that man's faults are usually the opposite of his natural qualities ; thus gentleness often becomes indolence, and firmness degenerates into harshness. The predominant fault is rooted in the character. We shall return to this subject later on.

Particular examen supposes, in the second place, courage, for we need courage to fight against ourselves in this vigorous way, to attack faults rooted, so to speak, in our very nature. Tell one who is imperious and proud that pride is his predominant fault,—" It is my nature," he will answer ; " I cannot change my nature."

When he says that his predominant fault is part of his nature he says what is very true; but he is mistaken in believing that he cannot correct and reform his nature, and that it is useless to try. It is, in fact, this very nature that he must attack; for it is the source which feeds so many infected streams, the trunk which nourishes so many branches bearing evil fruits. Only when we begin to attack ourselves in this vigorous way do we begin to accomplish something; before this our gains are trifling. In the third place, it is impossible to make the particular examen as St. Ignatius requires, without practising the virtues of vigilance over self, of interior recollection, of mortification of our passions; in a word without generous and persevering efforts. For these reasons we say that particular examen is something serious, though not difficult, considered in itself; for the law of God is not heavy: *Mandata ejus gravia non sunt* (1. John v. 3).

III. Particular examen is efficacious—first, because by means of it a man attacks his real enemies; second, because it enables him to meet them one by one in order to conquer them successfully; third, because it supposes in one who undertakes it a firm and persevering will never to give up so excellent a practice.

IV. Particular examen requires our best and most earnest efforts. The enemy of our perfection laughs at our vague general resolutions; he knows their result by experience. "If he that makes a strong resolve often fails, what will he do who seldom or but weakly resolves?" (Imit. 1. 19.)

Particular examen is not a vague resolution; it is a very special and consequently the most efficacious resolution we can take. It attacks, in fact, that nature which we may fiercely drive from us, says a profane author, but which unceasingly returns. It hides whole years sometimes to surprise us when we least expect it; it never dies, it only sleeps. Cease to watch over, to distrust yourself, and this nature, I mean your predominant fault, will awaken more powerful and attack you more violently than ever. Special faults grow and increase with our age—so much so that people, even people piously inclined but unaccustomed to overcome themselves, become, as they advance in life, insupportable to others. But if particular examen attacks the very foundation of our nature, is it astonishing that it requires our best and most earnest efforts?

Conclusion: If you wish to become perfect, *to know yourself*, attack your predominant fault by means of particular examen, according to the method offered you here by St. Ignatius.

"We must always resolve on something certain, and in particular against those things which hinder us most." (Imit. i. 19.)

We rarely overcome one fault perfectly. "If every year we rooted out one vice we should soon become perfect men." (Imit. i. 11.)

PRACTICE OF EXAMEN.[1]

Before the time of Examen.—We must choose and prepare our subject in such a way as to be able to mark the number of our failings.

In the morning we must endeavor to foresee the occasions of our fault; during the day we must endeavor to resist it, and when we fail, strike our breasts and make a sincere act of sorrow.

[1] By a director of souls.

At the time of Examination.—We must place ourselves in the presence of God, and give our minds completely to what we are about to do.

1st. Examine the graces we have received, and thank God for His love, in order that we may be excited to be generous in overcoming ourselves.

2d. Recall clearly to our memory the subject of our examen, and ask God for the grace to know our failings and to correct them.

3d. Examine our morning or our afternoon hour by hour; help ourselves by means of questions. Mark the number of our failings; compare them with those of the preceding day. We should not give too much time to this third point.

4th. Excite in ourselves deep contrition, and earnestly express it. Give to this and the following point an entire quarter of an hour, if possible.

5th. Foresee the occasions of future failings. Form definite resolutions covering only the period from one examination to another. Above all, pray for grace to be faithful to them.

Many souls find in the practice of remembering the presence of God the most efficacious means of overcoming their faults.

It is well from time to time to return for two or three days to one of the subjects which are, so to speak, a form of perfection, such as regularity, exterior modesty, purity of intention, equanimity of soul, the presence of God, or the spirit of prayer, humility, etc.

GENERAL EXAMEN.[1]

General examen should be made each evening. It is a practice commonly adopted by all persons truly desirous of advancing in virtue. Many, however, find it difficult; they find it dry and monotonous. Hence they acquit themselves of it superficially and unprofitably, or they omit it from time to time, and then end by abandoning it altogether.

The method offered here by St. Ignatius removes these objections by introducing a certain variety in the examination, which he divides into five points well fitted to console and strengthen the soul.

It will be well to make a few remarks on each of these points.

First Point.—We must return thanks to God for the benefits we have received. Few writers teach us to begin the examen by an act of thanksgiving. Yet what is more consoling and more encouraging than the divine benefits we have received? And when have we more need of courage than when we are about to require of our soul an account of its negligences and of its infidelities, when we are about to search and examine our weaknesses? Moreover, the thought of so many benefits will help us in the fourth point to understand our ingratitude.

Second Point.—Ask grace, etc., less by vocal prayers than by outpouring of the heart. Set

[1] Fr. Roothaan.

vocal prayers, recited from memory, frequently become a matter of routine and destroy the devotion of the soul. The heart, on the contrary, has an infinite variety of prayers; it never repeats. Then recognize our sins and banish them from our heart. It is not sufficient to know our sins; we must detest them; we must drive them from our heart, and treat them as enemies to whom no quarter can be given.

Third Point.—Ask an account of our soul. This examen should be made carefully, but without anxiety. It should not by any means exceed a fifth part of the time given to the whole exercise, since it is only one of the five points. Many persons reduce almost the whole examen to this point, which is the reason of the weariness and dryness they experience in this exercise, of the little profit they derive from it, and, not unfrequently, of their want of perseverance.

Fourth Point.—Ask pardon of God. We must excite ourselves to sorrow for our faults. Sorrow has the virtue of effacing sin. Then let our sorrow each day efface our daily offences.

Fifth Point.—Form the resolution to amend *with the assistance of grace.* This last point is the most important of the whole examen and perhaps the least understood in practice. In fact, why do we make the examination of conscience? To know our faults? No doubt; but for what further reason? In order that we may detest them. Certainly; in fact, I endeavor to know my faults that I may correct them; and to do this I need to renew each day *t*he firm resolution not to relapse into the same faults.

"According as our resolution is will the progress of our advancement be," says the author of "The Imitation;" which is very certain in the sense that we often remain far below our resolutions and rarely go beyond them. "If thou canst not continually recollect thyself, do it sometimes, and at least once a day; that is, at morning or evening. In the morning resolve, in the evening examine, thy performances, how thou hast behaved this day in word, work, or thought, because in these, perhaps, thou hast often offended God and thy neighbor."

We ought every day to renew our resolutions and excite ourselves to fervor, as if it were the first day of our conversion, and to say: "Help me, O Lord God, in my good resolutions and in Thy holy service, and give me grace now this day perfectly to begin, for what I have hitherto done is nothing" (Imit. I. 19).

With the assistance of grace: an absolutely necessary condition. "The resolutions of the just depend on the grace of God, rather than on their own wisdom, in Whom they always put their trust, whatever they take in hand" (Imit. I. 19).

CHAPTER X.

OF CONFESSION AND DIRECTION.

THE life of the body is preserved by food and repaired by remedies. In like manner the life of the soul depends upon confession and communion; confession is its remedy, and communion its life.

These two sacraments must be received with the requisite dispositions.

Examination of Conscience.—Examination of conscience is a necessary preparation for the Sacrament of Penance.

It consists of five points:

1st. Thanksgiving.

2d. Invocation of the Holy Spirit of light in order to know one's sins.

3d. A review of all one's actions, thoughts, and words.

4th. Sorrow for having sinned.

5th. Firm purpose of amendment.

See upon which of these five points you can dwell with most advantage.

This Exercise is to be Made Daily.—It is important to make a daily examination of conscience; it keeps the soul in a state of humility, and enables it to know itself. It wins new graces from Heaven by gratitude for those already received. It prepares the soul for confession, and prevents the omission of any grave sin in confession. It prevents vices from taking root in the soul. It renders contrition easy by frequent acts of sorrow; it regulates the future; it foresees the danger of offending God, and guards against the occasions of sin. In a word, it makes us more humble, more vigilant, more wise, more pure. and better prepared to meet death.

Are you faithful to your examen? For what reason do you neglect it?

A wise man foresees evil, guards against it as much as he can. You will be judged after your death. Forestall this judgment by judging yourself. If you excuse yourself, God will accuse you; if you pardon yourself. God will condemn you; while, on the contrary, He will defend you if you accuse yourself; He will pardon you if you condemn yourself.

Many complain of being unable to recall in the evening what they have done during the day; how then can they recall what they have done during a month or a year? This shows how very difficult it is to make a good confession without daily examination of conscience.

Thanksgiving is one of the most important parts of the examen. Consider the benefits God has bestowed upon you this day, and you will, without difficulty, conceive true sorrow for your faults. But avoid anxiety and trouble in searching for your faults. If you have committed any grave sin it will present itself at once to your mind. If you recall a fault of this kind, stop there, and conceive a great horror for it; consider the best means of repairing it; take a firm resolution to avoid it in future, and you will, in this way, have made a good examen.

Particular Examen.—It is particularly important to select one special fault to correct or one special virtue to acquire. This should be the principal subject of your examen. Many do nothing because they want to do too much; they declare war against all vices and destroy none.

This is an artifice of the Evil One to deceive and surprise them. Our forces are limited; we cannot do everything at once; and we weaken our forces by dividing them. They must be united to overcome the enemy.

It is well to attack but one at a time and never lay down our arms until it is vanquished.

What is the subject of your examination? What vice are you making war against? How long have you been fighting it? What advantage have you gained?

Confession.—The Sacrament of Penance is the second plank left us by God after shipwreck. Each time we confess our faults in the sacrament we acknowledge the wisdom of God by the acknowledgment of our ignorance; His power, by the manifestation of our weakness; His sanctity, by the declaration of our sins. We offer reparation to His greatness and majesty, which we have offended; we offer satisfaction to His justice; we humble our pride; we avert the chastisements we have merited; we sacrifice our honor, which we love most in the world; we purify the soul; we heal its wounds. We acquire a special right to the grace of God; we extirpate our vices; we secure our salvation; we afford peace and rest to our conscience.

Faults of those Over-eager to omit Nothing.—There are persons who believe that the excellence of their confession consists in remembering and accurately confessing all their sins and forgetting nothing. If anything escape them, they are troubled and believe their confession invalid. In this way they acquire a horror of the sacrament, believing that they never receive it properly. This scruple is dangerous, because it tends to keep people away from the sacrament and inspires them with aversion for this salutary remedy.

Are you one of such persons? Why do you torment yourself for a thing which is not in your power? Is it not God Who gives you knowledge of your sins? If it is absolutely necessary for you to declare them, He will cause you to remember them. He does not oblige you to say what you do not know. After giving a suitable time to your examination, be at peace. If your sins occur to your mind after confession, they will not, for that reason, remain in your heart, whence they have been driven by the absolution of the priest.

Fault of those who think they must feel Contrition.—Contrition to be true need not be sensible. If you do not feel sorrow for having offended God, beg Him to give it to you, and supply what you lack by sincere humility. Prostrate yourself before God, acknowledge your offences, and ask pardon for them. Go in good faith to confession without so much anxiety and self-seeking. Your kind Master sees your heart; He knows you do not wish to deceive, and the very fact of your going to confession proves that sin is displeasing to you and that you desire to amend.

Relapse should not discourage us.—One who relapses very easily into sins has reason to fear that his contrition was not very great. But, alas! the sacraments do not make us impeccable, and when our relapses are numerous and great they prove that we are neither vigilant nor faithful; then we must renew our resolutions to watch over ourselves more carefully and refrain from yielding to trouble or despondency.

We must listen to the Priest with Attention and Respect.—Do not imagine that you have made a good confession by simply confessing your sins. Listen attentively to the advice of your confessor, for his words are in a measure sacramental; they impart grace, they have a special virtue to heal your sick soul.

Of Absolution.—Do you know what takes place when the priest gives you absolution? Heaven opens, the Holy Spirit descends, the evil spirits are driven from your soul, which the Son of God has cleansed with His blood. You are released from your sins and the eternal punishment which you had incurred. You become again a child of God and heir to His kingdom; you receive infused graces and the gifts of the Holy Spirit. Humble yourself, then, before God; conceive great sorrow for your sins; imagine yourself on Calvary, where the blood of Our Saviour flowed upon your soul to cleanse and purify it; remain thus in respectful silence, filled with true humility and gratitude.

Of Satisfaction.—Perform the penance which the priest imposes; do not regard it as a penance, but as a very great grace which God bestows by permitting you to change in this way the sufferings of hell, which you have merited, into a brief and light expiation. The best penance is to avoid sin; and to do this we must hate it and punish ourselves for it.

Necessity of a Director.—Have you a director? Why have you not one? Do you know the way to heaven? Is there any one on earth who can guide himself? Sheep require a shepherd; you are not of the fold if you are without a guide.

Who can assure you that you are in the right way if not they to whom God has confided the government of souls, saying, "He that heareth you heareth Me; he that despiseth you despiseth Me"?

You are, you say, well versed in spiritual things. You should have more humility and distrust of yourself, for St. Bernard says: "He who is his own guide has a fool for a disciple, and does not need the devil to tempt him, for he is to himself the most perverse and most dangerous of evil spirits." Cassien adds: "It is impossible that the soul abandoned to the guidance of his superiors should ever err." Therefore it is necessary to have a director to whom we may reveal our conscience and from whom we may take advice.

Choice of a Director.—There are certain devout souls who can never find a director to their taste

They would change every month. Persons so difficult to please need a master to teach them the elements of the spiritual life by making them walk in the ways of humility and mortification.

The Spirit of Faith with which we should regard our Director.—It is very important never to separate the thought of God from one's director, and therefore to speak to him with great respect, to obey him faithfully, and to open our hearts to him with confidence and gratitude, so that if God permits us to be deprived of him we may not be overwhelmed by trouble and anxiety. God will always give us grace and light in proportion to our fidelity.

CHAPTER XI.

HOLY COMMUNION.

How we should prepare for it.—As the Eucharist is the most august of our sacraments, Holy Communion is the most important action of our lives.

Of the Sanctity required for Holy Communion.— Those who require perfect sanctity and extraordinary dispositions for approaching the Holy Table, thinking thereby to honor this sacrament, abuse and dishonor it, by rendering it useless to those who receive it and to those who refrain from it. In fact, if I am in a perfect state of sanctity what good will this sacrament do me, and when shall I receive it if I must have this sanctity?

Nothing could be more unreasonable than to require as preparation for a sacrament that which is the fruit and end of the sacrament. This beauty without stain, this perfection without blemish, this sanctity without spot, this grace, this perfect charity, are effects of the sacrament. It was to produce all these effects in our hearts by frequent reception of the Eucharist that it was instituted. Hence there is no justice in requiring such sanctity as a preparation for receiving it. If we measure our worthiness by the excellence of this sacrament, we should never receive it; if we measure it by our need, we should receive Communion daily. Jesus dwells in this sacrament, not to make Himself feared, but to make Himself loved. Bread is not food to be taken only at certain periods of the year, but every day. Why should He take this form if He did not wish to be our food? If He wished to be feared by men, would He not have taken a more awe-inspiring and majestic form? As we cannot do without this sacrament, Our Lord has made it easy for all to receive it. Draw near to the light and you will be enlightened; approach the fire and you will be inflamed; draw near to Jesus, Who is your life, your Sun, your Justice, your Sanctification; but go to Him without fear and He will examine you, He will instruct you, He will purify you, He will sanctify you.

Excessive Fear is Injurious.—One thing which prevents us from profiting by Communion is that we have no hunger or relish for this heavenly food. How can we approach it with love when our heart is filled with fear? and who could not but fear when he believes that it is an abuse of this sacrament to receive it with other than angelic purity?

Humility is an Excellent Preparation.—Endeavor to make a good preparation, Christian soul, and remember that the best of all preparations is a knowledge of yourself, of your poverty, and of your indigence, combined with a firm hope that Our Lord in His goodness will supply all that you lack. Do not, like Martha, be over-eager to serve your Saviour; rather, like Magdalen, await from your Saviour, in peace and silence, the food of your soul and the reformation of your heart.

Whether it is well to refrain from the Holy Table.—Do not keep away from the Holy Table through disgust or scruple. The soul is ill indeed that has lost all relish for this food. Salvation depends sometimes upon one Communion. How do you know whether this Communion may not be the one you omit?

Our Lord in this sacrament is not only the food of our soul, but also its remedy. How do you honor Our Lord by believing that you can do without Him and obtain sanctity without the assistance of His grace? How can you resist temptation without strength? and whence will you obtain that strength if not from this divine sacrament?

For those who receive Communion Frequently.—You communicate frequently, but do you receive the sacrament worthily? If you would rather die than receive Communion in a state of mortal sin, you have reason to believe that you do not commune unworthily.

Necessary Dispositions for receiving the Fruits of the Sacrament.—We may receive the principal effect of the sacrament, which is sanctifying grace, without receiving all the other fruits which it produces. To receive an increase of grace we must be free from mortal sin; to receive all the fruits of the sacrament we must be free from voluntary attachment to venial sin.

Who are they who profit by Holy Communion?—Do not judge that you are growing worse because you feel your evil inclinations more strongly. Communion does not take away all evil inclinations. They are left us to make us distrust ourselves and depend upon grace. If it does not prevent our feeling them, it prevents, as St. Bernard says, our yielding to them.

Whether we should receive Holy Communion when we believe we derive no Profit therefrom.—Humble souls usually believe they are going back instead of advancing. We cannot judge of our progress by our feelings. It is well that you should believe yourself the most wicked and the most unfaithful of creatures; but if you were so in truth, it would not prevent you from receiving Communion, provided you truly desire to do better. For how could you amend without grace?

Can we receive Communion when we have no Sensible Devotion?—Sensible devotion is not necessary to communicate worthily, since it does not always depend upon our will, and the greatest saints are frequently deprived of it even on the greatest feasts, as in the case of St. Teresa at Easter, either because the soul is attached to these little consolations, or because it expects to acquire them of itself. Whatever it may be, true devotion does not consist in these sensible feelings, but in a prompt and ready will to do what God commands and to avoid that which He forbids. Do what you can with the grace of God, and make up by your humility, as St. Bernard says, for what you lack in charity, and you will be well prepared.

The Best Preparation is Humility and Desire.— There are many beautiful practices for preparing ourself for Communion. The best, I think, after confession, consists in humility and desire. Humility makes us see our unworthiness; and desire, our indigence. The first tends to keep us from the Holy Table; the second sends us to it. One makes us say, with the centurion: "Lord, I am not worthy;" the other makes us say, as St. Peter did when the other disciples withdrew from the company of their Master: "Lord, to whom shall we go? Thou hast the words of eternal life."

Motives of Humility, of Love, and Desire.—To humble ourselves before Our Lord we need but ponder these words: "*Who art Thou, my God? and who am I?*" In order to desire to receive Him we must consider the honor and the advantage of going to this Holy Table, the infinite love which Jesus bears us, His desire to celebrate this passover with us, to enter into our hearts, and to impart His life to us.

The Intention we may have in Communicating.—Purify your intention. Approach the Holy Table to honor God, to obey His will, to accomplish His designs, to unite yourself to Jesus Christ, to give Him the life of your heart, to apply to yourself the merits of His passion, or for any other similar end.

Do not be over-anxious in your devotions. Remember that everything consists in humbling yourself and remaining in peace at His feet. Are you capable of receiving a God? Have you wherewith to entertain such a Guest? Beg God Himself, then, to prepare His dwelling.

There are many ways of occupying one's mind and exciting devotion before Communion. Some make use of the following thoughts: Who am I,

Lord, and who art Thou? What dost Thou come to accomplish in my heart? What shall I gain by receiving Thee? For what end do I receive Thee? Others go over the life of Our Lord, pausing upon the mystery which touches them most; for example: I am about to receive the Son of God, Who is seated on the throne of His Father, Who is adored by the angels, and Who took flesh for me in the womb of the Blessed Virgin. I am about to renew His incarnation by giving Him a new life in me.

If this thought does not occupy you, pass on to another and represent to yourself that you are about to receive Him Who was born in a stable, Who was visited by the shepherds, Who was adored by kings, Whom Simeon received in his arms in the Temple, Who was tempted in the desert, Who was transfigured on Tabor, Who worked so many miracles, Who gave sight to the blind, Who cured the sick, Who raised so many dead to life, Who never entered a house without leaving there marks of His kindness. Conceive a great desire to receive Him, and a firm hope that He will heal, sanctify, and enrich your soul with His merits.

Then pass on to His passion, and consider that you are about to receive Him Who, on the eve of His death, instituted this divine sacrament; Who sweat blood in the Garden of Olives; Who shed it from all the veins of His body in the pretorium of Pilate; Who shed the last drop of His blood on the cross; and that this same blood is about to inflame your heart and flow in your veins.

Remember also that He Whom you are about to receive loves you so tenderly that He was willing to die for you; that He comes to apply to you the fruit of His death and sufferings; that for you He was placed in the tomb, and that He is about to descend into your heart as He descended from the cross to the tomb; that you are about to receive this same body with its adorable wounds which He permitted His disciples to touch; that He is about to open His side and give you entrance into His heart.

Finally, consider that you are about to receive Him Who ascended into heaven, and Who is to judge the living and the dead. Is there not sufficient here to occupy you, and to excite your devotion?

Some find devotion in reading the Litany of the Holy Name of Jesus and pausing at the invocation which touches them most.

Thanksgiving.—Now if it is very important to prepare ourselves for Holy Communion, it is no less necessary to make good use of the time after Communion. O Jerusalem, if thou knewest Who it is that comes to thee, and the blessing thou canst receive from this visit!

If Jesus in coming to you is pleased to give you sensible marks of His presence, and moves your heart, profit by these precious moments. If you are distracted, tepid, and languid, do not be troubled, but beg God to supply what you lack and to effect in your heart all that He came to do. Food is digested in your body without your giving any thought to it, provided you do not disturb the operation of nature. Let grace do its work; if you do not hinder it by voluntary distractions, it will digest, so to speak, this heavenly food and transform you into Jesus Christ. He is the King of peace; His abode must be one of peace. Do not disturb His repose, and He will give you peace.

It is well immediately after receiving to remain a few moments in quiet, peaceful silence, listening to Our Lord's voice, or, rather, permitting Him to do what He wishes in your heart. Do not judge of the effect of Communion by your feelings. The most perfect operations of God are usually the least sensible. When the Bridegroom has entered, close the door of your heart and rest on His breast.

Love is eloquent; it needs no instruction to speak. It speaks most when it is young; it is more silent when it has waxed strong and reached its maturity. Speak much, tender souls, pray, weep, sigh, but do not fail to listen also to what Our Lord will say to you.

With regard to perfect souls, they should abandon themselves entirely to His love and quietly enjoy the presence of their Beloved. If they wish to speak let them content themselves with these words: "My God and my All." Even this is too much: "Let all flesh be silent at the presence of the Lord."

Those who have no facility in conversing with Our Lord may find some assistance from considerations similar to those which we proposed as suitable before Communion. For example: Behold, He Who was born in a stable, Who died on the cross for me, has come into my heart. Let them pause and make acts of love and gratitude.

There are some persons who make the presence of God most irksome to themselves; they are never so ill at ease as when in His company; no sooner does He enter their hearts than they fly from Him, turn their backs upon Him to talk with creatures: this is certainly unparalleled incivility. You do not know what to say to Him? Let Him speak. You cannot love Him? Can you not humble yourself before Him? Remain at His feet like Magdalen, and beg all the saints to thank Him for you; recite at least a few vocal prayers, and offer your divine Guest the best entertainment your heart affords.

CHAPTER XII.

THE OCCUPATIONS OF THE DAY.

We must acquit ourselves of the Duties of our State.—Whatever your state in life, the first and most important of your devotions is to acquit yourselves faithfully of its duties, as we shall explain more particularly in another chapter. Let each one, as St. Paul counsels, remain in the state to which God has called him, and let him acquit himself of its duties as imposed by God Himself. In this does our perfection consist, and it is upon the manner in which we have fulfilled the duties of our state or position that we shall be principally judged.

Reflect upon this important truth; see how you have acquitted yourself of the duties of your state. Do you consider it a state in which the providence of God has placed you; a state in which He wills you to find the graces He destines for you, as well as your peace and salvation, and in which He wishes you to honor and serve Him?

Count all that you do as nothing if it is not done for God. The trouble attached to your employment does not dispense you from it; if you do only what you please, can you be considered a servant of God?

Avoid Over-eagerness.—Over-eagerness and negligence are two faults which spoil a good action. What is your haste? Whence is this unquiet heart? Whence this natural impetuosity? It is not from God, for He does not dwell in the midst of such agitation and trouble.

Can you do anything without the assistance of God? Are you trusting in Him when you are so excessively anxious? Do you think He will bless what you undertake with such intemperate ardor? If He loves you He will never permit your intemperate designs to have the effect you desire; you must needs fail if you rely upon yourself. God desires the glory of your actions; you rob Him of it when you act with such precipitation.

Labor but without labor, I mean without anxiety or disquiet. Consider yourself as the instrument of the divinity, and all that you do will be divine. An instrument must be lifeless to be used to advantage. What could a painter do with a brush that moved of itself in his hands? Be dead to your desires, and all your actions will have the reward of eternal life. Let reason and grace guide you, and all that you do will be just.

Place yourself in the hands of God when you labor, bodily or mentally. Pause before you enter any path. Do not let nature take the initiative and precede grace. Do what you ought, not what you please. Regulate all your plans by your duties. In all your movements rely upon Him Who is immovable; preserve in all your actions a tranquil heart and mind. Hasten, if necessary, but never be precipitate.

We must avoid Negligence.—If over-eagerness is to be feared, negligence is still more so. The first comes from esteem and ardor; the second from contempt and sloth. One proceeds from a too ardent and the other from an indifferent heart. "He that is hasty with his feet shall stumble," says the Holy Spirit; but He curses him who does the work of God negligently.

Is it for God you are laboring? Does He not merit that you should serve Him with pleasure? Has He not bestowed sufficient blessings upon you? Has He not promised you sufficiently great rewards? Is He slow to render you service? Does His sun ever fail to shine upon you? What! The Creator serves His creature with pleasure, however wicked and unfaithful he may be, and the creature serves his Creator with reluctance?

Inconstant and Capricious Minds.—Do you take pleasure in your work? It is well that you should, but do not be attached to it. Purify your intention; labor, not because it gives you pleasure, but because God commands it. Let your pleasure be to please Him, and you will always work with pleasure. What should a servant think of if not of satisfying his master?

In performing your actions begin, not by the most agreeable, but by the most necessary; and let God be first in them all.

Amusements.—Play is a remedy to be taken only when ill, that is, when the mind is over-wearied by work. There are some, the Wise Man tells us, who imagine the life of man a play; they never work and would always rest. They are in health and would always take remedies.

Play for the relaxation of the mind is a laudable recreation. Play merely for gaining money is a shameful traffic. Play merely to pass the time is reprehensible idleness. We have not come into the world to seek pleasure, but to do penance; not to win money, but to win heaven. Play rarely, play little, play only a short time, play without over-eagerness.

Consider what you stake as lost from the first and it will not disturb you. If it is permitted to stake trifling sums to increase the interest of the game, give whatever you win to the poor.

Regulate your play and your pleasures; always bear in mind that St. Francis Borgia said: "We usually lose four things at play: time, money, devotion, and conscience." How do you spend your income? Are you parsimonious or extravagant in your dress, in your furniture, in your house, in your pleasure, in your table?

Meals.—We eat only to live; yet there are some who live only to eat. They can speak of nothing but entertainments, good cheer, a good table, and good wines. It would seem as though nature had erred in making them men; they should be animals.

Raise your heart to God as you go to the table; endeavor by purity of intention to convert this action, animal in itself, into a Christian duty. Grace before meals should never be omitted wherever you are. Its effect is more salutary than you think; if you neglect it, frequently food may injure more than it benefits you.

Beware of over-eagerness in eating, or of manifesting extreme pleasure or vexation when the food is well or ill prepared. Eat with the temperance and modesty which marked all the actions of Our Lord. Give to God the better part of what is served you, by depriving yourself for love of Him of something which especially flatters your palate.

If you neglect to thank God you do not merit that He should give you bread, and whatever your wealth you have reason to fear that you will lose it. God takes away from ungrateful souls blessings which they abuse and for which they are ungrateful.

Of the Word of God.—Do you take as much pains to nourish your soul as your body?

How do you profit by the word of God? You speak to Him through prayer; but it is God Who speaks to you through good books and sermons. The word of God is never without its effect; it either converts its hearers or renders them more culpable. Are you not too curious? Are you not of those who cannot read a good book unless its style is perfect; who can not hear a preacher unless his style is polished?

Seek in this tree of life the fruit rather than the flower. God, St. Paul tells us, has not willed to convert the world by eloquence, but by the fruit of His cross, which would have remained without effect if the apostles had employed the arts of oratory. It is not fine language which touches hearts, but the grace and unction of the Holy

Spirit. The wisdom of God spoke to man in parables and popular language; it will never convert you by means of studied discourses, but by the strength of its spirit and the simplicity of its words.

Seek the books and preachers who touch your hearts and not those who flatter your ear. Never let a day pass without reading a good book. Reading, says St. Bernard, seeks God; meditation finds Him; contemplation enjoys Him. Reading helps meditation, and meditation leads to contemplation. If you like the end, adopt the means; if you desire to taste heavenly things, frequently read and meditate upon them.

CHAPTER XIII.

OF A STATE OF LIFE.

How Important it is to be in the State of Life in which God wishes us.—After admiring the beautiful order of the universe and the wise economy of Divine Providence, persuade yourself that it is God Who has created this great variety of states and conditions on earth to unite all men by the bonds of necessity and dependence; to raise them to the knowledge of their principle by this multitude of employments; to reveal to them the greatness of His house and the treasures of His magnificence. For it is through the multiplicity of beings that we reach unity of being, and by following the course of the stream that we reach the source.

Every reasoning mind is filled with astonishment when it considers this great multitude of creatures who form the court of the King of heaven; when it contemplates their riches, their beauty, their functions, their order, their disposition, and their industry; but we must not stop here. To profit by this knowledge we must be further convinced that God, Who does everything with just weight and measure, as the Wise Man says, has from all eternity marked and destined for us a state in which He wishes us to serve Him; that He has attached to it our peace and made it the surest way of our salvation; our rest, because each thing is at peace when it is in its place; the surest way of our salvation, for the reason that the graces we need, and which are, so to speak, our wages, are given us according to the condition, the state, and the office in which God places us.

If the Church is an edifice, the faithful are the stones of which it is composed. If the Church is an army, the faithful are the soldiers. If it is a body, the faithful are its members. Now the stones of an edifice, the soldiers of an army, the members of a body, all have their place and employment, outside of which they are useless.

A man is happy when he performs his duties and faithfully follows the order marked by Divine Providence. He enjoys profound peace; he is under the protection of the Prince of order; he receives graces in abundance; graces which nourish him, graces which strengthen him, graces which cause him to grow in virtue, graces which lead him to perfection, because this food is proper and suitable to the disposition of his soul. As he is faithful to the law, the law is faithful to him. As he keeps order, order keeps him, defends and protects him. "Much peace have they," says David, "who keep Thy law, and to them there is no stumbling-block."

How we must choose a State in Life.—After considering this truth, reflect upon yourself, and see what your state is. If your state of life is not settled, and you have yet to choose it, pray God to make known the state in which He wishes you to serve Him. Listen to what He will say to you after Communion and during this retreat. See whither your inclinations lead you when your heart is at peace and undisturbed by passion. Reason is a divine light and a natural inspiration which never deceives those who follow it, particularly under the guidance of faith.

Consider, therefore, the end for which God has placed you in this world, which is to honor Him and to save your soul. Consider what state affords you the best means of attaining this end. Examine your disposition, your constitution, your character, your strength, your inclinations, your habits, the movements of your heart, the attractions of grace, the inspirations of the Holy Spirit.

Consider what you would wish to have done at the hour of death; what you would advise a friend to do in your place. And as it is difficult to distinguish the movements of nature from those of grace; and as the Evil One frequently transforms himself into an angel of light; and no one can judge in his own case, and there is danger of heeding the suggestions of self-love, the safest way, in order to proceed wisely in an affair of such importance, is to take the advice of a wise and experienced director; to make known to him the sentiments of your soul, and to abide by his advice, convinced that God will never permit you to be deceived when you act sincerely with His representative, through whom He makes His will known to you.

What they should do who are settled in a State of

Life.—If you are settled in a state of life, consider how it was that you entered it—through passion, interest, vexation, vanity, human respect? Did you consult God? Did you ask His light? Is your state good or evil? If good, you must perfect it. If evil, you must abandon it. If you are settled in a state of life and cannot leave it, remain in it, but in a spirit of penance, repairing as far as possible the fault you have committed, and bearing all the trials God sends you in it. Persuade yourself that you can only be restored to His favor by the chastisements of justice; that you can recover peace only by patience, innocence only by penitence; that suffering supplies the place of action; that the *only* source of salvation for you is humility and suffering; that peace will follow trouble; that calm will follow the storm.

Rules for Religious.—If you are a religious, whatever the means which brought you to religion, be persuaded that it has happened for the best, and that you are where God wills you should be. Does not the Son of God desire that all shall be perfect even as His Heavenly Father is perfect? and does He not say that the means of this perfection is to abandon our possessions, to deny ourselves, to take up our cross and to follow His example and counsels? This is the religious state. Therefore, though you have entered it thoughtlessly—that is, from no serious motive—yet you should believe it is the will of God, and that you are in the way of perfection. Make, then, a virtue of necessity. Embrace this state, however contrary it may be to your inclinations. Take upon your shoulders the sweet yoke of Jesus, and protest that you will bear it for love of Him all the days of your life.

Special States.—Graces are not only attached to the state and life in which God wishes us, but also to special places and employments prescribed us by obedience. Would you be a religious in an order to which God has not called you? Why would you wish to be in a house, in a position, in an office which God has not given you?

God's forethought embraces not only all mankind, but each of His creatures: to each one is assigned a special place, a special work; consequently your graces are attached to the place and the employment destined for you by Providence and indicated by obedience.

Reflections.—There are reasonable people who desire, it is true, only what is just, but desire it inordinately. They seek what is right unreasonably, that is, passionately.

Do you wish to live in peace and win blessings from Heaven? Ask nothing, refuse nothing, abandon yourself to the providence of God; be guided by obedience; trust in your superiors. As you have entered religion only to serve God, be convinced that you render Him no service which is pleasing to Him if you are not where He wills you to be, and if you do not do as He desires.

Oh, how happy is he who confides in God and abandons himself to His guidance! and how miserable is he who turns from God and follows the impulse of his passions!

CHAPTER XIV.

OF THE EXERCISE OF ONE'S CHARGE.

That we must Faithfully acquit ourselves of our Charge.—As you do not belong to yourself but to God, you should labor not for yourself, but for God. You will never labor more advantageously for yourself than when you labor for God's interest. You are laboring for His interest when you fulfil your charge as an office which He has given you, and acquit yourself of its duties with all the energy, watchfulness, and fidelity of which you are capable.

Make no distinction between your interests and those of God. You have but one interest, which is to save your soul, and your soul is God's only interest as well as yours. He thought of the salvation of your soul from all eternity; He labored for it from the beginning of the world; to accomplish it He descended from heaven to earth, was born in a stable, and died upon a cross. Do you appreciate this? Is it not worth your while to reflect upon it?

Our Talents are given us only to do what God commands.—A great ambition is a great cross. It is great folly to believe ourselves capable of all things. Our strength and our abilities are limited.

God, St. Paul tells us, divides His graces: when He sends us to labor in His vineyard He gives us exactly what we need. When He places us in any position He assigns us a fund of graces to enable us to acquit ourselves worthily of our charge.

How we should fulfil our Charge.—You will fulfil your charge faithfully if you receive it from God's hands, accept it by His orders, if you rely upon His grace, if you ask His blessing, if you aspire to no other charge, if you labor cheerfully, persistently, courageously, and perseveringly. Cheerfully, that is, without vexation; courageously, avoiding indolence; perseveringly, undeterred by weariness and vexations. With what fault does your conscience reproach you in the fulfilment of your charge? Are you where you should be? Do you do what you should and as you should?

We should not be Passionately attached to our Charge. —Do not judge that your charge is unsuitable to you because it does not please you. Inclination, it is true, is a mark of vocation, but it should be disinterested, peaceful, obedient, and free from all human respect and all ambition. Distrust an inclination which is turbulent, impetuous, rebellious, and impatient.

What True Devotion is.—Never separate God's service from the duties of your charge. Do not think that it is laudable to be at church when you should be at the palace, to pray when you should work. The most beautiful of all devotions is the fulfilment of your duties. Work without prayer is a vain occupation; prayer without work is false devotion. Satisfy your devotion after you have fulfilled your obligations. Precept is preferable to counsel, and duties to works of supererogation.

If you would succeed in your labors never separate work from prayer. Pray before work, pray during work, pray after work. The spiritual is to the temporal what the soul is to the body. What can the body do separated from the soul? "Seek first the kingdom of God and His justice, and all these shall be added unto you." Look after the principal, and the accessory will not be wanting.

Marks of Purity of Intention.—For whom do you labor? Are your intentions pure? Here are marks of a pure intention: to labor with a tranquil heart; to be ready to leave or continue a work you have begun; to labor as if only you and God were in the world; to be content to have no sensible and natural satisfaction.

CHAPTER XV.

OF VISITS AND CONVERSATION.

Visits should be Rare.—There are two kinds of visits: one necessary, the other optional. We must pay those that are necessary and regulate those that are optional; that is, the last should be infrequent, brief, profitable, and modest.

Solitude is such a great blessing that we should never abandon it except for something better. It preserves us from sin and unites us with God.

Example is powerful; nature is frail. Love springs from resemblance; conversation enkindles love; if you frequent worldly society, you are worldly or you will soon become so.

You wish, you say, to do good to others; I would advise you to begin your apostolate with yourself. Only he who has one foot firmly rooted in solitude may, like the compass, describe a circle and a figure without leaving his centre. We never converse with others without giving something of ourselves and receiving something from them. We give what we have of good, and take, perhaps, what they have of evil.

Do not trust to your virtue; it is soft wax which will melt before fire; it is a shield of glass capable of being shattered by the first arrow of temptation. The Evil One is powerful in dangerous occasions, and grace is weak; the heart is cowardly, passions are turbulent, objects alluring, inclination to is evil strong and violent. There is everything to fear for one who fears nothing.

Visits should be Brief.—If you are obliged to converse with others, leave your solitude only as the stone leaves its centre, as the magnet leaves the pole —with an inclination and desire to return. Let your visits and conversations be brief, and if you must give time to this kind of duties, let it be as little as possible.

I know no people more tiresome and more burdensome to others than they who imagine themselves least so. They are insupportable with their long stories, and exhaust the patience of those whom they visit. Moreover, how is it possible to speak at such length and do no harm?

In any case, it is better to let people see too little than too much of you; better that they should long for you than dread you. We appreciate what is rare; we disdain what is common. If your society is profitable, you will not bestow it so readily. If it is not profitable, you should not be so ready to inflict it upon others.

However good and innocent a conversation may be, it excites suspicion when it is too protracted.

We give nothing without receiving something, and what can worldly people give you except sentiments of vanity and idleness? These are two evil spirits which rarely leave them.

How can you expect God to dwell with you if

your heart is never at peace, if you are continually pouring it out upon creatures?

A bird which continually thrusts its head through the bars of its cage shows that its dwelling does not please it, that it longs to leave it. Happy is the man who can remain at home and is independent of society.

Visits should be Profitable.—If your position obliges you to go abroad somewhat, imitate St. Catharine of Siena, of whom it is said that no one approached her without becoming better. Let your conversation be holy and profitable.

Let there be nothing against God. This is St. Francis de Sales' great maxim, which we must always observe in conversation. Banish all raillery and detraction. Never amuse yourself at the expense of others. Would you be willing that your shortcomings should furnish entertainment to the company?

Do not be satisfied with doing no harm to any one; do good, if possible, to every one. There is nothing more earnestly recommended to us in the writings of the apostles than edification and good example. "Dearly beloved, I beseech you," says St. Peter, "let your conversation be good among the Gentiles, that they may, by the good works which they shall behold in you, glorify God." And in the same chapter he again tells the faithful: "According to Him That has called you, Who is holy, be you also in all manner of conversation holy." St. Paul gives the same exhortation to his disciple Timothy: "Be thou an example of the faithful in word, in conversation, in charity, in faith, in chastity." And he writes to the Philippians: " Only let your conversation be worthy of the Gospel of Christ."

From the fulness of the heart the mouth speaketh. When the apostles were filled with the Holy Spirit they began to speak. You must be filled with the spirit of the world, since you speak only of its vanities. There is a time, it is true, for all things, and you must beware of preaching untimely sermons, or of wearying your hearers even with good things. Your conversation should be seasoned with prudence. Honey is good, says the Wise Man, but we should not eat too much of it.

Visits should be Modest.—If you converse with others, and charity requires you to contribute to their amusement, never let it be at the expense of virtue or modesty. Be on your guard and watch over yourself, bearing in mind that there are no more dangerous occasions than such conversations. Avoid an imperious or oracular manner of delivering your opinion, as if there were no appeal from it; suffer others to differ with you without offence; do not take advantage of the modesty of others to monopolize the conversation and martyrize your hearers.

Speak but little, and speak well, and allow others the liberty you claim for yourself.

It is a mark of a trifling, ill-regulated mind to interrupt. A wise man speaks only in default of another, as it were, and to sustain the conversation. He follows the counsel of the Holy Spirit: " Where there is no hearing pour not out words." He knows that he needs the assistance of grace to speak wisely, and that God gives this grace only when He wills us to speak; hence if we speak otherwise, that is, if we interrupt and speak without regard to others, we can hardly fail to fall into some error or fault. Believe me, if you would learn to speak wisely, you must begin by learning to be silent. There are persons who speak more with the body than with the tongue, and employ more gestures than words. Gesture is intended to emphasize, and sometimes to take the place of speech; it is a mute language which speaks to the eye, and which is more readily understood by the heart than the mind. Speech is the interpreter of the mind, and gesture of the heart. But a profusion of gesture takes from the dignity of speech, and indicates, usually, an excitable mind.

If you do not allow yourself to be moved by passion, you will speak modestly and temperately, and your whole bearing will testify a temperate and well-regulated mind.

It is great wisdom never to give or to take offence; to suffer without making others suffer; to be a martyr without martyrizing others; to be able to observe a certain amount of restraint in our communications with others. There are persons who open their hearts to any one and every one; and others, again, who seem to be living behind a mask, either to surprise others or to guard against surprise themselves. Both extremes should be avoided; the first shows great want of discretion, the second proceeds from malice or distrust.

Cultivate ease and dignity of manner; be reserved without constraint, modest without affectation, obliging without flattery, merry without levity, serious without severity.

One never speaks wisely under the influence of passion. Good sense and piety counsel you to be silent under such circumstances, and even if you suffer confusion and mortification you will lose nothing thereby, but gain immeasurably by conquering your passion. Enjoy recreation or amusement with a pure intention; ask God to govern your tongue; keep yourself always in His presence; put a bridle on your tongue, and whatever the company in which you find yourself, never forget that God and His angels are present.

Do not be of those whose principles change with the times; rule your passions; do not abandon yourself to their shameful caprices. You are a man and a Christian. As a man you are guided by reason, as a Christian by grace. Both tend to preserve peace of soul, tranquillity of mind, and serenity of heart.

In your visits and social intercourse treat others with the kindness and courtesy you expect from them. Cultivate an equable manner, avoiding immoderate mirth or extreme solemnity; graciously grant a favor in your power, and when obliged to deny a request soften the refusal with kindness and marks of affection.

Fidelity to God obliges you to prevent evil discourses by adroitly changing the conversation, or by paying no attention to it, or by making it evident that it displeases you.

Do not be of those weakly complacent characters who praise everything, whether good or evil; or of those who indiscriminately censure and cavil at everything, and whom it is impossible to please.

Justice requires that you praise what is laudable; and charity, that you share in the joy of your neighbor.

Love, and do as you will. Love, I say, with that love which is charity, and your conversation will be like that of the angels, who bear with our defects, who counsel us in our doubts, who console us in our trials, who assist us in our miseries, who are with us only to help and benefit us. Bear yourself in like manner toward your neighbor, and your conversation will be angelic.

Friendship.—To love through instinct is to love as an animal; to love according to inclination is to love as a man; to love against inclination is to love as a saint; this is the supreme effort of Christian charity, and the triumph of divine love; for only God, says St. Thomas, can enable us to love one who does not please us; still more one who displeases us, who grieves and offends us.

CHAPTER XVI.

SILENCE.[1]

ENDEAVOR to secure yourself in the course of the afternoon fifteen minutes or a half hour of silence. During these moments think sometimes of the recollection of Jesus, Mary, and Joseph, and unite your work with theirs; at other times reflect upon the respectful silence which the saints observe in heaven, where they are completely rapt in God; sigh for this blessed repose.

Speak heart to heart with your angel at your side; thank him for his care of your salvation, promising him to respect and to faithfully follow his inspirations. Ask him to present the prayers and sighs of your heart to Our Lord.

You may also reflect upon the necessity of spending time profitably, and the strict account you will have to render, at the last day, of every moment of your life.

If you are alone recite some vocal prayers; but do not impose this silence upon those about you; if they speak to you answer without hesitation, without, however, prolonging the conversation.

Offer your silence to God to repair the faults

[1] P. de Gonnelieu

you have committed by your words, and also in expiation of the sins of the tongue committed in the world. If you fail in charity during the day, or answer impatiently, punish yourself by observing silence for the space of time necessary to say a *miserere;* it would be generous to impose this silence on yourself when you feel most desirous to speak. You have no idea how pleasing these little sacrifices are to our divine Master.

INTENTIONS FOR THE OBSERVATION OF SILENCE.[1]

We may have a special intention for each day of the week, and sanctify our silence, offering it as follows:

Sunday to the Holy Trinity, to honor the silence of Jesus in the bosom of His Father.

Monday to the Holy Spirit, to honor the silence of Jesus when He retired to the desert.

Tuesday to angel guardians, to imitate the silence of the angels before the Blessed Sacrament.

Wednesday to St. Joseph, to honor his silence and obtain an interior spirit.

Thursday to the Sacred Heart in the Sacrament of the Altar, where this divine Solitary observes a profound silence.

Friday to the mystery of the cross, to honor the silence which Jesus observed during His passion.

Saturday to the Immaculate Heart of Mary, to obtain the grace to imitate the silence of our holy mother.

[1] A director of souls.

CHAPTER XVII.

VISITS TO THE BLESSED SACRAMENT.

WE are pleased to be in the society of those we love. The Son of God delights to be with you. Do you delight to be with Him? Do you pay Him a visit each day? He remains upon earth to counsel you in your doubts, to console you in your trials, to strengthen you in your temptations. Do you believe that He is on our altars? Can you believe this and abandon Him?

Various Intentions in Visiting the Blessed Sacrament. Titles of Our Lord.—There are some who find devotion in considering Our Lord under various titles: Sunday as King, Monday as Father, Tuesday as Friend, Wednesday as Physician, Thursday as Spouse, Friday as Redeemer, Saturday as glorious Conqueror and Vanquisher of demons.

We should make acts of faith, hope, love, confidence, thanksgiving, etc., in conformity with our present dispositions and the special title we are considering. They who receive Communion daily may follow this same method and receive Our Lord under a special title each day.

Different Circumstances of the Passion.—Others consider Our Lord in the course of His passion, of which this sacrament is a representation.

Monday, in the Garden of Olives, struggling with sorrow, and inviting you to struggle with Him. Tuesday, in the house of Annas and Caiphas, bearing ignominy and insult, and inviting you to bear injuries after His example. Wednesday, before Herod, classed with Barabbas, and mocked as a fool, teaching you to bear to be derided and contemned for His sake. Thursday, in the scourging and crowning with thorns, telling you how you must suffer for Him. Friday, bearing His cross to Calvary, and begging you to bear it with Him and to die with Him. Saturday, in the tomb and in limbo, exhorting you to descend thither with Him. Sunday, risen in Galilee, or in heaven, promising you that you will reign with Him.

Virtues and Mysteries of Our Lord.—Others finally, after the example of P. de Gonnelieu, consider a virtue, a mystery of Our Lord corresponding to the day of the week.

Sunday: Contemplate Jesus gloriously risen. Ask, with confidence, a share in the joys of His glorious resurrection, and for this end receive the trials of life with submissive patience.

Monday: Honor Jesus in His state of victim in the Sacrament of the Altar; immolate yourself completely to His love by sacrificing to Him your passions, your ill-regulated desires, thoughts, and affections, and unite yourself with the expiation which Jesus offers to God His Father.

Tuesday: Honor the faithful obedience of Our Lord, Who descends upon the altar at the voice of the priest, and take the resolution to obey all your superiors for love of Him.

Wednesday: Meditate on the patience of Jesus in the Blessed Sacrament, where He endures the outrages and ingratitude of bad Christians. Ask pardon for your guilty brethren and for yourself, and beg the grace to bear without complaint the offences and trials which fall to your lot.

Thursday: Adore Jesus humbled, ignored, despised, and abandoned by men, for whom He is daily immolated. Bear Him company by uniting yourself with all your soul to His meek and humble heart.

Friday: Honor the love which impelled your divine Saviour to give Himself without reserve, in order to transform you into Himself. Return His love with true devotion.

Saturday: Thank Him for the liberality He has manifested toward you in the many graces He has bestowed upon you in your Communions. Ask pardon for the abuse you have made of them, and resolve again to love Him without reserve, and to serve Him with your whole heart.

CHAPTER XVIII.

SPIRITUAL RECOLLECTION.[1]

It is to this point, my dear Philothea, that I wish to draw your particular attention, since in it consists one of the most assured means of your spiritual advancement. Recollect as often as you can, in the course of the day, by any of the four ways I have marked out for you, that you stand in the presence of God: observe what He does, and what you are doing, and you will find His eyes perpetually fixed upon you with an inconceivable love. Then say to Him: "O my God! why do I not turn my eyes toward Thee, as Thou always lookest on me? Why dost Thou think incessantly on me, O my God? and why do I seldom think on Thee? Where are we, O my soul? Our true place of rest is God, and where do we find ourselves?"

As birds have their nests on trees, to which they retire at need, and the deer thickets and forests in which they hide from pursuit, or enjoy the cool shade of summer, so will we, Philothea, choose some place every day, either on Mount Calvary or in the wounds of Our Lord, or some place near

---

[1] "Introduction to a Devout Life."

Him, as a retreat to which we may occasionally retire, to refresh and recreate ourselves amidst our exterior occupations, and there, as in a stronghold, defend ourselves against temptations. Blessed is he that can say with truth to Our Lord: "Thou art my place of strength and my refuge, my defence from storms, and my shadow from the heat" (Ps. lxx. 3, Isa. xxv. 4).

Remember, Philothea, to retire occasionally into the solitude of your heart, while you are outwardly engaged in business or conversation. This mental solitude cannot be prevented by the multitude of those who surround you; for as they are not about your heart, but your body, your heart may remain in the presence of God alone. This was the exercise which the holy King David practised amidst his various occupations, as he testifies in the following, as well as in the several other parts of his psalms: "O Lord, I am always with Thee. I beheld Thee, Lord, always before me. I have lifted up my eyes to Thee, O my God, Who dwellest in heaven. My eyes are ever toward Thee, Lord."

And indeed our conversation is seldom so serious or our occupation so absorbing as to prevent us from withdrawing our hearts occasionally from them, in order to retire into this divine solitude.

When the parents of St. Catharine of Siena deprived her of every opportunity, place, or leisure to pray and meditate, Our Lord inspired her to make a little oratory in the depth of her heart, whither she could retire in spirit amidst the painful labors which her parents imposed upon her. And she received no inconvenience from the attacks of the world, because, as she said, she shut herself up in her interior retreat, where she comforted herself with her heavenly Spouse. She found this practice so profitable that she afterwards counselled her spiritual children to adopt it.

Retire, therefore, from time to time, into the solitude of your soul, where, separated from all creatures, you may speak heart to heart with God on the affairs of your soul, as a friend speaks to a friend. Say with David: "I am become like to a pelican of the wilderness: I am like a night raven in the house. I have watched, and am become as a sparrow, all alone on the house top" (Ps. ci.). These words, taken in a literal sense, show us that this great king spent solitary hours in the contemplation of spiritual things. And taken in a mystical sense they reveal three excellent retreats whither we may retire to be with Our Saviour. The raven in the dark, silent house brings to mind the desolate stable where Our Saviour lay hidden from the world, expiating and mourning our sins. The pelican of the wilderness, which with her own blood nourishes and gives life to her young, indicates Calvary, where Our Saviour shed the last drop of His blood for us. The sparrow flying heavenward recalls the ascension of Our Saviour when He gloriously ascended from this earth to heaven. Let us frequently retire in this way to contemplate Our Saviour under these various circumstances. Blessed Elzear, Count of Provence, having been long absent from his devout and chaste Delphina, she sent a special express to him, to inquire after his health, by whom he returned this answer: "I am very well, my dear spouse, but if you desire to see me, seek me in the wound of the side of our dear Saviour, for it is there only that I dwell; there will you find me; if you seek me elsewhere, you will seek in vain." This was a Christian nobleman indeed.

CHAPTER XIX.

OF ASPIRATIONS, EJACULATORY PRAYERS, AND GOOD THOUGHTS.[1]

WE retire into God because we aspire to Him; and we aspire to Him that we may retire into Him: so that aspirations to God and spiritual retirement are the mutual support of each other, and both proceed from the same source,—viz., devout and pious thoughts.

Make then, Philothea, frequent aspirations to God by short but fervent elevations of your heart. Admire the infinite excellence of His perfections; implore the assistance of His power; cast yourself in spirit at the foot of Jesus crucified; adore His goodness; converse with Him frequently on the affairs of your salvation; present your soul to Him a thousand times a day; contemplate His clemency and His sweetness; stretch out your hand to Him, as a little child to his father, that He may conduct you; place Him in your bosom, like a fragrant nosegay; plant Him in your soul, as the standard under which you will fight the enemy; rouse and appeal to your heart in innumerable ways, to enkindle and excite in it a passionate and tender

[1] "Introduction to a Devout Life," Book II., ch. xiii.

affection for your Spouse. Ejaculatory prayer was strenuously recommended by the great St. Austin to the devout Lady Proba. And, Philothea, if we accustom our soul to treat familiarly with God in this way, it will be altogether perfumed with His perfections. Now there is no difficulty in this exercise, as it is neither difficult nor incompatible with other occupations, since in these spiritual and interior aspirations we only make short deviations which, instead of preventing, rather assist us in the pursuit of the object we have in view. The pilgrim, though he stops to take a little wine to refresh himself, interrupts not his journey by doing so, but, on the contrary, acquires new strength to finish it with more ease and expedition, resting only that he may afterwards proceed the faster.

Many have collected a store of vocal aspirations, which may be very profitable; but I would advise you not to confine yourself to any set form of words, but to pronounce, either with your heart or your lips, such as love spontaneously suggests; for it will furnish you with all that you can desire. It is true there are certain words which have a peculiar force to satisfy the heart in this respect, such as the aspirations interspersed so copiously throughout the psalms of David; the frequent invocations of the name of Jesus; the ejaculations of love expressed in the Canticles, etc. Spiritual hymns will also answer the same purpose when sung with attention.

They who love with a human and natural affection have their hearts and thoughts incessantly engaged by the object of their passion, and their lips continually chant its praise. When absent they lose no opportunity of testifying their affection by letter, and meet not a tree on the bark of which they do not inscribe the name of their beloved. In like manner, such as truly love God can never cease to think of Him; they live and breathe only for Him; their only thought is the pleasure of loving Him; His praise is ever on their lips, and, were it possible, they would engrave the sacred name of Jesus on the breast of all mankind.

To this all things invite them, as there is no creature that does not declare to them the praises of their beloved; and, as St. Austin says, after St. Antony, everything in the world speaks to them in a silent yet very intelligible language in favor of their love. All things excite them to good thoughts, which give birth to many animated notions and aspirations of the soul to God. Behold some examples:

St. Gregory Nazianzen, walking on the sea-shore, observed how the waves, advancing upon the beach, left behind them shells, little periwinkles, stalks of weeds, small oysters, and the like, which the sea had cast upon the shore, and then, returning with other waves, took part of them back, and swallowed them up again, while the adjoining rocks continued firm and immovable, though the billows beat against them with so much violence. Upon which he made this salutary reflection: that feeble souls, like shells and stalks of weeds, suffer themselves to be borne away sometimes by affliction, and at other times by consolation, at the mercy of the inconstant billows of fortune; but that courageous souls continue firm and unmoved under all kinds of storms; and from this thought he proceeded to those aspirations of David (Ps. lxviii.): "Save me, O God : for the waters are come in even unto my soul. O Lord ! deliver me out of these deep waters. I am come into the depth of the sea: and a tempest hath overwhelmed me." At that time he was in affliction for the unhappy usurpation of his bishopric attempted by Maximus.

St. Fulgentius, Bishop of Ruspa, being present at a general assembly of the Roman nobility, when Theodoric of the Goths made an oration to them, and beholding the splendor of many great lords, ranked each according to his quality, exclaimed: "O God, how glorious and beautiful must the heavenly Jerusalem be, since earthly Rome appears in so much pomp! For if in this world the lovers of vanity be permitted to shine so bright, what must that glory be which is reserved in the next world for the lovers and contemplators of truth !"

St. Anselm, Archbishop of Canterbury, by whose birth our mountains have been highly honored, was admirable in the application of good thoughts. As this holy prelate was proceeding on a journey, a hare pursued by hounds ran under his horse, as to a place of refuge, suggested by the imminent danger of death ; whilst the hounds, barking around, durst not attempt to violate the sanctuary to which their prey had recourse. A sight so very extraordinary made the whole company burst into laughter ; but the saint, weeping and sighing, cried out : "Alas ! you laugh, but the poor beast does not laugh; the enemies of the soul, after hunting and driving it on, through various turnings and windings, into every kind of sin, lie in wait for it at the narrow passage of death, to catch and devour it; but the soul, being terrified, looks for succor and refuge on every side; and if it find none, its enemies mock and deride it." When the saint had thus spoken, he rode on, sighing.

Constantine the Great wrote with great respect to St. Antony; at which the religious about him being greatly surprised, the saint said: "Why are you astonished that a king should write to a man? Be astonished rather that the eternal God has written His law to mortal men; nay more, has spoken to them by word of mouth in the person of His Son."

St. Francis, seeing a sheep alone amidst a flock of goats, said to those about him: "Observe the poor sheep, how mild it is amidst the goats; our blessed Lord walked thus meekly and humbly among the Pharisees." At another time seeing a lamb devoured by a hog, he exclaimed in tears: "Ah! little lamb, how vividly dost thou represent the death of my Saviour!"

The illustrious St. Francis Borgia, while yet Duke of Gandia, frequently recreated himself at the chase, during which amusement he was accustomed to make a thousand devout reflections. "I admired," said he afterwards, "how the falcons come to hand, suffer themselves to be hooded and to be tied to the perch; and yet men are so rebellious to the voice of God."

The great St. Basil said that the rose in the

midst of thorns makes this remonstrance to men: "That which is most agreeable in this world, O ye mortals! is mingled with sorrow; nothing here is pure; regret always follows mirth; widowhood, marriage; care, fruitfulness; and ignominy, glory. Expense follows honor; loathing comes after delight; and sickness after health." "The rose is a fair flower," said this holy man, "yet it makes me sorrowful, reminding me of my sin, for which the earth has been condemned to bring forth thorns."

A devout soul standing over a brook on a very clear night, and seeing the heavens and stars therein represented, exclaimed, "O my God! these very stars which I now behold shall be one day beneath my feet, when Thou shalt have lodged me in Thy celestial tabernacles; and as the stars of heaven are here represented, even so are the men of this earth represented in the living fountain of divine charity." Another, seeing a river flowing swiftly along, cried out, "My soul shall never be at rest till she be swallowed up in the sea of the divinity, her original source." St. Francisca, contemplating a pleasant brook, upon the bank of which she was kneeling in prayer, being rapt in ecstasy, often repeated these words: "The grace of my God flows thus gently and sweetly like this little stream." Another, looking on the trees in bloom, sighed and said: "Ah! why am I alone without blossom in the garden of the Church?" Another, seeing little chickens gathered together under the hen, said: "Preserve us, O Lord, continually under the shadow of Thy wing." Another, looking upon the flower called heliotrope, which turns to the sun, exclaimed: "When shall the time come, O my God! that my soul shall faithfully follow the attractions of Thy goodness?" And seeing the flowers called pansies, which are beautiful but without fragrance, he said, "Ah! such are my conceptions, fair in appearance, but of no effect, producing nothing."

Behold, Philothea! how one may extract good thoughts and holy aspirations from everything that presents itself amidst the variety of this mortal life.

Unhappy they who withdraw creatures from their Creator, to make them the instruments of sin; and thrice happy they that turn creatures to the glory of their Creator and employ them to the honor of His sovereign majesty, as St. Gregory Nazianzen says: "I am wont to refer all things to my spiritual profit." Read the devout epitaph of St. Paula, composed by St. Jerome; how agreeable to behold it interspersed with those aspirations and holy thoughts which she was accustomed to draw from occurrences of every nature!

Now as the great work of devotion consists in the exercise of spiritual recollection and ejaculatory prayers, the want of all other prayers may be supplied by them; but the loss of these can scarcely be repaired by any other means. Without them we cannot lead a good active life, much less a contemplative one. Without them repose would be but idleness and labor vexation. Wherefore I conjure you to embrace this exercise with your whole heart, without ever desisting from its practice.

CHAPTER XX.

ST. FRANCIS DE SALES' MANNER OF PERFORMING HIS ACTIONS.[1]

I AM reliably informed that St. Francis de Sales, in the performance of exterior duties, represented to himself similar actions in the life of our perfect model, Jesus Christ. In conferring Holy Orders he beheld Our Lord consecrating priests and apostles. When he administered the sacraments, he thanked Him for instituting them, and for the great benefit the faithful derived from them. When he visited the sick he represented to himself Our Saviour visiting the mother-in-law of Peter and the daughter of the prince of the synagogue. When he conversed with companions, he remembered that Our Saviour repulsed no one. When present at any social gathering, he contemplated Him at the marriage-feast of Cana in Galilee. When he found himself alone, he recalled Our Lord's solitude in the desert. When suffering under persecution, he contemplated Him forced to fly from the persecution of Herod. When he honored his parents, he thanked God for deigning to be subject to Mary and Joseph. In

---
[1] P. de la Rivière, S.J.

times of joy he adored Him on Mount Tabor. In times of suffering and spiritual dryness he contemplated Him on the cross on Calvary.

In a word, whatever he did, whatever befell him, he kept his thoughts fixed upon his tender Redeemer, from whom he learned innumerable wise things and pious sentiments.

Part Second.

THE INTERIOR LIFE.

"The presence of God which sanctifies our souls is that indwelling of the Trinity which penetrates to the depths of our hearts when they are submissive to the divine will; for the presence of God which we enjoy through the exercise of contemplation effects this intimate union in us only as do all other things which come to us in the order of God. It holds, however, the first rank among them, for it is the most excellent means of uniting one's self with God when He wills that we should use it." ("Abandonment to Divine Providence.")

"Our life may be estimated by our prayer, and our prayer by our mortification." (P. Crasset.)

"To place ourselves in the presence of God, it is necessary that we make some effort, or that God Himself attract us; but to remain in it requires neither effort on our part nor attraction on the part of God. If we simply stay where He is pleased to have us, and because He is pleased to have us there, we remain in His presence." (St. Francis de Sales.)

FIRST TREATISE.

THE SOURCES OF OUR IMPERFECTIONS AND THEIR REMEDIES.[1]

There are four general sources of our imperfections which require to be carefully considered.

I. *Forgetfulness of the End.*—The first is that we think not at all, or very little, of the end of our creation and our vocation. We live as if we were placed in this world only to live, and not to serve God and save our souls.

We are satisfied with taking good resolutions and writing good purposes. Paradise is not obtained by desires, but by deeds.

Remedy for this Forgetfulness.—To remedy this disorder, frequently consider whence you come and whither you are going. You come from God, and you are going to God. A traveller always keeps his destination before him. A marksman keeps his eyes fixed on the target. Let the eyes of your soul be always fixed upon your end, and frequently ask yourself, What have I come into this world to do? What have I come into religion to do? Is it to pass away time or to employ it well?

II. *Neglect of the Means.*—The second source of our imperfections and our infidelities is that,

[1] P. Crasset, S.J.

though we think of our end and desire to attain it, we do not take the necessary means. It is by means of our actions that we become perfect and that we gain heaven. Now a good action requires to be not only beautiful and regular in appearance, but must be good interiorly; that is, it must be actuated by a pure, upright, disinterested intention; it must be animated by an interior spirit, which is to the action what the soul is to the body. Our life is such as our actions, and the perfection of our life depends on the perfection of our actions.

Remedy for this Neglect.—To correct this fault accustom yourself to perform your actions through a virtuous motive, with an upright, pure, and holy intention, with all the application of your mind, and all the affection of your heart, as if each action were the last of your life, reflecting that God's eyes are fixed upon you, and that He awaits this service from you. Frequently bring to mind the following thoughts, which will help you to perform them well: that God wills you to contribute to His glory by this action; that He contemplates this action; that He attaches a special grace to this action; that by this action He will recognize whether you love Him; that you are rendering Him a service by performing this action well.

That His wisdom has regulated this action from all eternity.

That His infinite greatness ennobles this action.

That His adorable sanctity consecrates this action.

That His sovereign will ordains this action.

That you satisfy His love by performing this action well.

That your peace of heart depends on this action.

That your merit is contained in this action.

That you will offend God if you fail to perform this action.

That you will be deprived of the grace which ought to follow this action.

That your salvation, perhaps, depends on this action.

That you should, therefore, think only of performing this action well.

III. *Want of Recollection.*—The third source of our imperfections is want of recollection and of attention to ourselves. We are pleased to converse and to remain with those we love. The heart flies to the place of its treasure and thinks only of what it desires. If we love God we shall think unceasingly of Him and willingly remain in His company. And as He is in the depth of our souls, if we love Him our hearts will never go abroad, or will return at once if they chance to wander. But alas! we must needs go abroad for we find nothing in our interior which pleases us, hence we are always abroad seeking consolation of creatures. A dissipated soul is like the wandering sheep, which is eventually devoured by the wolf.

Remedy for this Third Fault: a Spirit of Prayer.— To avoid this misfortune, keep yourself always in the presence of God, and preserve a spirit of recollection in all your exterior occupations. Let your soul walk after the manner of your body, keeping one foot firm and motionless while the other advances; when your mind labors, let your heart be in repose and remain motionless in its centre, which is the will of God, from which it should never deviate.

Before beginning an action always see whether it is in order, whether it is pleasing to God, whether it is for Him you do it, and then ask His blessing.

During the action raise your mind from time to time to God, renew the purity of your intention; do not let your heart be wholly absorbed by the work or marred by natural satisfaction. Restrain the ardor of passion, which seeks to penetrate all actions, and if it must accompany you, let it not precede, but follow reason; let it not rule as master, but obey as a slave. You will know that you are performing an action for God, if you readily abandon it when necessary, and suffer interruption with patience.

After you have accomplished the action, return to the solitude of your heart and rest a brief moment on the breast of Our Lord before passing on to another. Do not imagine that you have lost the presence of God because you have been a few moments without thinking of Him; it is not possible in this life for the mind to be always occupied with God, and this thought might even divert you from your work. But the heart should never depart for a moment from its love and its obedience.

Bear this well in mind, that you are in the presence of God as long as you do His will, and that you are thinking of Him when you are thinking of acquitting yourself faithfully of the duties He has imposed upon you. He wishes you to discharge your duties faithfully, which you cannot do unless you apply all your mind to them. For this reason, if the thought of God prevented me from applying my mind to this present writing, I should be obliged to reject it as a distraction. Therefore do not imagine that you have wandered from the presence of God, or that God has withdrawn from you, because you have not thought of Him for a time; if you have done His will, you have continued in His presence, and you will lose it only when you do something contrary to His will. You are united in heart and mind to God when you apply yourself to doing well what He wills, and your intention is such that if you were asked for whom you were doing this action, you could at once reply, for God, to obey Him and to please Him. Remember that you are only as distracted as you will to be; if you have not wished to be distracted, you have not been.

IV. *Want of Mortification.*—The fourth and principal source of our imperfections, to omit all the others which would make these reflections too long, is that we are fond of the pleasant things of life and have a horror of mortification.

Within us we have self-love, which always seeks sensible pleasure; without us, the Evil One, who tempts us; the world, which attracts us; objects which flatter us; occasions which encompass us. Therefore if we are not always on our guard and if we do not close the doors of our senses to all these enemies, they will soon become masters of our hearts.

There is a strange opposition between the soul and the body, between the spirit and the flesh, between grace and nature. That which strengthens one weakens the other; that which gives life to one is death to the other. Therefore, to preserve the life of grace, we must never cease to mortify the inclinations of nature.

It is not sufficient to mortify ourselves for a time and in one thing; we must, if possible, mortify ourselves in everything and at all times, with prudence and discretion. One untimely indulgence makes nature more proud and insolent than a hundred victories weaken it. A clock must be wound regularly, a garden must always be cultivated, the hands must be constantly washed, the hair must be constantly combed. If you cease for a time to mortify your passions you will no longer find anything in your soul. "My brethren," says St. Bernard, "that which is cut down springs up again, that which is extinguished rekindles, that which sleeps wakens again." To preserve the interior spirit of devotion, we must prevent the soul from diffusing itself abroad, by closing to it the doors of the senses, by encompassing it, as the Prophet says, with a hedge of thorns. We rouse nature instead of subduing it. All our efforts tend to strengthen it instead of to weaken it. This is too inconvenient, we protest; this devotion is too severe, it interferes with my health, it would make me lose my mind. It does not suit me. I could not live in that way. Then acknowledge that you are not a reasonable man; that you are not a Christian; that you are not one of the elect; to be predestined one must resemble Jesus Christ, walk in His footsteps, and imitate His example. Acknowledge, further, that you have not the spirit of Jesus Christ, since you obey the flesh, which continually wars against it. Acknowledge, finally, that you renounce the crown of paradise, since it is only for those who have fought the flesh and mortified themselves.

O Christian soul, did you come into this world to live as the beasts? Where will you be placed in paradise? In what rank? In what order? Among the martyrs covered with wounds? Among the confessors exhausted with penance? There is no saint that has not crucified his flesh with its vices; and you, cowardly deserter of the cross, you ease-loving, effeminate soul, you would dare to take your place among these valiant warriors, these noble conquerors who spent their lives in combat and won innumerable victories?

Remedy for this Fourth Fault: a Spirit of Mortification.—The remedy for all these disorders is to persuade yourself that, having come into this world only to save your soul, and into religion only to sanctify yourself, you are obliged, whether in one or the other, to practise mortification; since without mortification and without that holy hatred of yourself, you can be neither a Christian nor a saint, nor can you attain either perfection or happiness.

Begin then to cause Jesus Christ to live and reign in you by the mortification of your passions.

Die to the life of the senses by refusing them all that they desire contrary to the commands of God and the dictates of reason. Mortify your tongue, never speaking in anger, or in the time of silence, or when you have a great desire to speak. Mortify your eyes by keeping them cast down and by refraining from curious glances. Mortify your ears by closing them to vain discourses, idle words, uncharitable, frivolous, or dangerous conversations. Mortify your flesh by granting it only what is purely necessary, unless reason or obedience dictate otherwise. As a rule, deny yourself anything that you passionately desire; and, in return for the sacrifice, God will flood your soul with the torrent of His delights, and overwhelm you with ineffable consolations. **Taste and see that the Lord is sweet.**

SECOND TREATISE.

MORTIFICATION.

I. TRUE IDEA OF MORTIFICATION.[1]

The true idea of mortification is, that it is the love of Jesus, urged into that shape partly in imitation of Him, partly to express its own vehemence, and partly to secure by an instinct of self-preservation its own perseverance. There can be no true or enduring love without it, for a certain amount of it is requisite in order to avoid sin and keep the commandments. Neither without it is there any respectable perseverance in the spiritual life. The rest which forms part of the normal state of the spiritual life is not safe without it, because of the propension of nature to seek repose in natural ways when supernatural are no longer open to it. Mortification is both interior and exterior, and of course the superior excellence of the interior is beyond question. But if there is one doctrine more important than another on this subject, it is that there can be no interior mortification without exterior; and this last must come first. In a word, to be spiritual, bodily mortification is indispensable.

[1] "Growth in Holiness."

II. NECESSITY OF MORTIFICATION.

Some have spoken as if bodily mortification were less necessary in modern times than it was before, and consequently that the recommendations of spiritual writers under this head are to be taken with considerable abatement. If this means that a less degree of mortification is necessary for holiness now than was necessary for past ages of the Church, nothing can be more untrue, and it comes up to the verge of condemned propositions. If it means that increased valetudinarianism and the universality of nervous diseases, combined with other causes, discreetly point to a change in the kind of mortifications, the proposition may be assented to, with jealousy, however, and wary limitations. The Lenten Indults of the Church may be taken as an illustration.

But this false doctrine is so deep in the minds of many that it is necessary to combat it before we proceed further. The degree of mortification and its idea must remain the same in all ages of the Church, for penance is an abiding mark of the Church. To do penance because the kingdom of heaven is at hand is the work of a justified soul. To get grace, to keep it, and to multiply it, penance is necessary at every step. And when we say that holiness is a note of the Catholic Church, we show forth the necessity of mortification; for the one implies the other, the first the last. The heroic exercise of penance must be proved to the satisfaction of the Church before she will proceed to the canonization of a saint; and the quite recent beatifications of Paul of the Cross and Marianna of Gesú show how completely unaltered the mind of the Church remains on this point. Marianna's life is nothing but one unbroken series of the most startling austerities, which make us shudder from the inventive cruelty which they display. The life of St. Rose of Lima, by the side of those American virgins, looks soft, comfortable, and easy. It seems as if Paul were raised up to alarm the stagnant eighteenth century, and to renew before the eyes of men the austerities of St. Benedict, St. Bruno, St. Romuald, or St. Peter Damian. He reanimated the old severe monastic spirit, in contempt of all modern usages and mitigations, and for a hundred years his children have trodden in their father's steps with undecaying fervor. The existence and primitive vigor of the austere Passionists is one of the greatest consolations of the Church in these effeminate days.

We must remember also that, according to the teaching of Scripture, it is quite a mistake to regard, as some unthinkingly do, the practice of mortification as a counsel of perfection and a work of supererogation.

When carried to a certain degree, or when expressed in certain ways, it is doubtless so. But mortification in itself, and to a certain degree, and under given circumstances, is of precept and necessary to salvation. This is not only true of the self-inflicted pains which are sometimes of obligation in order to overcome vehement temptations, or of those various mortifications which are needful too in order to avoid sin; but a definite amount of fasting and abstinence, irrespective of the temptations or circumstances of individuals, is imposed by the Church on all her children under pain of eternal damnation. This expresses the idea of penance for its own sake, and the necessity of it, as one of the functions of the Church, as a soul-saving institute. When, therefore, men say that they do not practise mortification, but leave it to those who wish to be saints, they may, on being questioned, show that they are sound in doctrine and do not mean the error which their words, strictly taken, imply; but we may be sure that the very use of such loose language is a proof that a real error about mortification is deeply imbedded in their minds.

Indeed, modern luxury and effeminacy, which are often pleaded as arguments for an abatement of mortification, may just as well be called forward to maintain the opposite view; for if it be a special office of the Church to bear witness against the world, her witness must especially be borne against the reigning vices of the world, and therefore in these days against effeminacy, the worship of comfort, and the extravagances of luxury.

If the Church has to witness always against the reigning vices of the world, each soul has likewise, if not to witness, at least to defend itself against them. And how shall it defend itself against the worship of bodily comforts except by depriving itself of them? Changeable as the world is, it is unchanging too. The world, the flesh, and the devil are practically the same in all ages; and so, practically, mortification has the same offices to perform. Whether we consider the soul in the struggles of its conversion, in the progress of its illumination, or in its variously perfected degrees of its union with God, we shall find that bodily mortifications have their own place, and their proper work to do, and are literally indispensable.

III. REPLY TO VARIOUS OBJECTIONS.

But let us look for a moment at the various objections urged against this. First, we are told that the health of the world is not what it was, and if there is an equal or even greater longevity, the normal state of health is more uniformly valetudinarian, and that if inflammatory attacks are less frequent, nervous complaints, on the other hand, are more prevalent, and that the relaxation of Church discipline on the subject shows her appreciation of these facts. All this is true, and doubtless many most important deductions are to be drawn from it. Still I maintain it is more concerned with the kind of mortification than the degree. The conduct of the Church in the mitigation of fasting is as wise as the conduct of Leo XII. was marked with the usual practical sagacity of the Holy See, when he caused the possibilities of the old observance of Lent to be medically investigated. Moreover, the plea of health, while it is always to be listened to, is to be listened to with suspicion. We must always be jealous of the side on which nature and self are serving as volunteers. Great, then, as we must admit the consequences of a state of valetudinarianism to be on the spiritual life, a general and plenary dispensation from corporal austerities is not one of them; and we must remember also that our forefathers, who troubled their heads little enough about their nerves, and had no tea to drink, were accustomed to hear from Father Baker, who only gave utterance to the old mystical tradition, that a state of robust health was positively a disqualification for the higher stages of the spiritual life.

A second objection, and one sometimes urged in behalf of priests and religious, is that modern hard work is a substitute for ancient penance. The fewness of the clergy and the multitude of souls have certainly brought upon the ecclesiastics of this generation an overwhelming pressure of work; and it is true of them, as it has always been of religious orders engaged in the apostolate, that the measure of bodily austerity to be expected of them is very different from that which we expect from contemplatives and solitaries. I do not say, therefore, that this objection expresses no truth, but only that it will not bear all the weight men put upon it. Certain kinds of penance are incompatible with hard work; while at the same time the excessive exterior propensities which hard work gives us are so perilous to the soul that certain other kinds of penance are all the more necessary to correct this disturbing force. All great missionaries, Segneri and Pinamonti, Leonard of Port Maurice and Paul of the Cross, have worn instruments of penance. The penalties of life, as Da Ponte calls them, are doubtless an excellent penance when endured with an interior spirit, and worth far more than a hundred self-inflicted pains.

Yet he who maintains that the endurance of the former is a dispensation from the infliction of the latter will find himself out of harmony with the whole stream of approved spiritual teaching in the Church; and the brevity of his perseverance in the interior life will soon show both himself and others the completeness of his delusion. Without bodily penance, zealous apostolic work hardens the heart far more than it sanctifies it.

A third class of objectors tells us to be content with the trials God sends us, which are neither few nor light. If they told us that the gay suffering and graceful welcome of these dispensations were of infinitely greater price than the sting of the discipline or the twinge of the catenella, most true and most important would the lesson be, and to many a hot-headed spiritual suckling quite indispensable. Youth, when it is strong and well, full of fervor and bathing in devotional sweetness, finds almost a physical pleasure in tormenting its flesh and pinching its redundant health. There is little merit in this, as there is little difficulty and less discretion. And at all times one blow from God is worth a million from ourselves. But the objectors fall into that mistake of exaggeration which runs through so many spiritual books. Because A is more important than B they jump to the conclusion that B is of no importance at all. Because the mortifications which God sends us are more efficacious and less delusive, if rightly taken, than the mortifications we inflict upon ourselves, it does not follow but that these last are not only an important, but even an indispensable element in the spiritual life. We may answer them briefly as follows. Yes, the best of all penances is to take in the spirit of interior compunction the mortifications which the wise and affectionate course of God's fatherly providence brings upon us, but unless we have practised ourselves in the generous habit of voluntary penances, the chances are very much against our forming this interior spirit of penance, and therefore of getting the full profit out of the involuntary trials God sends us.

Besides these objections there is another latent in many minds which should be noticed. Our present habits of life and thought lead to an obvious want of sympathy with contemplation. It has no results on which we can look complacently, or which we can parade boastfully. Everything seems wasted which is not visible; and all is disappointment which is not plain success. It is supernatural principles especially which are at a discount in modern days. Now it is easy to see how this want of sympathy with contemplation leads to a misappreciation of austerity. They are content with each other, and both enter deeply into the region of supernatural operations. To think lightly of either is to be out of harmony with the mind of the Church, and to injure our own soul, whatever may be its vocation, by narrowing the range of its supernatural vision.

From all these considerations it may warrantably be concluded that there is nothing in modern times to dispense us either from the obligation or counsel of bodily mortification; that, on the contrary, there is much in modern habits to enforce the obligation and to urge the counsel, and that all the modifications to which the actual circumstances of modern life point concern themselves wholly with the kind of mortification and not at all with the degree.

IV. BENEFITS AND ADVANTAGES OF MORTIFICATION.

Something remains to be said on the uses of mortification. These are ten in number, and all of them deserving a serious consideration. Its first use is to tame the body and bring its rebellious passions under the control of grace and of our superior will. Full half the obstacles to a spiritual life are from the body and the treacherous succor which its senses give to our baser passions. These must be, I do not say altogether removed, but effectually crippled, before we can hope to make much progress. We never find in any one a real earnestness of mind or seriousness of spirit where honest attempts are not being made to keep the body in subjection. The reason why men are religious under sorrow and not at other times is that they do not practise bodily mortification, whereas sorrow afflicts and rebukes the flesh, and so for the time performs the functions of mortification. Sorrow acts on the soul through the body as much as through the mind.

The second use is to increase the range of our spiritual vision. Sensitiveness of conscience is one of the greatest gifts which God gives us in order to a spiritual life. The things of God, says the Apostle, can only be spiritually discerned. The process of our purification by grace depends on our increasing clearness of vision as to what is faulty and imperfect. From the discernment of mortal sin we come to that of venial sin, from venial sin to imperfections, from imperfections to less perfect ways of doing perfect things, and from that to a delicate perception of the almost invisible infidelities which grieve the Holy Spirit within us. And if bodily mortification is not the sole means by which this sensitiveness of conscience is obtained, it is one of the chief, as well from its own intrinsic method of operation, as from its power to impetrate the gift from God.

This brings me to the third use of mortifications of all kinds, which is to obtain power with God. Suffering easily becomes power in the things of God. The price He sets upon it is shown by the fact that the world was redeemed by suffering, and that suffering gives their palm to the martyrs and their crown to the confessors. The gift of miracles followed hard upon austerity. When we complain that we have no power with God, that our prayers remain unanswered, that our efforts to root out some besetting sin are unavailing, and that we give way to temptations and to surprises of temper or loquacity, it is for the most part because we are not leading mortified lives. It is in this that mortification so amply repays us for the pain it gives. For not only is it an immense gain to have power with God, but the obvious connection between the mortification and the power enables us not so much to believe in supernatural things as to handle them with our very hands and feel their weight. Indeed, even a temptation may come from this. If, then, for the sake of our own spiritual growth and the interest we feel in the glory of God, the triumph of faith, and the salvation of souls near and dear to us, we desire to obtain power with God, we must habitually and constantly practise mortification.

Its fourth use is to intensify our love. It is of the nature of love to thrive on no food so well as on the evidence of its own vigor; and nothing testifies to us so surely our love of God as the infliction of voluntary austerities upon ourselves; and while it manifests our love it augments it also. Pain, too, of itself prepares the heart for the emotions of love by softening it and making it childlike. And where the object loved and contemplated is of sorrow and suffering, as Jesus is, love impels us more or less vehemently to imitation. Do we complain that our love of our dear Lord is slackening? Forthwith let us mortify ourselves in something, and the smouldering embers will break into a bright flame. As sure as power follows mortification, so also does love.

Its fifth use is to make us unworldly, and to inundate us with spiritual joy. Nothing is in itself so unworldly as mortification, because it is the killing of everything that the world most prizes and cherishes. It breaks off all the inordinate attachments to creatures which we may have formed, and it hinders us from embarrassing ourselves with new ties; for mortification is found by experience to be so difficult that we dread to increase the breadth of the region over which we are compelled to extend it. And what is each new attachment but a fresh horde of savages to be brought painfully beneath control? As to spiritual joy, it flows like a tide into some empty place. In proportion, therefore, as our hearts are void of earthly attachments,—and an attachment may be defined to be an affection which is not duty,—in the same proportion are they capable of enjoying the sweetness of God. Hence it is that mortified persons, when discreet, are always mirthful. The heart is lightened, because the burden of the body is taken off it. Nothing can make us unworldly but mortification. Have we never seen persons clouded round with sorrow so deep and dark that we approached it reverently as we would a sanctuary, and yet it has not made the sufferer unworldly? That blessed office is the monopoly of mortification.

Its sixth use is to hinder our making a great mistake, which is leaving the *via purgativa* too soon. This is perhaps the chiefest danger in the whole of the spiritual life. Many try to go so fast when they first begin, that they lose their breath and give up the race altogether; and even if they do not, they cannot leave behind what they wish to leave before the appointed time. They are like men running wildly to outstrip their own shadow. It cannot be. Nature wants to be out of her novitiate. Meditation would fain be thrust up into affective prayer, and the captivity of little things longs to expatiate in liberty of spirit. The bruised flesh asks to be let alone, and interior mortification requests to be allowed its primitive vagueness, and to remain undefined. Weekly communion gravitates to daily, and the soul, a little tired of looking after itself, inclines to convert the world. If there is difficult navigation anywhere in the spiritual life, it is here. See! the reefs are strewn with wrecks, and the waves wash up at every tide the bodies of half-made saints, of broken heroes and frustrated vocations. No harm comes of keeping long in the lower parts of the spiritual life. All possible evil may come of mounting too quickly. An evil when it is mortified first looks dead. It feigns death as beetles do. If it succeeds in deceiving us, and we pass on, we shall rue it bitterly. It is only the old story: look well to your foundations, dig them deep, and build broad, and plan your building magnificently large, as if you were a prince. Mortification, of all things, helps us to do this. Its difficulty brings out our weakness. One while clumsy, another while cowardly, we are content to be kept down, when daily failures are telling us what would happen on the giddy heights above us. But how long shall the *via purgativa* last? Who can tell? It depends upon fervor. Anyhow, we must count it by years, not by months.

The seventh use of mortification is to be found in its connection with prayer. How many complaints are we daily hearing of the difficulties of mental prayer! If we do not mortify ourselves, why complain? Listen to this vision which Da Ponte relates as having happened to a person whom he knew. He gives it at length in the third tract of his "Spiritual Guide." God showed this person the state of a tepid and idle soul, which is given to prayer without mortification. She saw in the middle of a wide plain a very deep and strong foundation, white as ivory, about which a fair, ruddy youth of admirable beauty was walking. He called her to him, and said: "I am the son of a powerful king, and I have laid this foundation that I might build a palace for you to dwell in, and to receive me whenever I come to visit you, which I shall do frequently, provided you always have a room ready for me, and open as soon as I knock. In time, however, I shall come and live entirely with you, and you will be delighted to have me for a daily guest. Judge, however, from the magnitude of this foundation what the edifice is to be. Meanwhile I will build, and you must bring me all the materials." The lady began to be sore amazed and afflicted, for she deemed it impossible that she should of herself bring all the requisite materials. The young man, however, said: "Do not be afraid; you will be quite able to do it. Begin to bring something at once, and I will help you." So she began to look about for something, but presently stopped and fixed her eyes on the young man, whose beauty delighted and refreshed her. Yet she took no pains to please him. She feared him very much when she saw that he was watching her. Nevertheless, she did not blush at her disobedience. While she was thus loitering, she saw that the foundation was being gradually covered with dust and straws by the wind, and sometimes such whirlwinds of dust arose that she could not see the foundation at all. Sometimes floods of rain covered the whole with mud, which gradually spread over them, and caused a rank vegetation of weeds to sprout up. At last nothing of the foundation remained but the spot which the young man's feet covered, and at last a sudden whirlwind covered him, and the foundation disappeared from her sight beneath a heap of filth. The lady was very much afflicted to find herself alone, especially as she was soon surrounded by ruinous heaps of lime, sand, and stone. She bewailed her tepidity and idleness; but believing that the young man was still hidden in some of the cavities of the foundation, she cried out in a loud voice: "Sir, I am coming; I am bringing materials; I pray you come forth to the building; for I am deeply penitent for my sloth and delay." While she was in these dispositions, the vision was thus interpreted to her: The foundation signifies faith and the habits of other virtues which Christ infuses into the soul at Baptism, desiring to build upon them a fair edifice of lofty perfection, provided the soul cooperates with Him by bringing the necessary materials, observance of the divine precepts and counsels, which by aid of the same Lord it can do. But the soul is often so delighted with meditating on the mysteries of Christ that it becomes tepid and idle in the imitation and obedience of Him, and through this inattention and slovenliness the habits of virtue are gradually obscured by venial sin, and the eyes of the soul so dimmed that they cannot see Our Lord. In punishment of this sloth He sometimes allows the soul to fall into a mortal sin, which stains and destroys everything. Then, by the mercy of God, it repents, finds the stones of contrition, the lime of confession, and the sands of satisfaction all round it, and calls on Jesus with a loud voice to pardon the sin and to begin the building for the second time.

The eighth use of mortification is to give depth and strength to our sanctity, just as gymnastic exercises give us muscle and play of strength. This is connected with what was said a while ago of not trying to get out of the *via purgativa* too quickly. When Simeon Stylites first began to stand upon his column, so Theodoret tells us, he heard a voice in his sleep which said, Arise and dig! He seemed to dig for a time, and then ceased, when the voice said to him, Dig deeper! Four times he dug, four times he rested, and four times the voice cried, Dig deeper! After that it said, Now build without toil! There can be no doubt but that the digging was the humbling toil of mortification. There is such a thing as a thin, meagre piety, a religious sentimentality which cannot go beyond the beauty of taste or the pathos of a ceremonial, a devotion for the sunshine but not for the storm; and the fault of the lank, crazy edifice that is raised by it is the absence of mortification in its original construction.

The ninth use of mortification concerns bodily austerities. Without exterior mortification it is idle to expect that we shall ever attain the higher grace of interior mortification. It is the greatest of delusions to suppose that we can mortify judgment and will, if we do not mortify our body also. Interior mortification is certainly the higher; yet in some sense exterior is harder. It is harder because it comes first, and has to be exercised when we have as yet scarcely any empire over ourselves. It is harder because it is more sensible. It is harder because our victories are at best mean to look at, and our defeats palpable and discouraging. It is harder because habit helps us less. If our bodily penances are rare, each one has the difficulties of a new beginning. If they are frequent, they fall on unhealed wounds. Whereas with interior mortification the victories always look dignified, the defeats are surrounded by such a host of extenuating circumstances as veil their disgrace. We must remember that throughout our spiritual life we have our body for our companion, and none but a very few privileged saints have ever quite subdued it. Moreover, body has to be saved as well as soul, and so it is not true that, in devotion, exterior things are only a means to interior. They have, besides that instrumental character, an import and significancy of their own. There have always been two classes of heresies with regard to spiritual theology; and I cannot think of one heresy which has not come either from a disunion of the interior and the exterior, or a dwelling on one of them to the neglect and depression of the other. I tremble when people speak much of interior mortification; it sounds like a confession that they are leading comfortable lives. On the other hand, when men exaggerate the importance of bodily austerities, the chances are that they do not practise them at all, or that, practising them, they rest in them with complacency, and so are fakirs, not Christians, having no spiritual life which can deserve the name.

The tenth and last use of mortification is, that it is a most excellent school for the queenly virtue of discretion. The truly mortified man will as little think of not listening to discretion as he would think of listening to cowardice. Discretion is a habit of hitting the mark, and there must be a supernatural truth in the eye and a supernatural steadiness in the hand in order to attain this. Mortification is the grand subject-matter of these trials of discretion; and the virtue will show itself in obedience, humility, self-distrust, perseverance, and detachment from penances themselves. This was the trial to which the bishops put Simeon Stylites. They sent a messenger to bid him come down from his pillar. If he hesitated they would know his extraordinary vocation was not from God. But the words were hardly out of the messenger's mouth than he put one foot down from his column. In his docility they recognized the call of God and bade him stay.

V. DISCRETION IN THE USE OF MORTIFICATION.

The details of mortification belong more to the direction of particular souls. Each one requires a legislation for himself. There seems, however, to be a consent among spiritual writers that while pleasures, passions, and pains are the three great fields of mortification, a certain order ought to be observed in our application to them. Pleasures should be mortified first, passions next, and pains be taken last. They do not mean by this that there are three distinct and successive classes of penances, and that we must practise one till we are out of the other, any more than writers when they divide mental prayer into twelve or fifteen states mean that we go out of one into another, as if they were separate rooms. All that is meant is, that upon the whole a certain order is to be observed, and upon the whole one object to be sought at a certain time rather than another one.

Mortifications are divided into exterior and interior. Of the exterior there are five principal classes. First, afflictive penances, such as fasting, discipline, hair-shirt, catenella, cold, and wakefulness. Of these the one which most requires jealousy is that which concerns loss of sleep, and next to it the bearing of cold. For the results of these to the health may be and often are permanent. And generally of all these penances two things may be observed: first, that no one should ever take them out of his own head, without counsel and obedience; and secondly, that perseverance in them is of far greater moment than either quantity or quality. It has often been noticed that when a person becomes spiritual, one of the very last infirmities which leaves him is an unmortified pleasure in eating and drinking. There is something wonderfully humbling in this; and we must pay particular attention to it, trying to mortify ourselves in something at every meal, and not to eat between meal-times.

The second class of exterior mortifications consists in the custody of the senses, in order to rebuke levity and curiosity, and in these singularity and affectation should be guarded against.

Under the third class comes the patient bearing of illness and pain, and especially the acceptation of death in the spirit of penance.

Under the fourth class come fatiguing and self-denying works for the good of our neighbor, or the relief of the poor, or the exaltation of the faith.

Under the fifth comes all that is penal in the common tasks and daily vicissitudes of life: the obligation of work, the inconveniences of poverty, the weather, and like things, all which may become meritorious by being endured in an interior spirit of penance, and united to Our Lord's endurance of them in His thirty-three years.

Under the head of interior mortifications comes first of all the mortification of our own judgment, or razionale, as St. Philip called it. Can there be a harder task in the whole of the spiritual life? If you ask me how it is to be done, I answer—the words are easy, not so the practice: Distrust your own opinion, and acquire the habit of surrendering it in doubtful things. In matters about which you are clear, speak modestly and then be silent. Try never to have an opinion contrary to that of your natural and immediate superiors. Let their presence be the death of your own views. With your equals try to agree in matters of no moment, and, above all, have no wish to be listened to. Judge favorably of all things, and be ingenuous in giving them a kindly turn. Condemn nothing either in the general or the particular, but make all things over to the judgment of God. When reason and virtue oblige you to speak, do so with such gentleness and want of emphasis that you may seem rather to despise than value your own opinion. Mortifications of the will form another class. The tongues of others fill a third to overflowing. Spiritual desolations are a fourth, and horrible temptations, specially allowed by God, a fifth. All these have their own symptoms and require their own method of treatment, which it would be out of place here to investigate. There is little left for the work of sanctification to do when our will is conformed to the will of God and endures humbly and sweetly the adverse wills of others. The strife of tongues is a mortification from which few can hope to escape, especially if they are endeavoring either to do good to others or aiming at a high sanctity for themselves. It was one of the ingredients in Our Saviour's chalice, and was considered by the Psalmist as so afflictive that he prayed God to hide him from it beneath the shadow of His wings. Spiritual desolation, so hard to bear, gives both courage and humility to our relations with God, while unusual and obstinate temptations purify the soul, as in a very crucible, from all remains of earthly dross.

VI. DANGERS TO BE AVOIDED.

But if mortification has its difficulties, it has its dangers also. Many mortifications are preceded by Vainglory, who blows the trumpet before them. Other mortifications she accompanies; and some even receive from her all their life, animation, and perseverance. It is as if this evil spirit had a standing commission from her master: Whenever a soul is about to practise a mortification, there be thou also! The remedy for this is to put all our mortifications under obedience. It is difficult then for either vainglory, ostentation, affectation, wilfulness, or indiscretion to fasten upon our penances and corrode their precious life. And they are the six chief dangers of mortification. Neither must we forget to be on our guard against a superstitious idea of the value of pain growing up in our minds alongside of our austerities. Many mortifications remain mortifications when the pain of them has passed away; and the value of them depends upon the intensity of the supernatural intention that was in them, not on the amount of physical pain or bodily discomfort. Mortification is a putting something to death, and the passion that is dead already is more mortified than one that is only dying, and yet the last feels pain, while the first is past all feeling. It is astonishing how many are unconsciously deceived by this superstitious notion of the value of mere pain; not that it is without value; but it is not the gem, it is only the setting of it. It is this error which has given so much vogue outside the Church, and sometimes also to unwary persons in it, to the delusion of thinking that perfection consists in always doing what we dislike, which implies that our affections and passions will never be brought to like the things of God or be in harmony with grace. Thus you will hear of persons having a scruple whether they ought to be kind to others because they have so much sensible pleasure in it, or visiting the poor for the same reason, or following a particular bent of devotion. Some even impose it as a rule upon the souls they guide—in almost every instance with as much absurdity as indiscretion. In the only sense in which sound mysticism would allow of such a maxim, it would require a special and clearly-marked vocation, and it would be as rare as the call to make St. Teresa's and St. Andrew Avellino's vows always to do what was most perfect. Yet the Church stopped at those vows when she was called upon to canonize the saints, and would not proceed till evidence was given her of a special operation of the Holy Ghost. No one ever became a saint, or anything like one, by ceasing to cultivate the sweeter parts of his character or his natural virtues because the doing so was so great a pleasure. Yet Jansenism thought that the secret of perfection lay in this single charm. It is a most odious and uncatholic idea of asceticism.

VII. DELUSION TO WHICH MORTIFICATION EXPOSES US.

To the difficulties and dangers of mortification we must add a word on its delusions. It is a fertile subject. Guilloré, who has treated of the subject at length and with his usual severity, sums it all up by describing the four classes of persons which are most subject to these delusions. The first class embraces those who have always led an innocent life, and on that account easily dispense themselves from austerities; and not being drawn to them themselves they make no attempt to draw others that way. They do not see why they should maltreat a body which is so little rebellious, and inflict on it such constant pain when it teases them with but an occasional disturbance. The second class contains those who, though their lives have been far from innocent, are nevertheless from softness of temperament disinclined to austerities. They can hardly believe that anything which is so far above their cowardice, as this persecution of self, can be necessary and indispensable. Useful they are willing to admit it to be, but surely not necessary; for in that case where should they be? And are their intellectual views of perfection, or their sentimental aspirations after it, to end in smoke? The third class comprises those who have greatly offended God, and therefore think that they must set no bounds to their austerities. Hence they go beyond the limits of sage reason on one side and the inspirations of grace on the other. The fourth class numbers men of fiery zeal and hot-tempered enthusiasm, whose peace is in war and their rest in struggle, and who satisfy nature by the chastisement of their bodies. But when the blood runs or the face grows pale, they are miserably deceived if they consider that to be a true spiritual mortification which has only been the rude satisfaction of a natural and impulsive passion.

THIRD TREATISE.

PRAYER.[1]

CHAPTER I.

THE EXCELLENCE AND NECESSITY OF MENTAL PRAYER.

PRAYER, the holy fathers tell us, is an elevation of our soul to God by the union of our mind with supreme truth and of our heart with supreme goodness. It is a respectful homage which we render to the divine grandeur and majesty by the submission of all our powers.

St. Chrysostom, in his beautiful homilies on prayer, says that prayer is to the soul what the nerves are to the body, walls to a city, arms to a soldier, wings to a bird, respiration to animals. We judge a body to be dead, he says, when it no longer breathes, and we must believe a soul to be dead when it no longer prays.

To be sure, he speaks of prayer in general, inasmuch as it includes mental and vocal; but as mental prayer is the soul and the principal part of this

---

[1] P. Crasset, S.J.

exercise, if it is necessary to pray it is necessary to meditate, particularly as vocal prayer without it is not true prayer, but a vain and reprehensible occupation.

At the same time, it is not this kind of meditation that we are about to speak of here, but of purely mental prayer, which is undoubtedly preferable to vocal, except where the latter is of precept and of obligation.

Certain celebrated doctors quoted by Suarez believed mental prayer to be necessary for all classes of persons, and that they could not be saved without it.

This is going too far. It is probable that they meant by meditation the elevation and the reflection necessary to receive the sacraments worthily, to conceive sorrow for our sins, to ask for extraordinary graces from God, and to produce, at times of precept, acts of faith, hope, and charity.

However this may be, it cannot be denied that mental prayer is necessary to those who wish to lead, I do not say pious, but even Christian lives, whether they are beginners, or have already made considerable progress, or have attained perfection.

Beginners must acquire purity of heart by frequent confession and continual mortification; confession effaces sin and mortification destroys its principle; now both require the assistance of meditation.

A penitent must hate his sin, and to do so he must understand its malice. How can he understand it without reflection, without consideration, without meditation? I do not speak of the examination of conscience he must make on the Commandments of God and of the Church, which is a manner of meditation as profitable as it is necessary.

Neither can we practise mortification without the assistance of mental prayer, for mortification is a thing that does violence to nature, and is very contrary to our inclinations; it tends to subdue and destroy nature; and as the natural instinct of all creatures is self-preservation, it is evident that if the soul does not rise above itself by means of prayer, it cannot conceive that holy hatred so necessary to enable it to deny itself what it loves and to embrace what it fears.

What we say of beginners applies also to those more advanced in the spiritual life: without prayer the first cannot cut off their vices, and the second cannot acquire virtue. It is in prayer that the soul discovers the beauty of virtue, is inflamed with love for it, and incited to practise it.

The great Cardinal Bellarmine, as celebrated for his piety as his learning, says that it is prayer, so to speak, which gives life to all the other virtues and preserves them in the soul.

It enlightens our faith by bringing us in contact with objects from which the senses tend to withdraw us and to which they blind us.

It sustains our hope by giving us familiar access to God, and by uniting us with our principle.

It causes us to recognize the vanity, inconstancy, and infidelity of creatures; inspires us with horror of the world, and inflames us with love for God by the knowledge and experience which it gives us of His goodness.

It gives us a knowledge of ourselves, which teaches us wise lessons of humility, makes us realize and appreciate our nothingness, and reveals to us the greatness and sanctity of God, before Whom our imaginary virtues have no existence, beauty, form, or measure.

Finally it leads us into those sacred solitudes where the soul enjoys its God in the peace and repose of holy recollection. It conducts us, in spirit, to hell, where we behold the place which might have been ours; to the cemetery, to look upon our final resting-place on earth; to heaven, to behold the throne which is destined for us; to the valley of Josaphat, to behold our Judge; to Bethlehem, to look upon our Saviour; to Tabor, to behold our Love; to Calvary, to behold our Exemplar.

A volume would hardly suffice to enumerate all the treasures of grace which the faithful soul finds in meditation, and the consolations in all its trials which it receives from God.

No doubt there are persons who are unable to give a considerable portion of time each day to meditation, but I am convinced that we can never attain Christian perfection unless we supply for meditation in some way, either by pious reading, or the instruction of confessors, or the teaching of sermons.

It is not necessary to demonstrate that the perfect must be souls given to prayer, since it is prayer which unites them to God, in which union their perfection consists. Thus there never have been saints who were not devoted to prayer; it was their occupation and their consolation. Their lives, we may say, were an unceasing prayer, as the Son of God commands; their every breath was a prayer, which makes me conclude with St. Augustine that to live well we must pray well; just as to pray well we must live well. This is a necessary condition of the prayer of which we are treating.

CHAPTER II.

DISPOSITIONS FOR PRAYER.

Poverty is eloquent; to pray well we must know our misery. There is no advocate at the bar who pleads his cause better than the poor man seeking relief in his necessity from a rich patron. If we are cold in our prayer it is because we do not realize our misery or appreciate our need.

And yet, just as there is no man without desires, there is no man without needs. The rich of this world are full of them; kings are more dependent than their subjects; they need more assistance than a poor workman; he is dependent only upon the labor of his own hands, but a sovereign is dependent upon all his subjects; which shows that exalted positions are only a form of brilliant servitude. It was David's appreciation of his misery which made his prayer so eloquent, so powerful, and so constant.

It is the same with the rest of mankind; as there

is no one without needs there is no one who does not know how to pray and to recommend his necessities to God; but how many will you find who know how to converse with Him? When Moses had conversed with God he could no longer converse with men, and he prayed God to dispense him from bearing His orders to Pharao. But we find, on the contrary, many clever minds who converse brilliantly with men, but find it impossible to converse with God. Why is this? It is because their hearts are engaged in sin and filled with affection for creatures. "Where the heart is there is its treasure." We like to converse with those we love, hence it is not astonishing that one who has no love for God should do all he can to avoid His presence and His company. But when a soul is detached from all created things, it is impossible to express or conceive of the delight which it finds in prayer.

The apostles formerly said to the Son of God: "Lord, teach us to pray." Strange request! There is nothing more miserable than a man who does not recognize his wretchedness; he is full of needs and knows not how to reveal them. Behold the effect of sin, which blinds our mind and debauches our will!

But what is still more deplorable is that there are many who recognize their misery, yet seek no relief; they feel their wretchedness and cannot declare it; they come before God and have nothing to say to Him. Their prayer is a continual distraction of mind and dissipation of heart.

To remedy an evil so common and so deplorable, we would facilitate for all souls the practice of prayer. We find innumerable precepts concerning prayer in books; the shortest way, in my opinion, is that of detachment and mortification. Prayer is a fire that is fed with the wood of the cross. How can a heart, agitated by passions, a prey to all the desires of a sensual, avaricious, ambitious nature, remain at peace in the presence of God? Grace is a quality so pure and so delicate that it can have no intercourse with the senses. Therefore to rise to heaven we must be detached from earth, and to unite ourselves with God in prayer we must separate ourselves, by mortification, from all creatures.

How can we practise mortification if we do not know how to pray? you ask, for prayer is as necessary to mortification as mortification is to prayer. True, and for that reason they must never be separated; however painful or laborious we find prayer, we must never abandon it, inasmuch as this labor is very great mortification, and disposes the soul to receive great graces. When we practise what we know, God teaches us what we do not know. Do what you can and God will do what you desire. But to do what we can we must know what we ought to do. That is what we shall teach in the following chapters.

CHAPTER III.

VARIOUS KINDS OF PRAYER.

There are, besides vocal, seven degrees or kinds of mental prayer.

The first is called meditation.
The second, affective prayer.
The third, the prayer of silence.
The fourth, the prayer of union.
The fifth, the prayer of privation.
The sixth, the prayer of transformation.
The seventh, the prayer of quiet.

In the prayer called meditation the soul considers, ponders, and digests Christian truths; it dwells upon the life and death of Our Lord, upon His actions, His sufferings, His doctrine, His example. This prayer, the basis, the foundation of all the others, is the gate of the sanctuary through which we must enter. It would be extremely rash, St. Bernard tells us, for a newly-converted soul to seek the embrace of the Bridegroom before it has kissed His feet by penance and His hands by the practice of good works. When it has labored long and faithfully in the acquisition of virtues, then it may sigh for a favor which we hardly venture to desire in this life, so much is it above the merit and condition of man.

The soul, therefore, must meditate before it loves, must labor before it rests, seek before it possesses. But when the mind, after the enjoyment of great light, no longer finds wherewith to occupy itself in meditation, then it may pass on to affective prayer, incessantly sighing and yearning for this divine Bridegroom Whose worth it has learned and Whose goodness it has experienced.

From this prayer of aspiration it passes to the prayer of silence ; for when it is wearied with crying, speaking, meditating, sighing, seeking, calling, there follows a silence in the heaven of its soul, by which it learns, like St. Augustine, that it is seeking without that which it possesses within ; it is in this mysterious silence that it sees things and hears secrets which it is not permitted to reveal to men.

This is a great favor, but it is followed by a still greater ; for the mind being, as it were, excluded from this divine sanctuary, the Spouse enters the heart ; all the doors of its interior and exterior being closed, He unites Himself with the soul by a secret touch which St. Louis de Blois calls *substantial*. For the soul, after this union, believes firmly that it has substantially touched the divinity, inasmuch as it was not through the sense of sight, or hearing, or smell, or taste, or spiritual odor, that it felt God present, but by that of touch, which has this in common with the corporal sense that it produces immediate contact with the object. Just as a friend, during the night, feels and knows when his friend touches him, though he does not seem to see him, so the soul, its mind plunged in profound obscurity, insensibly feels in its heart and touches its Spouse through a knowledge which St. Bonaventure calls experimental, immediate, and substantial ; and this union, inexplicable and even inconceivable to those who have not experienced it, is the spiritual marriage of the soul with God, the nuptials of the Lamb which render it a fruitful mother in virtues, merits, good works, and spiritual children, which it unceasingly produces through the unction of the Word, which is that of its divine Spouse. Blessed are they who are called to this feast, to these nuptials of the Lamb!

This operation endures only a short time, but the memory of it is a balm which rejoices the mind and the senses, though they have scarcely any knowledge of it. The bereft spouse, at thought of it, sighs without wishing to sigh, weeps without wishing to weep. She remains so filled with God that she cannot speak; and though the operation is past, she cannot doubt that God is in her heart and her heart in God. In the presence of this divine Spouse, Who reposes in the depth and the centre of her soul, she becomes sometimes inflamed with a love so violent that if she did not moderate her transports she would swoon away.

But, inasmuch as this state is infinitely delightful and may be called paradise on earth, if it lasted for a long time the soul would not merit anything, any more than the blessed in heaven; at least, finding its repose and happiness in this life, it would hardly think of the other. For this reason Our Lord deprives souls, some suddenly, others gradually, of these extraordinary delights and plunges them into a state of privation.

It would be impossible to depict the astonishment of the poor loved one when it finds itself suddenly plunged into this horrible darkness, abandoned to the fury of its passions, and thrust from such a paradise into an abyss of misery. At first, it believes itself lost and imagines it has committed a great sin which has offended its Spouse and obliged Him to withdraw from its presence. It weeps, it sighs, it groans, it languishes; it yearns to return to its former state, but it cannot; it finds an armed cherubim at the gate of this paradise to refuse it entrance; it makes strenuous efforts to produce acts, but to no effect, inasmuch as its Spouse, Who is hidden in its heart, holds its powers bound, and prevents them from being diffused abroad. Oh, what need the soul has at such times of an experienced person to assure it that all is well, and that it has entered into the life of the spirit and the kingdom of grace, where the senses have no part! When a soul is faithful and tranquil in this state of privation, the divine Spouse never fails to make Himself seen and felt like the sun which scatters the clouds which concealed it; this is the moment of ecstasies and rapture; the joy of the soul is so great that it would be beside itself, did it not moderate its transports and permit itself to be guided. It cannot conceive how it could have believed itself separated from Him Who was in the depth of its heart; it is filled with confusion because of its infidelities, and after the experience it has had of its love, it passes into the prayer of transformation, where it becomes one in spirit with God by the annihilation of its judgment, its will, its acts, its powers, and of its being, so to speak; just as wood after being dried and purified is changed and converted into fire—with this difference, that the wood changes its nature, and that of the soul is preserved however penetrated it may be with God. Henceforth its prayer is that of sweet and tranquil rest in God without care, desire, movement, or seeking of any kind, like the streams which at the end of their long course rest in the bosom of the ocean, like the blessed who enjoy God and are lost, so to speak, in Him, and have no thought or care for themselves.

This is the state to which the soul attains when it is faithful to the exercise of meditation and the practice of mortification, when it abandons itself to the providence of God and relies on no creature. As my aim in this treatise is to instruct only beginners and to facilitate for them the practice of prayer, I shall not dwell upon the higher or extraordinary prayer, or how it must be regulated, but only on the ordinary prayer called meditation.

CHAPTER IV.

MEDITATION.

This prayer is necessary to beginners and requires rules, methods, and precepts; it is composed of four parts, called preparation, consideration, affection, and resolution.

This subject is treated of at length by all the spiritual fathers; I give a brief summary of it for the benefit of those who have not read or cannot read fuller treatises.

I. PREPARATION.

It is tempting God to begin our meditation without preparation, and manifest want of respect to present ourselves before Him with careless indifference. As our intelligence is limited, we can do nothing well without previous preparation. Great actions require great consideration, and great enterprises great preparation. Now what is greater, nobler, more important, than to converse with God on the affairs of our salvation? Therefore we must never go to meditation without preparation. Preparation is required in everything: artists prepare themselves to execute their conceptions; orators to deliver their discourses; politicians to carry out their policy; wise men to carry out their designs.

There are two kinds of preparation: one is remote, the other immediate.

Remote preparation consists in three things:

1. In keeping the mind recollected during the day.

2. In preserving the heart pure from sin and free from passion.

3. In reading the subject of meditation.

As I am instructing beginners, I do not pretend to lay down rules for perfect souls. There are mystics who do not hesitate to say that they have no need to prepare themselves for meditation. This, I think, is speaking unwisely; they mean, no doubt, that they are always prepared for meditation, which is true, for they are always united to God, and their subject is always present in their minds and is contained in these three significant words, God, all, nothing.

As to the immediate preparation, it includes three things very necessary to a good meditation.

1. A lively faith in the presence of God, which we may call the soul, the sun, the fire of meditation; the soul which animates it, the sun which enlightens it, the fire which inflames it.

There are two ways of placing ourselves in the presence of God; one by considering, like St. Stephen, Our Lord, either in heaven, whence He looks down upon us, or in the Blessed Sacrament, where He lives for us. This representation of the sacred humanity may be useful for beginners, provided it require no great exertion of the mind or effort of the imagination.

The other manner of placing ourselves in the presence of God is more spiritual: it consists in believing and recollecting that we are before God and that God is before us; that we are with God and that God is with us; that we are in God and that God is in us; that His immensity fills all things, and that we are filled therewith to the very depth of our being, as St. Augustine says; that, therefore, we can never be separated from the being of God, though we may sever ourselves from His love.

2. After placing yourself in His presence, adore Him with profound respect, prostrating yourself, body and soul, before Him. Then offer Him your meditation and the time you intend to devote to it, protesting that it is for love of Him, and to please Him, that you are about to perform this ac-

tion; be prepared to spend the time of meditation in light or in darkness, in consolation or desolation, seeking no other satisfaction than that of pleasing God. This resignation is important for receiving God's graces and remaining in the state in which He may place you. If, when you have done your best, you leave meditation satisfied, it is a mark that you have entered upon it with a pure intention; but if you are sad and despondent, it is a mark that you have sought your satisfaction and not that of God.

3. The last thing required as preparation is to invoke the Holy Spirit, acknowledging that you are not capable of a good thought if He does not inspire it; of applying your mind if He does not restrain it; of elevating your heart if He does not attract it; of loving Him if He does not inspire and animate you.

II. CONSIDERATION.

The consideration forms, so to speak, the body of the meditation. The Prophet Jeremias says that the whole earth is desolate because there is no one that enters into himself and considers the great truths of religion. And David tells us, "Blessed are they who search the testimonies, the commandments of God, for they will find the fountain of living water, and the treasures of grace contained in them." "Blessed," he says elsewhere, "is the man who hath not walked in the counsel of the ungodly, nor stood in the way of sinners, nor sat in the chair of pestilence: But his will is in the law of the Lord, and on His law he shall meditate day and night. And he shall be like a tree which is planted near the running waters, which shall bring forth its fruit, in due season." Thus does he begin the first of all his canticles.

The manner of making the consideration varies according to the subject of the meditation and the person meditating. If the subject is some mystery or action of Our Lord's life, we must examine all the circumstances; for example, if we are meditating on the Passion, we must consider Who it is Who suffers, what He suffers, where He suffers, how He suffers, for what purpose He suffers.

If it is a virtue upon which we are meditating, we must consider its nature, its characteristics, its beauty, its advantages, its necessity, the means of acquiring it, and the occasions of practising it. If it is a vice upon which we are meditating, we must endeavor to learn the malice of it, the evil effects of it, and the remedies to be applied to it.

In regard to the person meditating, there are people who cannot readily discourse in meditation, either because they are convinced of all the Christian truths, or because they have no facility in reasoning, or because of a dull intelligence or a too lively imagination.

They who are convinced of the truths of religion should give themselves more to affections than considerations. They would do well also sometimes to remain quietly in the presence of God, listening to His voice in the depth of their soul, or sitting at His feet like Magdalen, or waiting, like the paralytic, until the waters are stirred, sending forth loving sighs from time to time, and begging Our Lord to give them His love.

They who have difficulty in reasoning or discoursing may make use of the method of Louis de Grenada or of St. Francis de Sales, who counsel beginners, particularly women, to keep a book before their eyes, to read the first point, and if it suggest no good thoughts, to begin again and to read the first two lines with great attention, as if it were Our Lord Himself Who spoke in them; then to pause and ponder a little upon what they have read, and to produce some affection conformable to the subject; after these two lines, to read two more, considering the truth proposed in them, reflecting upon their lives and producing sentiments of gratitude or of sorrow for their sins. When they find something which touches them, they should pause, and before going any further, derive all the profit they can from it.

If they find nothing to occupy them, let them have recourse to other methods, which we shall teach later on.

Persons possessed of a lively imagination should fix the mind upon some mystery, or place, or figure, representing the mystery as actually taking place before them. Thus, if the nativity of Our Lord is the subject of our meditation, we must imagine ourselves in the stable of Bethlehem; if His death, upon Calvary; if His transfiguration, upon Tabor. If we meditate upon hell, we must descend in spirit to this place of torment; if upon death, we must picture ourselves upon our bed about to render up our soul to God. If it is a truth we are considering, we must imagine Our Lord instructing us, or think of Him under some figure relating to the truth we are contemplating. This kind of representation serves to fix the imagination, and St. Ignatius makes it a prelude to the consideration.

But we must beware, as I have said, of forcing the mind; on the contrary, if at the beginning of the meditation we feel drawn to the presence of God, we must remain there without entering into the subject. If the same happens during the meditation, we must cease to discourse, and abandon ourselves to the operation of the Holy Spirit. This is the advice given by St. Ignatius himself in his "Exercises."

III. AFFECTIONS.

Considerations are formed by the understanding, and affections by the will. Sterile reflections serve only to make a man vain and wicked, but affectionate reflections make him humble and holy. The light of the sun would be a vain ornament to the earth if it did nothing but shed its light upon it; it must also warm and fructify it. As God desires principally our hearts, affections are much more noble and more necessary than considerations.

Affections are the good desires and movements of the soul produced by the consideration of some subject; such are the acts of all the virtues, of faith, of hope, of charity, of adoration, of admiration, of praise, of thanksgiving, of offering of one's self, of sorrow for sin, of confusion at our past life, etc.

As it is by means of such acts that the heart is detached from creatures and united with God, we must endeavor to produce them as much as possible, without, however, making any violent effort. If you cannot produce acts of charity, produce acts of humility; this virtue, St. Bernard says, compensates for want of charity. Suffer if you cannot pray; make a meditation of patience instead of consolation. Above all, be at peace and do not be troubled, but be convinced that the most excellent of all prayers is to do the will of God, and to be satisfied wherever He places you.

IV. RESOLUTIONS.

Our resolutions are the most important of all the affections of the soul, and must be made whether the meditation has been one of consolation or one of dryness. There are some who spend the time of prayer in learned speculations; others in tender affectionate sentiments; others in obscurity of mind; others in dryness and aridity of heart; some are always moved to tears, others never weep. Others, again, have a complacent admiration for virtue, but never come to the practice of it; others make many and excellent resolutions, but which are never followed by any results. Aristotle says that they who study ethics without being any the better therefor are like a sick man who delights to hear his physician discourse upon his malady but will take no remedy.

A meditation without fruit is an amusement of the mind and a very dangerous form of idleness. We must not judge of meditation by the tender sentiments we have experienced, but by the profit we have derived from it, or at least by the sincere desire we have to do good and to practise virtue. When you leave meditation, however dry it may have been, with the desire, the resolution, to correct your faults and to do God's will, your time has not been lost. The sacraments do not render us impeccable, much less meditation; but it ought to prevent our falling so frequently or so grievously, and incite us to greater ardor in the practice of virtue.

There are two kinds of resolutions; one general, the other particular. General resolutions are, for example, to love God with our whole heart, to practise virtue, to avoid anger, to conform ourselves in all things to the will of God. Particular resolutions determine the time, place, circumstances; as, for instance, to mortify ourselves on certain occasions; to practise meekness and patience under certain circumstances; to conform our will to that of God in some loss, humiliation, or sickness.

General resolutions are not bad, but we must make special ones also, particularly against the vice to which we are most addicted, and to which we must lay siege in meditation, directing all our batteries against it. At other times we may resolve to perform a certain number of acts of virtue during the day; if you derive this fruit from meditation you have no reason to fear that it is not well made. But bear in mind four things:

First, that our affections, whether sweet and sensible or dry and cold, must be followed as much as possible by resolutions, which are their proper fruit.

Second, that we must not make many resolutions at a time, but confine ourselves to one well fixed in our mind. A skilful sportsman never goes after several hares at a time; he confines himself to one.

Third, that we must begin by what is easy before undertaking what is difficult; correct our exterior before reforming our interior; for he who is not faithful in little things will not be in great; while, on the contrary, if you acquit yourself faithfully in little things God will help you to accomplish great.

Fourth, that we must not make resolutions for life, but sometimes for a month, or a week, and chiefly for the present day; if we fail in carrying out our resolution, and we fall as before, we must not lose courage, but rise at once and repair our fault at the first opportunity.

V. CONCLUSION.

The conclusion or colloquy includes three things: thanksgiving, offering of ourselves, and petition.

We must first thank God for the honor of being allowed in His presence, for the lights we have received, and the good desires He has inspired.

Second, we must offer Him our soul, our body, our mind, our heart, all that we possess, all that we hope for, particularly the good resolutions we have formed in meditation.

Third, we must ask His blessing and the grace to accomplish what He inspires, representing to Him our weakness, our inconstancy, our infidelity, our malice; addressing ourselves sometimes to Our Lord, sometimes to His blessed Mother, sometimes to the saints to whom we have most devotion, and who excelled in the virtue we need.

Fourth, after meditation we must endeavor to keep ourselves in the presence of God and to preserve a recollected spirit, frequently returning during the day to what has touched us most, that we may thus preserve our devotion and be constantly reminded of our resolution. This is what St. Francis de Sales calls the spiritual bouquet.

CHAPTER V.

DISTRACTIONS.

St. Bonaventure truly says that spiritual exercises consist in knowing three things: what God is, what man is, and how man is to unite himself with God. There are several kinds of union, one of which is prayer; but it is difficult to preserve it, for the reason that the Evil One does all he can to disturb it: he torments us with distractions and evil thoughts; then he persuades us that we ought to abandon prayer, that we are losing our time; that to pray as we pray is not to please but to offend God; that it is better not to pray at all than to pray with so much irreverence; that our mind is too active, our imagination too lively, our occupations too numerous, that we cannot reason and discourse on such subjects; that God is cold and indifferent to us; that it is better to leave this exercise to those who have little else to do, and content ourselves with ordinary devotions. Credulous souls are only too often deceived by such temptations, and abandon God through fear of displeasing Him.

To remedy so great an evil, we must be convinced of three things:

First, that of all the remedies which we may apply to distractions in prayer the worst and the most pernicious is to abandon meditation; the Evil One urges it, knowing that when he has cut off the source of grace the soul must languish and die for want of nourishment.

Second, that there is a great difference between consolation and devotion: consolation usually has to do with the senses, devotion has its seat in the heart; consolation passes away, devotion remains; we may have consolation without devotion, as we may also have devotion without consolation. When a soul in great aridity is contented and abandons itself to the will of God, it possesses devotion in a sovereign degree; for true devotion, according to St. Thomas, is a firm disposition of the will to do generously, promptly, and constantly all that God asks of it. Thus we may say that there is no one more devout than one who has no consolation, who feels no devotion, provided he is faithful to meditation, and is content with whatever disposition God sends him, whether to punish him or to sanctify him.

Third, that distractions and dryness are by no means the unmitigated evils we imagine, but, on the contrary, a precious mine capable of affording us rich treasure, if we only use them aright.

CHAPTER VI.

CAUSES OF DISTRACTIONS AND ARIDITY.

I should need a large volume to give all that the fathers have said on this subject. St. Bonaventure estimates six causes, Gerson seventeen; they may be reduced, however, to three: God, man, and the Evil One.

All that God does is for our good; His object is our salvation, whether He remains with us or whether He withdraws from us. The absence of the sun is almost as necessary to the earth as its presence; one makes the day and the other the night; the night is not as beautiful as the day, but it is quite as necessary. Now God withdraws from us in prayer for several reasons.

The first is to keep us humble. Pride is a strange thing in man; he can do nothing of himself and yet he prides himself on all that he accomplishes; he is nothing but misery, yet thinks he has no need of mercy.

If God bestows any favor upon him he thinks it

the result of his own merit or labor, and robs its Author of the glory due Him; if he catches a fish, he offers sacrifice, as a prophet says, to his net instead of to God; if he gains a victory, instead of kissing the hand of the Lord Who has won it, he kisses his own, which Job says is a grievous sin, an impiety like to that of a man who denies God.

Now it is to make man know his misery and his dependence that God withdraws His consolations; He deprives him of tender and sensible graces to make him feel the need of them; in darkness he discovers what he is; in aridity he learns to appreciate and to ask for what he has not. "My God," said the great St. Augustine, "let me know myself and let me know Thee." We cannot know God if we do not know ourselves, and we learn to know ourselves in the school of poverty.

Here we also learn the value of grace. Things are valued in proportion to their rarity. Abundance, Tertullian says, impairs and vitiates itself; to know the worth of a possession we must have lost it. If we always had this manna from heaven, perhaps we should weary of it like the Jews; but when we are deprived of it we begin to appreciate its worth; consequently we seek it more fervently, we ask for it more humbly, we find it with greater pleasure. We guard it with greater circumspection, fear, and watchfulness. I fear much, says St. Bernard, that ungrateful souls will be abandoned by grace, which they regard, not as a favor, but as a rightful possession of which they are sovereign master and proprietor. The saint refers to the grace of devotion of which God frequently deprives souls, leaving them always what is necessary to resist temptation and to do His will.

This privation is painful, but at the same time necessary not only to keep us humble and make us appreciate grace, but also to enable us to increase our merits; for, as I shall show presently, we merit but little in meditation or prayer filled with tender affectionate sentiments; it is not a state which raises the soul above itself; it is gratifying and satisfies nature; the state in which we merit is that of pure love, of humility, of patience, and rarely is charity pure in sensible fervor, humble in elevation, patient in pleasures.

It is for this reason that Our Lord, as He one day told St. Teresa, leaves souls in darkness, desolation, and aridity. The saint was astonished to hear enlightened souls complain of aridity, knowing it to be a state in which the soul gives greater honor to God, acquires more merit, and practises all virtues with greater perfection.

It is also a time when God recognizes those who are faithful to Him and who truly love Him. Many, in the abundance of grace, declare, like David, that nothing shall ever change or overcome them, and no sooner do they lose their abundance than they are immediately cast down and troubled. Others, at the festival board, declare, like St. Peter, that they will never deny their Master, but when temptation comes abandon Him like the apostle. The weakness of man is inconceivable and his presumption still more so. He blinds himself with his own lights, he forgets his poverty the moment he has left it, he is no sooner restored to health than he imagines himself immortal; hence God afflicts and tries us, not to learn what we are, for that is well known to Him, but to make us know ourselves. Thus did He try Abraham, recognizing His servant's fidelity in his prompt obedience. "Because thou wast acceptable to God," said the angel Raphael to Tobias, "it was necessary that temptation should prove thee." Therefore we have no reason to dread these states of aridity as we do, since God permits them to keep us humble, to prove our love, to make us appreciate grace, and to increase our merits. No doubt some will say, "I should have no difficulty in bearing this state if I were sure it came from God; but what troubles me is that these distractions come through my own fault, through my negligence and in punishment for my infidelities." Even if this were true, you must not lose courage, but patiently endure the trial you think you have merited, making up by your humility for what you lack in charity.

It is true that distractions do frequently come from ourselves, from the activity of our mind, from the strength of our passions, from bodily infirmity, from a wandering imagination, or as the result of unfaithfulness or of attachment to creatures. But all these distractions are innocent, provided we do not dwell upon them. Only those which have their seat in the heart are culpable, for these are deliberate and voluntary, at least in their principle.

Still another source is dissipation of mind during the day; if we are constantly occupied with vain and dissipating reflections, it is difficult to rid our selves of them during prayer. Hence the fathers and the masters of the spiritual life tell us that we must dispossess ourselves of all earthly things if we would be filled with spiritual, and that we must keep ourselves during the day what we would be in prayer.

When I say this I refer particularly to the heart and not to the mind. There are persons whose only efforts are against their thoughts, and who never think of combating their passions. Their hearts are filled with earthly attachments, disquieting desires, and yet they hope to enjoy the repose and peace of detached souls. This cannot be. They must dispossess the heart to free the mind, they must be free from the tyranny of passions to pray without distractions; for the heart follows its treasure, and is wont to dwell on what it loves.

There is a certain state where the soul is so fully convinced of the beauty and excellence of the Christian virtues that it can no longer reason in meditation, and as it has labored much it asks only to rest, even as the beloved disciple who reposed on the breast of his Master while the others partook of the repast prepared for them. The distractions which arise in this state do not come from an evil source; they are, on the contrary, a mark of robust spiritual health, and indicate that the soul needs change of disposition and method. Thus, if your heart is detached from creatures, and if you are faithful to your spiritual exercises, this state of aridity and dryness will afford you a rich harvest of grace and cause you to exclaim with the Wise Man: "I have labored a little and have found much rest to myself." Blessed indeed are they who die in the Lord; they will find the treasure of their good works, they will enjoy the fruit of their labors, the God of peace will wipe away their tears, they will never more know care or anguish, grief or pain.

A third cause of our distractions is the Evil One. He appreciates the profit a soul derives from prayer; hence he leaves nothing undone to make us weary of it, to make us abandon it. To this end he persuades us that it is a waste of time, that prayer such as ours, instead of pleasing, offends God; or he overwhelms us with drowsiness, plunges us into melancholy, fills us with vexation, harasses us with abominable thoughts; if we yield to the latter he has accomplished his purpose; if they fill us with horror, he persuades us, by exaggerating our aversion and fear, that we have sovereignly displeased God, and that to rid ourselves of such abominations we must abandon meditation, since it is then that these phantoms take possession of our mind and imagination. Alas! only too many souls are deceived by these suggestions of the Evil One, and fly, like Cain, from the presence of God.

Now that we have learned the causes of this evil, let us endeavor to apply the proper remedy.

CHAPTER VII.

WE MUST NEVER BE TROUBLED BECAUSE OF DISTRACTIONS AND ARIDITY.

In order to bear joyfully, or at least patiently, the privation of sensible sweetness and divine consolations, we must be convinced of two truths: one is, that the evil of these states of desolation and dryness is not what we imagine; and the other, that they benefit the soul and enable it to acquire much merit.

The first truth does not need to be proved, but illustrated. There is no doubt that a sin to be such must be voluntary; hence your distractions, if you do not yield to them, cannot but be innocent, even though they continue all the time of your meditation.

You will tell me, perhaps, that they are voluntary as to their cause, and that you give occasion to them; but even though this be true, it is no reason for yielding to discouragement and abandoning prayer; for either you know or you do not know their cause. If you do not know it, you must regard them as a temptation of the Evil One, a disposition of grace, a trial of your virtue, an occasion of merit, a physical infirmity, none of which prevent your prayer from being a very pleasing sacrifice to God. If you recognize the cause, ask pardon of God for it and promise to remove it, accept what you suffer in a spirit of penance, and believe me, you will make an excellent meditation.

It is an unwise proceeding to apply one evil to remedy another. If you have yielded unrestrainedly during the day to dissipation of mind is, it any reason for flying from God after you have offended Him? Should we abandon ourselves to the wilds of the forest because we have wandered ever so little from the right path? It is a mistake to think that distractions always come from dissipation of heart. I have shown the contrary in the preceding chapter, and even were it the case, what does it avail to be troubled? Trouble increases instead of lessening the evil, besides adding to the disturbance of your mind, instead of restoring it to recollection.

You say that you do nothing in meditation. I cannot agree with you. I am of the opinion, on the contrary, that you never accomplish more than when you think you have done nothing. To convince you of this second truth, I must observe again that the time of consolation, though more pleasing than that of desolation, is not a time in which we accomplish most for our spiritual interests or acquire most merits. In consolation we receive God's favors, in desolation we give Him what He asks of us; in one we plan, in the other we labor; in the first we enjoy God, in the second we combat for Him. Do you not think it is higher and nobler to give than to receive; to labor than to sleep; to combat than to follow our pleasure?

To resist temptation is to suffer a species of martyrdom for the faith, for charity, for religion, for justice. It is to sacrifice our soul, our body, our heart, our mind, and all our passions to the glory of God, Who witnesses our combats, ever ready to crown our patience. It is to produce, in the noblest and most heroic manner, acts of all the virtues: of faith in darkness of spirit, of hope in abandonment, of charity in weariness, of poverty in spiritual destitution, of patience in suffering: this is what you do, and you call it nothing!

A soul, as I have already said, merits hardly anything in consolation. It cannot be sure of producing a single act of supernatural virtue; for we call supernatural that which is above nature, which surpasses its powers. Man naturally believes only that which he understands, hopes for only that which is possible to him, loves only that which pleases him. Hence his faith is supernatural when he believes what he does not understand; his hope is supernatural when he hopes for that which he cannot accomplish or compass; his charity is supernatural when, for love of God, he loves that which does not please him. To believe in the midst of spiritual darkness, to hope in the midst of infirmity, to love despite all obstacles, is to perform acts of virtue which are beyond the power of nature, and which can be done only through the assistance of God.

And this is what a soul does which continues faithful and peaceful in these painful states of privation and aridity: it believes a God present Whom it cannot see; it hopes in Him against all hope; it abandons itself to One by Whom it believes itself abandoned; it loves Him despite the weariness and anguish in which He plunges it; it bows to His severe and crucifying designs; it suffers a martyrdom of love; it humbles itself at sight of its misery; it is content with its poverty and blesses God, like Job, when it beholds itself despoiled of all its spiritual possessions, covered with wounds and ulcers, and persecuted by devils, striving to make it break forth into murmurs and complaint.

Oh, if a soul knew how it honors God in a prayer of patience, if it knew the treasures of merit it amasses every moment, it would never wish to change this state! Not that we must reject consolation when God offers it; it is a heavenly dew necessary to tender souls not yet firmly rooted in virtue; only we must endeavor not to be attached to it. The peace of great souls is not founded upon these sensible favors, but upon the order and good pleasure of God, Whose will constitutes their happiness and their only consolation. Theirs is a life of the spirit and of grace uninfluenced by nature and the things of sense.

Now, what is more natural than to believe that which we see? To hope for that which we may touch? Who would not believe God present if he felt His divine operations in his heart? Who would not hope in God if he experienced His caresses? Who would not love God if he were unceasingly consoled by Him? It is not in light, therefore, that we practise supernatural faith, but in darkness. It is not when God flatters us that our hope is divine, but when He afflicts us. It is not in consolation that we love God with a pure love, but in desolation. Yes, believe me, you never do more than when you think you have done nothing; you never merit more than when you think you have merited nothing, inasmuch as in these painful states we produce, as I have shown, acts of divine faith, of supernatural hope, of pure charity, of general mortification, of Christian humility, of blind obedience, and of heroic patience: it is then that man pays God the homage of his whole being, and offers Him the sacrifice of all his passions. Then why should we be troubled, or lose courage, or abandon meditation?

You cannot, you tell me, think of God. Then be satisfied to love Him and to conform your will to His, accepting the state in which He places you. Your mind wanders? There is no great harm in that, provided you do not let your heart follow, but keep it steadfast. Alas! I have no consolation in prayer. What, is it for that that you come to meditation? Do you deserve that God should console you, you who have so grievously offended Him, and whose place is among the reprobate? But what greater consolation can there be than to do God's will, to be in His presence, to manifest your fidelity and your love for Him? I am always distracted. If your distractions are voluntary, you offend Him; if they are against your will, you honor Him, you please Him, you love Him: everything is pleasing to God except sin, and there can be no sin when the will is lacking. A prayer of suffering is better than a prayer of enjoyment. It is a sweet perfume which rises to heaven and fills paradise with its fragrance. Let us keep these words of St. Augustine always in mind: "You please God if God pleases you; He is satisfied with you if you are satisfied with Him."

I am satisfied with God, but I am not satisfied with myself. And why are you not satisfied with yourself, unless you take pleasure in being miserable? You are told that God is satisfied with you provided you are satisfied with Him, and you do nothing but worry and murmur. It is not against yourself that you murmur, but against God, for leaving you without consolation, for not treating you, it seems, according to your merits.

Moreover, since you do what you can, I do not see what reason you have to be dissatisfied with yourself. Far from it, you reply; it seems to me that I never do all that I might. You take pleasure in tormenting yourself. Tell me, could you do more than you are doing at present? If you could, why do you not do it? If you could not, why are you troubled?

The enjoyment of God constitutes the happiness of heaven and earth, with this difference—the happiness of heaven is unalloyed, that of earth is mingled with sorrow: in heaven we shall worship a God of happiness, on earth our God is a Man of sorrows. Our union with God in this life must resemble that of the sacred Humanity with the Word: the superior part of the Humanity was happy, the inferior suffered; its moments of happiness were few, its heart was continually plunged in an ocean of bitterness, for it had come to expiate in suffering the pleasure which men take in sin.

This is the state of holy souls in this life: according to the spirit nothing could be more pleasing, according to the senses nothing more painful. It is true that God, from time to time, permits them to taste that happiness which eye hath not seen, which ear hath not heard, and which hath not entered into the heart of man; but this endures only for a short time, for this life is a time of probation and merit. The kingdom of God, St. Paul tells us, does not consist in these sensible consolations, but in justice and peace and joy in the Holy Ghost, Who peacefully dwells in a heart. Therefore, though you are distracted in mind, if your heart only remains steadfast, you have nothing to fear. Your mistake is, that you confound these two kinds of distractions, and you do not distinguish between two kinds of union; one of the heart, and the other of the mind. Be convinced of this, that you may be intimately united with God in heart, though your mind may be distracted, and that all the involuntary distractions in the world cannot distract you and separate you from His love.

I understand this perfectly, some good souls will say, and yet I am not satisfied; there is a feeling of disquiet in the depth of my heart which fills my meditation with bitterness. Whence is this? The cause is not difficult to find; you do not come to meditation alone, self-will accompanies you. You wish to give uninterrupted attention and you are not willing to suffer distractions; you want to burn with fervor and you are not willing to endure coldness; you wish to enjoy light and you are not willing to be left in darkness; you wish and you do not wish ; you do not find that which you wish, and you find that which you do not wish. What wonder that you are troubled! Banish this self-will, and your trouble will cease ; purify your intention before entering upon meditation ; do not seek your own satisfaction, but that of God ; accept whatever state it may please Him to place you in, and be convinced that all states are good in which there is no sin ; that you can find God wherever self is not to be found ; that He fills your heart in proportion as you empty it of all earthly things ; that being spirit, He wishes to be adored in spirit ; that sensible unions are dangerous ; that fruitfulness follows sterility ; that after the night comes the morning, and that the best of all prayers is to die to your desires and to mortify your passions. In this way you will restore peace to your soul and dissipate the gloom which possesses it. But as all distractions do not come from the same causes, there are still other remedies to be applied.

CHAPTER VIII.

REMEDIES FOR DISTRACTIONS.

Every one complains of distractions, and few are willing to apply the remedy. We like the cause and dislike the effect ; we wish to be recollected in prayer and dissipated at all other times. Is not this desiring what is impossible?

We have said that distractions come from three

sources—from God, from man, and from the Evil One. When they come from God we must endure them; when they come from the Evil One we must repel them; when they come from man we must apply a remedy.

There are two kinds of remedies. The first precede prayer, the others accompany it. The remedies which precede it are numerous; among others, recollection of mind, purity of heart, mortification of the senses, victory over the passions, flight from companions, detachment from all possessions, honors, and created pleasures, interior silence, and the annihilation of all desires.

It is astonishing, says Pope St. Gregory, that we who are so unmortified presume to aspire to contemplation. We are full of ourselves and we would be filled with God! We exercise no restraint over either our body or our heart; we grant our senses all that they ask; we gratify our eyes with curious objects, our mind with innumerable vanities; we spend our time in vain and idle conversations; we give ourselves up to dissipation of heart every day, and we think we can establish ourselves in recollection at once and when we will. This is impossible.

To establish and preserve ourselves in interior peace, we must be ever on our guard and continually watch over the movements of our heart. There are few persons truly dead to all their desires; hence the majority, in prayer, are like a ship tossed on the waves and impelled hither and thither by every wind. Yet such souls ought not for this reason to abandon prayer; they have greater need of it than they who are quietly anchored, so to speak, in the spiritual haven. But what must I do, you ask, to banish these importunate thoughts? You must, first, place yourself in the presence of God and renew the thought of it from time to time. Second, when you go to prayer you must free your mind of all affairs likely to distract it, and conceive a great desire to converse with God ; then turn to your subject, and propose to yourself the truth upon which you wish to meditate.

I do this, you answer, but to no purpose as far as my mind is concerned ; it is impossible to keep it a moment in the presence of God; it is an idle truant constantly escaping and returning only at long intervals. This is what makes me weary of prayer and leads me to think I am not fitted for it.

This is a common complaint with a great many souls. The way to remedy the evil is to find the means of occupying our minds and enkindling our hearts in this time of dissipation, coldness and dryness.

CHAPTER IX.

FIRST MEANS OF DEVOTION.

Perfect prayer does not consist in thinking much, but in loving much; and, generally speaking, activity in prayer does not equal passive endurance. There is a species of contemplation in which the soul suffers divine things; suffers the wanderings of the mind, the weariness and despondency of the heart, the follies of the imagination, the harassing temptations of the Evil One. This is to suffer divine things; it is a kind of contemplation which is not pleasing to nature, but which is very meritorious and which gives great honor to God.

But besides this exercise of patience there are excellent practices which will enable us to spend the time of prayer peacefully and profitably, should we find ourselves unable to apply our mind to our subject.

The first means of devotion is a manner of prayer, partly mental and partly vocal, which St. Ignatius teaches in his "Exercises," and which St. Teresa tells us she used to advantage for a long time. It consists in reciting slowly some vocal prayer and pausing upon each word to derive from it all the spiritual sustenance it may afford us.

Thus, when you say the Lord's Prayer, pause after the words *Our Father*, and endeavor to appreciate the tenderness and love which the title implies. Then make an act of faith in God as your Father. Consider by how many titles you are His child—viz., by creation, by conservation, and by justification. Then address your soul thus: My soul, if God is thy Father, why dost thou not love Him? If God is thy Father, why dost thou not hope in Him? Why dost thou not make known to Him thy needs? God is thy Father and thou fearest to die of hunger! He has given His blood for thee and thou thinkest He may refuse thee bread! O my God and my Father, I hope in Thee! O best of fathers, what an unworthy child Thou hast! I am truly grieved for having offended, persecuted, dishonored Thee as I have since I came into this world. Father, I have sinned against Thee, and I am not worthy to be called Thy child; but let me be numbered among Thy servants. I will cease to offend Thee; henceforth I am determined to love Thee.

If these words serve to occupy you, do not go any further. When you have gathered from them all they afford you, pass on to the next, *Who art in heaven*, and consider how great and powerful God is Who dwells in this magnificent heaven; that this beautiful paradise, this magnificent dwelling, is your inheritance, and that, therefore, you must not fix your heart upon the paltry things of earth. Develop this evangelical field, and it will afford you a treasure of grace which will enrich you and open to you a source of living water which will refresh you.

After the "Our Father" you may take the "Hail, Mary," or the "Creed," or a psalm, and analyze it in the same way. You may also recite the Litany of the Holy Name of Jesus, and, pausing upon each title given the Son of God, produce acts of faith, of hope, of love, of contrition, of thanksgiving, or of any good sentiment the words suggest. For example, when you say, *Jesus, God of peace, have mercy on me*, pause and consider that Jesus is a God of peace, that He only can give peace to your heart. Then say, O my soul, why dost thou seek to find peace among creatures? O God of peace, give peace to my poor heart, for it is frequently troubled and disquieted. Oh, when shall

I rest in Thy heart, which is the centre of my peace? O sweet Jesus, give me Thy peace, Thy love, Thy blessing; speak, and command the waves to be still; appease this tempest, which hinders Thy repose and mine! O my soul, love only Jesus, since He only can give thee peace and satisfy thy desires.

You will find this manner of prayer most profitable, and it may also serve to excite your devotion after Communion. You cannot fail, among all these beautiful titles of the Son of God, to find one which touches your heart and appeals to the present position of your soul. When you have found it, let your mind dwell upon it like a bee upon a flower, extracting from it all the honey of devotion it contains.

You may also read with respect and attention devout sentences from Scripture or from the "Imitation;" they certainly will afford you thoughts which will excite your devotion either during meditation or after Communion.

CHAPTER X.

SECOND MEANS OF DEVOTION.

As the end of prayer is to correct our faults, we should consider that as the best prayer which inspires us with the greatest horror of sin and the greatest desire to avoid it. Prayer, it seems to me, may be compared to an orange-tree which bears leaves, flowers, and fruit; there are some persons who amuse themselves with culling the leaves, others with wreathing the flowers into bouquets, but the wisest gather the fruit and eat it with pleasure.

Now the fruit of prayer consists, principally, in a knowledge of our faults and in the resolution to correct them; thus we make a good meditation when we make a good examination of conscience. St. Ignatius has also taught us this manner of prayer. He tells persons not yet accustomed to meditate, and who are desirous to begin a new life, to examine their conscience on the commandments of God and the Church; to dwell upon each one for a short time, considering what it commands, and how just, salutary, easy, and reasonable it is; then to consider how they have observed it, and at sight of their failings against it to make acts of contrition for the past and to resolve to do better for the future.

We may make the same examination on the seven deadly sins, by considering their malice and conceiving great sorrow for having offended God so grievously.

Persons accustomed to make meditation may have recourse, with advantage, to this remedy when they find themselves in a state of dryness or desolation. Let them consider their own sins, particularly the vice to which they are most addicted; let them search the causes and the evil effects of their sins, and, after conceiving a horror of them, determine upon the means of avoiding them in future. If they leave meditation firmly resolved to adopt these means of amendment, they may be sure that they have made an excellent prayer.

There are others who find much profit and consolation in dwelling on the graces God has conferred upon them, and the dangers from which He has delivered them. Those who are more advanced in prayer may make use of this consideration to excite their love for God and their sorrow for their sins, contrasting the benefits they have received from Him with their indifference, their coldness, their cowardice, their infidelities, and their ingratitude: this will certainly afford occupation for the space of half an hour.

CHAPTER XI.

THIRD MEANS OF DEVOTION.

A soul sometimes finds itself in certain states in which nothing can console it; everything grieves and afflicts it; it seems to be suspended, as the patient Job says, between heaven and earth, unable to derive consolation from either. St. Bernard, who experienced such a state, gives an admirable picture of its misery, which ought to console all sufferers.

Perhaps the most grievous suffering of the soul in these states of darkness and desolation is the temptations which are so violent that it cannot be sure that it has not consented to them. I could bear this anguish, it says, if I were sure I did not consent to these abominations; but it seems to me that I utter all these thoughts that assault my mind, that I consent to all that I feel. There are two remedies for the suffering caused by this cruel uncertainty. One is to submit our judgment to that of our director, to fear only what he fears, and to despise all that he despises. There is no safe path in the spiritual life but that of submission and obedience.

The other remedy is to have some exterior sign to indicate that we embrace what is good and reject what is evil. Thus, some souls finding themselves violently tempted, or unable to produce any of the acts proper to meditation, take a crucifix and say: "My God, I declare before heaven and earth that whenever I kiss my crucifix it is to adore Thee; whenever I press it to my heart, it is to protest that I love Thee. Whenever I bow my head, deign to accept it as an act of humility; whenever I strike my breast, as an act of contrition; whenever I raise my eyes to heaven, as an act of resignation to Thy adorable will. When I utter the name of Jesus, it is to protest that I reject all the suggestions of the Evil One, and that I detest all that displeases Thee." God, as you know, does not need these exterior signs to understand the dispositions of your heart; He knows, without our telling Him what we wish and what we do not wish: this, therefore, is only to reassure timid souls and to restore their peace of mind; for, as the body acts only through the impulse of the soul, these exterior acts must necessarily proceed from the heart even though it seem to have no part in them. And as God is satisfied with our good desires, you will have the merit of acts that you cannot make, and spend the time of meditation most profitably.

Others, again, adopt still another method: their prayer is one of desire when they feel unable to pray as they would wish. If they find themselves constantly distracted and unable to preserve their recollection, or to free themselves from a state of coldness and indifference, or to excite any pious sentiments in their hearts, they raise their eyes to heaven and say: "My God, I would, in truth, do more for Thee than I do. Oh, that I could love Thee with my whole heart! Oh, that I could praise and honor Thee like the blessed in heaven! Would that I could make my prayer like that of the many good religious now in prayer before Thee! My God, I am not worthy to assist at the banquet of prayer with them; grant me but the crumbs which fall from their table. Oh, that I could pray with their fervor and attention! I offer Thee their prayer and that of Thy beloved Son to compensate for all that mine lacks."

This is an excellent and most meritorious prayer; it is like that of the countryman travelling with St. Ignatius. On their arrival at an inn, the saint and his companions knelt down to pray; the good man fell on his knees and said: "My God, I desire to do what these holy men are doing, and to pray as they pray." God rewarded the good man's humility with a great gift of prayer.

CHAPTER XII.

FOURTH MEANS OF DEVOTION.

You will tell me, no doubt, that these desires are soon over, and that you do not know what to do with the rest of the time; but there are still many other ways of spending it with great merit.

Do as the Son of God did in the Garden of Olives; He spent several hours repeating the same words: "Father, not My will but Thine be done." You cannot think a prayer unworthy of you which was worthy of God and which has been consecrated by His heart and His lips. It is a prayer of union than which you could offer none more perfect.

Then recall to mind all that grieves and afflicts you, and say with profound respect:

"My God, behold this chalice of weariness and desolation in which my lips are steeped, and which is in truth most bitter. I beg Thee, if it be possible, let it pass from me, but not my will but Thine be done.

"My God, behold this chalice of sorrow and humiliation which is presented to me; my heart faints and quails at sight of it. I beseech Thee that I may not drink it, yet not my will but Thine be done.

"My Father and my God, I am threatened with a grievous malady; it appalls and terrifies me. If it be possible, let this chalice pass from me, yet not my will but Thine be done."

Bring to mind in this way all that troubles you or is likely to grieve you, and, despite the repugnance of the senses, conform yourself to the will of God. I do not know that you could offer a better prayer than this.

CHAPTER XIII.

FIFTH MEANS OF DEVOTION.

If you cannot converse with God, invite creatures to praise and bless Him with you: this will not be a distraction, but a holy occupation which is the theme of our most beautiful canticles.

Say, for example: "All ye works of the Lord, bless Him, praise Him, and glorify Him forever. Angels of heaven, bless and praise God. Ye sons of earth, chant the praises of your Saviour and Lord; love Him with all your hearts."

Bring before you in this way the whole universe, and invite all creatures, animate and inanimate, to bless God like the men in the fiery furnace. Unite yourself with this concert of loving praise, and honor God to the best of your power by your humility and your patience. Bless and extol His infinite perfections, His goodness, His beauty, His wisdom, His power, His munificence, His mercy, His justice, His meekness, His patience, His grandeur, His majesty, His magnificence. Consider these attributes one by one and offer them the homage of your heart, saying: "O my God, how loving Thou art! Oh, how great is Thy beauty! How great is Thy goodness! How great and powerful Thou art!" Endeavor to be penetrated with the admiration which these words are fitted to excite, and say: "Bless the Lord, O my soul: and let all that is within me bless His holy name. Bless the Lord, O my soul: and forget not all that He hath done for thee: He forgiveth all thy iniquities: He healeth all thy diseases. He hath redeemed thy life from destruction: He hath crowned thee with mercy and compassion: He renews thy strength like the eagle's."

Continue in this way with all the perfections of God, pausing upon those which make most impression on your heart.

But the most beautiful and most consoling prayer for a sorrowful and despondent soul is to go in spirit to all the scenes of Our Lord's life and to thank Him for all that He endured for us.

Enter in spirit into the stable of Bethlehem, and adore Him with the shepherds; admire His humility, love His meekness, hope in His goodness, draw near to the manger, and if you find yourself incapable of any good thought, remember that the animals honored Him by their mere presence as best they could. Repeat the sweet canticle of the angels; give glory to God, and ask peace for your heart.

Then from the mystery of the nativity pass on to the adoration of the magi; go to the Temple and offer the infant Saviour to God with Mary; fly with Him into Egypt; shut yourself up with Him in the poor house of Nazareth; study His life there:

then His public life, His fasting in the desert, His preaching in Judea, His walking upon the waters, His healing of the sick, His raising of the dead. But, above all, follow Him through all the stations of His passion, from the Garden of Olives to Mount Calvary ; thank Him for all that He endured for you ; hear His gentle reproach to His sleeping disciples : "What! could you not watch one hour with Me? Watch ye, and pray that ye enter not into temptation." A suffering soul will find inestimable consolation in contemplating these sorrowful mysteries.

CHAPTER XIV.

SIXTH MEANS OF DEVOTION.

When we have learned how to love God we have acquired a noble science. There are many who cannot meditate, but few who cannot send forth loving sighs. These sighs, which voice the yearning love of the soul, are in reality the most beautiful, the most fervent, the most eloquent of all prayers : they are the prayer of souls wounded by the love of God, and aspiring to union with Him ; they can no longer speak ; their love is poured forth in sighs. "Daughters of Jerusalem," they cry, "stay me up with flowers, compass me about with apples, because I languish with love." This is all that breaks from time to time the beautiful silence of the soul where the heart alone speaks and where its every breat his a sigh of love.

Now, though this prayer is the final disposition

for union with God, and the occupation of those who can no longer meditate, yet all souls can practise it : it constitutes what we call ejaculatory prayers, which are loving darts which speed from our heart to the very heart of God.

It is also a prayer which knows neither art nor method ; it is taught by love ; to practise it the heart must be in no way constrained, but left free to say to God all that it wills. The language of love, St. Bernard says, is barbarous to one who understands it not ; but it is the language of the court of heaven, where charity reigns.

Though spontaneous acts are always best, we are not obliged to refrain from seeking to make others, particularly at seasonable times. For example, when we are suffering from aridity or distractions, or when we find nothing to occupy us, then the soul should seek its entertainment in loving. The aspirations should be short, particularly when they come from a heart wounded with the dart of love.

O my God and my All, when shall I be wholly Thine ? when wilt Thou be wholly mine ?

O God of my soul, how happy I am to be Thine ! O my Glory, my Life, why can I not love Thee as Thou shouldst be loved ?

My God, my God, why hast Thou forsaken me ? Ah ! I need not ask. I have truly deserved to be abandoned.

My heart is ready, my God ; my heart is ready : not my will but Thine be done.

O Jesus, look upon me with compassion and bless me !

Oh, why did I ever offend Thee, God of my heart and Father of my life?

Oh, when shall I love Thee, when shall I embrace Thee, when shall I possess Thee?

In this way we may produce any number of aspirations according to the disposition of our soul; and even though in times of aridity we seem not to feel the sentiments which they express, they will, nevertheless, be pleasing to God.

CHAPTER XV.

SEVENTH MEANS OF DEVOTION.

I must repeat again that the end of meditation is, not to meditate, but to love; hence affections, as they detach the heart from creatures and unite it with God, avail more than speculations and reasoning. We cannot love without meriting, but our meditations are not always an occasion of merit. Meditation is a means of exciting affection. When we have attained the end, the means are no longer necessary; if you can love, I dispense you from meditating.

Love is the disposition, the occupation, of souls who have long resisted their passions, who are persuaded of all the truths of religion, and who have made much progress in virtue; such souls, as I have said, have nothing more to do but pour forth their love in sighs and desires till they find the object of their desires in the enjoyment of the

Beloved. It is but a moment—a moment so brief and yet so long!

Souls advanced in prayer have no need of method or rule in the production of these affections; they should simply abandon their heart to the impressions of love and the movements of the Holy Spirit. But beginners who find themselves unable to meditate should, until they are more accustomed to the exercise of prayer, have recourse to a book containing all these acts of the various virtues.

CHAPTER XVI.

LAST MEANS OF DEVOTION.

Though the practices taught in the preceding chapters are fitted to occupy the most distracted mind and to inflame the most tepid heart, yet, as there are states where the soul is unable either to think of or to speak to God, and feels the utmost aversion for pious exercises, our final counsel is to make, in such case, an exercise of humility and patience.

The prayer of the humble is so powerful before God that it may be said to be irresistible. Achaz was a wicked king; but when he humbled himself, God was compelled, as it were, to lay down His arms, and when urged by a prophet to punish him He declared that, Achaz having humbled himself, it was not in His power. But when patience is united with humility, there is no anger which it will not appease, no scourge which it will not avert, no grace which it will not obtain, no power which it will not disarm, no strength and consolation which it will not merit.

Oh, how powerful in heaven is the cry of a humble soul! How it forces God's mercy and goodness! "Blessed," says St. Paul, "be the God and Father of Our Lord Jesus Christ, the Father of mercies and the God of all comfort, Who comforteth us in all our tribulations." St. Bernard bids us observe the words of the Apostle: God is not the Father of special mercy, but of many mercies; He is not the God of special comfort, but of all comfort; He comforts us not in special tribulation, but in all our tribulations; He is the plenitude of goodness, charity, and mercy, desiring only to be poured upon us.

Now, upon whom of all men does God look with most pleasure? Upon the humble in mind and heart, who believe themselves unworthy of all consolation, and who feel it too great an honor that He suffers them in His presence.

The streams of divine consolation flow not upon the mountains, says St. Bernard, but in the valleys. Patience is a virtue whose work is to finish and perfect—that is, to impart perfection to its possessor, as St. James says.

If it is God's glory we are seeking in prayer, there is nothing which honors Him so much as humble patience and patient humility; if it is our own merit, there can be no merit without humility and patience; if it is our perfection, humility must be its foundation, and patience its crowning glory.

We cannot always discourse in meditation, we cannot always reason, we cannot always weep; but we can always humble ourselves. We cannot always have consolation, but who is there that cannot always practise patience?

Humble yourself, then, Christian soul, when your meditations seem to you cold and fruitless; when you are assailed by distractions and temptations; humble yourself in all your trials; acknowledge that you can do nothing without the assistance of God's grace, that you are nothing but ignorance, weakness, and malice. Do not be satisfied with acknowledging that of yourself you can do nothing, but confess that you deserve nothing but chastisement; beware of complaining or murmuring as if God treated you with more severity than you deserve. Descend in spirit into hell, and consider whether your present position, your present trials, are not more endurable than that which your sins prepared for you there. Is it not God's presence which constitutes paradise? The saint's enjoyment of this presence is unalloyed; if yours is mingled with trials and difficulties, it has the advantage of affording you new merits and graces.

Avoid idleness. At the same time be convinced that you are not idle when you are not voluntarily distracted; that you accomplish much when you suffer much; that a prayer of consolation is not equal to a prayer of patience; and that if you do what you can, God will give you what you desire.

Great graces are the result of great struggles; great consolations follow great temptations. St. Teresa was sixteen years practising the prayer of patience, and merited by her fidelity to receive a great gift of prayer and extraordinary communications from God. If she had lost courage, if she had abandoned meditation, she never would have attained the prayer of union.

But you tell me God has abandoned you so long; that you are like the mountains of Gelboe—cursed by God—upon which neither the rain nor the dew of heaven ever fell; that God is displeased with you. Do not heed these discouraging thoughts. God is leading you through this hard and stony desert to the promised land flowing with milk and honey. He is establishing you in humility in order to fit you to receive the great favors He intends to bestow upon you. He is despoiling you in order to enrich you, and to make you merit what He yearns to give you.

Your whole duty consists in fidelity, and in never abandoning meditation, however painful or difficult you find it. If, when you are unable to pray, the Evil One asks you what you are doing, tell him that you are doing the will of God; that you persevere in this present duty because He commands it; that it is only too great an honor to be allowed in His presence; and that, if you can do nothing, you will at least learn to suffer.

Happy soul that can say at the hour of death, "I have never, whatever my occupations or distractions, failed to make my meditation." I am sure that a soul that can say this will not wait until the hour of death to be introduced into the promised land.

Some will tell you that they leave God for God

—that is, to serve Him, to preach, to hear confessions, to visit the poor, to comfort the sick. Alas! I fear they leave God to seek themselves. A good meditation furnishes matter for a good sermon; our hearts must be filled with that which we would impart to others; we must be united with God to win others to Him. Can we save souls without the assistance of grace? And is not meditation the channel through which it flows to us? Some allege, in extenuation, their inability to meditate; but this is, in truth, only a want of faith, of confidence, of charity. It is not tempting God to do what He commands, and to unite ourselves with Him by means of prayer. It is tempting Him, on the contrary, to expect His blessing and His assistance when we abandon the means He has prescribed for obtaining them; it is fighting without arms, guiding without light. In fact there is much reason to fear that these persons so zealous for the glory of God are over-zealous about themselves, and would rather lose their meditation than risk losing a little of their reputation.

O my God, one loses nothing in Thy service; too much dost Thou honor those who honor Thee. I shall always keep in mind this maxim of one of Thy faithful servants: "I would rather lose my reputation than my meditation, and preach a poor sermon than make a bad meditation."

Then be faithful, devout soul, to your spiritual exercises, whatever repugnance you may experience, however numerous your occupations. When you fall into some infidelity, do not lose courage, but repair it by your patience. Our homage is due to the justice of God as well as to His other perfections; our suffering pays this homage. His justice debars us from His merciful graces, but when it is satisfied, God is free to lavish His favors upon us. Our humility and patience satisfy His justice; they are the victims to be immolated on its altar; hence we are gaining immeasurably when we think all is lost.

Finally, remember that where there is least of nature grace reaps the richest harvests; that the operations of God are only the purer for being less sensible; that you are never nearer to God than when you think yourself furthest from Him; and that if you are faithful in this purgatory of desolation you will enter before you die into the paradise of consolation, where you will sing the praises of God, and where you will say, with the son of Sirach: "Behold with your eyes how I have labored a little and have found much rest to myself."

FOURTH TREATISE.

THE DEVOTION OF CALVARY.[1]

FIRST INSTRUCTION.

HOW IMPORTANT IT IS TO MEDITATE ON THE PASSION OF OUR LORD JESUS CHRIST.

I CALL the devotion of Calvary meditation on the Passion of Our Saviour. The prince of the apostles, instructing the faithful and desiring to render them victorious over all evil spirits, recommends them above all things to arm themselves with the thought of the sufferings of the Son of God as with a buckler impervious to all their attacks. "Christ," he says, "having suffered in the flesh, be you also armed with the same thought." St. Paul, writing to the Hebrews, exhorts them to use the same arms both to defend themselves in combat and to strengthen them in trials. "Think diligently upon Him that endured such opposition from sinners against Himself, that you be not wearied, fainting in your minds."

In truth, the thought of a God dying for sinners detaches the heart from affection for the world,

[1] P. Crasset, S.J.

inspires it with horror for the pleasures of sense, renders the trials of this life sweet and pleasing; it heals the wounds of the soul by the precious blood which flows from those of His body; it conquers the temptations of the Evil One and puts him to flight; it fills the Christian with divine consolations; it enlightens his mind and inspires him with firm hope of his salvation, through the knowledge it gives him of God's goodness and of the infinite price of the blood shed for him on the cross.

It is a devotion so dear to the heart of our divine Master that He instituted the great sacrifice of our altars to perpetuate the memory of it; and St. Paul, His disciple, after being raised to the third heaven, protests that he knows nothing but "Jesus Christ, and Him crucified;" as if he learned in his exalted state nothing greater, more sublime, and more necessary to the world than the knowledge of Jesus crucified and the devotion of Calvary.

Yet this knowledge is not to the taste of all. There are some who, it would seem, cannot adapt themselves to this devotion, sometimes because their hearts are attached to worldly possessions, honors, and vanities; or they are eager for the pleasures of the senses, which are not to be found on Calvary; or they cannot bear the reproach of this great example of patience; or, finally, because they cannot apply their minds to these sorrowful mysteries, or they do not move their hearts. This is the usual complaint of certain pious persons who, with strange inconsistency, seek only consolation in meditating on the Passion of Our Lord, and would drink the delicious wine of grace contemplating their Saviour's bitter draught of vinegar and gall.

To assist souls aspiring to perfection who find it difficult to meditate and to apply their minds, I have undertaken in this little work to give an easy and profitable manner of considering the sufferings of Our Lord.

SECOND INSTRUCTION.

A NEW MANNER OF MEDITATING ON THE PASSION.

The masters of the spiritual life teach several ways of meditating with fruit on the Passion of Our Saviour.

The first is that of St. Bernard, who wishes us to consider it, not as something that is past, but as actually present before us. This is also the manner of the Church: she represents all the mysteries of our religion to us as taking place the day she commemorates them: "This day," she says, "is born unto you a Saviour." To-day He died on the cross; to-day He rose from the dead; to-day He ascends into heaven.

The second is to believe that He suffered not only for all men in general but for each one of us in particular; that He thought of us in the midst of His greatest sufferings; that we were continually present to Him through all His Passion. It was after this manner that St. Paul meditated on this great sacrament of piety: "He loved me." he says, "and delivered Himself for me."

The third manner of meditating on the Passion is taught us by St. Bonaventure, that great lover of the cross and glorious imitator of Jesus crucified. He would have us, after considering all the sufferings of Our Saviour, enter into ourselves and recognize that we are the cause of all that He endured, that it was our sins which caused Him to die on the cross. This truth of faith is fitted to move the hardest heart.

The fourth and easiest manner consists in pondering all the circumstances of the Passion presented in these beautiful lines, which I found in the works of P. Suffren, who, I think, is the author:

RECOGITATE.

Quis patitur? Christus, Verbum, sapientia Patris.
Quid patitur? Spinas, verbera, sputa, crucem.
Pro quibus haec patitur? Pro nostra hominumque salute.
Cur patitur? Semper ne patitur homo.
A quibus haec patitur? Ab amica stirpe suorum.
Haec quando patitur? Cum mage fortis erat.
Haec ubinam patitur? Medio telluris in orbe.
Quomodo dic patitur? Discere nemo potest.
Fortis, amans, mutus, patiens, mansuetus obedit.
Sic patiente Deo, tu quoque disce pati.

RECOLLECT.

Recollect, again, again,
O ye blood-bought sons of men!
Who this Sufferer? Christ, the Word,
The wisdom of the Father, *God*.
What the suffering? Scourge and spear,
Thorns and spitting, cross and bier.
For whom this woe? Oh, think again!
For our salvation, for us men.
Why this suffering? So that we
Suffer not eternally.

> From whom comes this sore distress?
> From the men He died to bless.
> When this suffering? In the hour
> Of His manhood's brilliant flow'r.
> Where this suffering? In that town,
> The centre of earth's true renown.
> How He suffered tell to-day!
> Ah! no human tongue can say.
> Strong, loving, mute, in patient wise,
> Meekly, obediently, He dies.
>> O ye blood-bought sons of men!
>> Seeing your God endure such pain,
>> Learn to follow His bleeding feet,
>> And kiss the cross, and find it sweet.
>> (*Translated by* MISS S. L. EMERY.)

Besides these four ways of meditating on the Passion there is still another, which seems to me easier and perhaps simpler than those we have just been considering. It consists in applying the reason and two of the senses, sight and hearing.

To understand it we must imagine we are assisting at a tragedy, where we do three things: we look, we listen, and we think. We look at what the actors are doing; we listen to what they say; and we reflect on their actions and their words. It is through these two senses that the pleasure and pain of such spectacles enter. We weep when we see a great prince unjustly persecuted; we rejoice when the scene changes and fortune becomes more favorable to him. Then the mind resolves to practise his virtues and to imitate his example, which is the object of the tragedy.

St. Gregory Nazianzen has written a tragedy in verse on the Passion of Our Lord Jesus Christ. When you go to meditation persuade yourself that you are about to assist at this tragedy, at which the angels wept, the sun was darkened, the rocks were rent and trembled to their very foundation. We must look at what takes place in each scene; hear what is said; and reflect upon what we see and upon what we hear.

St. Augustine says that when the Roman stage represented a struggle between two friends who wished to die one for the other, the spectators were moved to tears. And can we behold unmoved the Son of God, the Monarch of the world, our best Friend, voluntarily suffering for us the most cruel and shameful death? Shall we be insensible to His sufferings? "O all ye that pass by the way, attend, and see if there be any sorrow like to My sorrow." It is Jesus Christ Who speaks here and Who teaches us by the lips of Jeremias how we should meditate upon His Passion. "*Attend*"—that is, give ear, apply the sense of hearing; "*see*"—apply the sense of sight; "see if there be any sorrow like to My sorrow"—apply the mind, consider if there be any sorrow equal to that which I endure for thee. St. Ignatius, the founder of our society, calls this kind of meditation the application of the senses. He applies all five; I appeal only to two, to which I add the operation of the mind.

Now, to facilitate this holy exercise we must observe the following rules:

I. We must know the history of the Passion—that is, what is said and what is done in each mystery.

II. We can divide the Passion into seven parts, for the seven days of the week, meditating upon two mysteries each day, one in the morning and the other in the evening. Persons who make only one meditation, and to whom one mystery furnishes matter for one or for several days, may devote two weeks or even the whole month to the meditation of all the Passion; and they should begin in the same way each week or each month.

III. We must beware of entering upon meditation to seek sensible favors and consolation; our purpose must be to honor Jesus Christ, by our presence to console Him for the part we have taken in His sufferings, to learn from His example, and to be incited to practise His virtues.

IV. After reading the history of a mystery of the Passion we should quietly consider what is taking place and listen to what is said as if we were present at the sorrowful spectacle; then apply the reason to the consideration of the mystery; then produce affections and resolutions in conformity with the mystery.

V. If the reading of the history excites a sentiment of devotion in your heart, dwell upon it and go no further. If it is unmoved, pass on to the meditation of the mystery. Begin by applying the sense of sight; then hear what is said; then consider the circumstances of the mystery.

If the heart continues unmoved, it is well to recite certain prayers fitted to produce affections. Finally determine upon the practices and resolutions: they are the chief fruit of meditation; therefore they must never be omitted.

VI. The devotion of the Passion may serve not only as meditation, but also furnish a devout means of assisting at Mass, particularly when you are to receive Holy Communion. Consider Our Saviour in your heart, in the mystery you have been contemplating adore Him, and thank Him that He willed to endure so much for love of you. You may apply the devotion in the same way in your visits to the Blessed Sacrament. You will find much consolation in contemplating Our Saviour in the mystery which has been the subject of your morning meditation.

THIRD INSTRUCTION.

WHAT THEY SHOULD DO WHO CANNOT MEDITATE ON THE PASSION.

I find there are two classes of persons who excuse themselves from meditating on the Passion of Our Saviour.

The first are those who are not yet accustomed to meditate, and who, from want of study, or capacity, or intelligence, or ability to reason, or because of a lively imagination, or, finally, because of a hard, insensible heart, cannot fix their minds on these mysteries.

There are directors who counsel such persons to abandon all subjects of meditation and to make no effort to think of anything. This may be good advice for souls advanced in perfection, but is very pernicious for beginners: it introduces the soul into a state of criminal idleness and of false peace instead of nourishing it with good thoughts and holy affections. It is contrary to all the principles of nature, of grace, and of faith. It ruins the foundations of the spiritual life and opens the door to innumerable illusions and distractions. It deadens the passions instead of conquering them. It lulls vices instead of stifling them. It flatters nature, and instead of raising the soul to true perfection brings it to the verge of dangerous precipices. It is not necessary to give the opinion of spiritual authorities on this subject. Common-sense and our natural intelligence are sufficient to show us that we can rest only after we have labored; that we reap only after we have sown; that we find the treasure of the Gospel only by searching for it; that we become masters only after we have been disciples.

Fear is the beginning of wisdom and the foundation of holiness. The conversion of the sinner does not usually begin through love, but through fear of God's judgments. Only Moses dares ascend Mount Sinai and enter into the mysterious darkness where one beholds God face to face and converses with Him as friend with friend. The gross and carnal people beheld the light at a distance and trembled at the sound of the terrible thunders. They were even forbidden to approach the foot of the mountain under pain of death; which shows us that only pure and holy souls may aspire to this union.

This is the doctrine of St. Thomas, of St. Augustine, of St. Bonaventure, and of all theologians. They teach that it is with grace as with nature, where the instrument must be prepared even to penetrate matter. St. Bernard considers souls most audacious, presumptuous, and rash who, though still unpurified from their vices, dare to aspire to the position of spouse and ask that the divine Bridegroom "kiss them with the kiss of His mouth." He tells them they should kiss the feet of Jesus by penance before venturing to kiss His hands, and afterwards kiss His hands by good works before they may kiss His mouth. In a word, he would have them purge the mind of its errors by the meditation of Christian truths, and the heart of its evil inclinations by continual mortification; he would have them pray, seek, desire, send forth continual sighs, and struggle without respite against their passions, before they aspire to the repose of contemplation. Therefore they who aspire to perfection must begin by meditating on the great truths of religion in order to detach themselves from the world, and to recognize its false maxims. They must ponder and carefully weigh the end for which God has placed them in this world; consider such truths as death, judgment, the eternity of punishment, the malice of sin and the punishment which God has inflicted upon it since the beginning of the world, the small number of the elect, the vanity and infidelity of creatures, the graces they have received and the account they will have to render of them. When such reflections have inspired them with great horror of sin, they should contemplate Jesus Christ, the great Model and Exemplar Whom God commands us to imitate. Let them meditate upon His actions and His words, but principally on His Passion, to excite themselves to the practice of virtue, as well as to be strengthened in their struggles and consoled in their trials.

But they must bear in mind two things. One is, to be faithful to their meditation and never to abandon it, whatever difficulties they experience; the other is, never, as I have said, to seek their own satisfaction in meditation, but only the honor and glory of God, Who has manifested an extreme desire to have us compassionate His sorrows. If He strikes their hearts with the rod of Moses, that is, with the cross, were they of rock, they will break forth into a torrent of tears, and they will find in the wounds of the Saviour the oil and honey of devotion. Jesus is the Way, the Truth, and the Life. He is the Way for beginners; He is the Truth for those who are advanced; He is the Life for the perfect. This, it seems to me, is what they have to do who are not versed in spiritual things and who aspire to perfection.

FOURTH INSTRUCTION.

WHAT THEY SHOULD DO WHO HAVE CEASED TO BE ABLE TO MEDITATE ON THE PASSION.

There are others to whom, at one time, no devotion appealed more tenderly than that of Calvary; they drank with joy of the living water from this divine source. And then a time comes when they fall into such insensibility towards these divine mysteries that they can no longer apply their minds to them or relish their sweetness. The touching objects which formerly moved them to tears no longer make any impression upon their hearts. In vain do they seek this divine source; it is as if it were dried or closed to them; it awakens no sentiment of compassion or devotion in their hearts. What are souls to do who find themselves in this state?

The most enlightened masters of the spiritual life are of the opinion that if such persons are fully convinced of all the truths of our holy religion, if they have long striven against their passions, and if they are perfectly abandoned to the providence of God, they may remain peacefully in His presence, and repose quietly on His breast, without constraining either their heart or their mind to make any effort. For we must not imagine the repose of such souls to be pure idleness. The mind is never inactive. It acts in this state, but in a quiet, spiritual, imperceptible manner which is known only by souls whom God has raised above the senses; who have been introduced, as Holy Scripture says, into the "wine-cellar" of the Bridegroom. St. Francis de Sales compares such souls to persons in a ship, who make more progress even in sleep than the best traveller can accomplish in walking and running. If you ask what a soul does in this mysterious repose, I will tell you in a few words.

I. It mortifies all its passions and represses all the movements of nature in order not to disturb the operations of the Holy Spirit, Who never fails to fill a soul with His divine presence when He finds it void of creatures. The full effect of His power is realized by a heart that does nothing to hinder His divine operations.

II. It repels all distractions that are presented to the mind, and shuts out the image of all objects likely to divert it from its intimate union with God.

III. It inflicts a species of martyrdom on nature, silencing all its thoughts, stifling all its desires, and suspending all its operations, that it may be possessed, moved, and animated only by God.

IV. It loses itself, buries and annihilates itself, in God. It dies to itself, seeking only the accomplishment of God's will, which it learns through the one who governs it, through the attraction which it feels, and through its inability to pray in any other way.

V. It offers God the sacrifice of all its powers, its thoughts, its desires, its actions, being like a victim that is slain, burned, and consumed on the altar of His love. It never ceases to keep its heart void of self and of all creatures, that it may be filled with the spirit of God.

VI. It presents itself before God as an unwritten page upon which He may imprint what figures and characters He will; as a blank, immovable canvas upon which the divine Artist may trace His own image; as a spotless mirror upon which the heavenly Sun sheds all its rays and transforms it into another sun like itself.

VII. It sleeps so calmly and profoundly on the breast of its Spouse that the hours seem as moments, and it comes forth from this repose as strong and robust as a man from bodily sleep, and who, though apparently idle during these hours of repose, is, nevertheless, renewing his powers and does not deem the time lost though the whole night has been given to uninterrupted sleep.

VIII. It remains lost in the divinity of God like a river which has reached the ocean, on the mighty bosom of which it is borne and rests after its weary course over mountain and vale.

IX. It is united with God, in a measure, like the saints in heaven—that is, in a close and immediate union.

X. It produces, in an eminent degree, acts of all the virtues: of faith, plunging into the mysterious darkness which envelops the throne of God; of hope, relying upon no creature, yet finding no sensible support from either heaven or earth; of charity, seeking God only and desiring no sensible consolation; of humility, humbling and annihilating itself in the presence of God with the knowledge of itself; of poverty, having nothing and desiring nothing; of mortification, keeping all its passions enslaved; of patience, suffering all the distractions which the Evil One creates in its mind to disturb its peace; of conformity to the will of God, abandoning itself to His guidance and desiring only to please Him. And so it is with all other virtues: the soul practises them in an eminent degree though it seems to be in a state of inaction and sleep.

But the principal occupation of the soul in this mystical repose, and which includes all that we could say on the subject, is the enjoyment of God. Acts of virtue are good in their time and for all kinds of persons; but there are some more perfect than others. An act of love of God is incontestably the noblest of all; but among acts of love there is one which in merit and dignity exceeds all the others—viz., the enjoyment of God, for it unites the soul to its final end, which constitutes the perfection and happiness of man. But this enjoyment is not a sudden brief emotion like the other acts of love produced in the fervor of devotion; it is a peaceful, tranquil repose in God like that of the blessed in heaven. This manner of prayer, therefore, may be called a continual and uninterrupted exercise of the love of God, through which the soul enjoys its sovereign good and its final end, in the repose of all its powers, in the annihilation of all its desires, and in the abandonment of itself to all the designs of God, which St. Francis de Sales calls "remitting one's soul into the hands of God."

This is what a soul does in that prayer, which persons of more learning than experience censure as idle. They are prompted by the zeal which impelled Martha to tax her sister Mary with idleness as she sat at the feet of Our Saviour, listening to the ineffable words which fell from His lips. St. Bernard wisely remarks in regard to such persons: "If any one censure the repose of the soul in contemplation as idle, be sure he is a carnal man with no knowledge whatever of the workings of the spirit of God. Let him heed Our Lord's words to Martha: 'Mary has chosen the best part, which shall not be taken away from her.'"

They who censure this repose confess, frankly enough, that they have no experience of it and pride themselves on roundly acknowledging it. Yet the same St. Bernard and all spiritual writers after him insist that this science is acquired only by experience, and that they who have no experience of it have no knowledge of it, and can no more judge of it than the blind can judge of colors.

Now, is it wise, is it just, to censure a thing of which we have no knowledge, and to condemn what we do not understand?

FIFTH INSTRUCTION.

IN WHAT MANNER PERFECT SOULS MAY MEDITATE ON THE PASSION OF OUR SAVIOUR.

This instruction will make the preceding instruction more clear, and afford, I hope, much consolation to certain souls who grieve that they cannot meditate on the Passion of Our Lord.

I call, with St. Jerome, a perfect soul not one that discovers only virtues in itself, that, like the Pharisee, is distinguished from the rest of men only by its penances and good works, but one that perfectly recognizes its nothingness and its imperfection; that feels the weight of its misery, of its passions, and of its evil habits; that considers itself as filled with vices and faults; that believes itself the most unfaithful, the most ungrateful, the basest of creatures; that, far from being satisfied with itself or dazzled by the splendor of its virtues, regards itself as an abyss of poverty, weakness, and malice; that distinguishes itself from others only by its humility, its obedience, its disinterested service, its confidence in God and its abandonment to His providence, and, above all, by a sincere, constant, firm desire to do God's will in all things, however they may thwart its natural inclinations. This is what I consider being holy and perfect; for humility is the foundation of perfection, and one who is humble truly believes, with St. Paul, that he is the greatest of all sinners. Now, whatever certain mystical writers may say to the contrary, I hold, with St. Bonaventure and St. Teresa, that souls in a state of union and raised by God to an eminent degree of contemplation may, when the divine Spouse does not bind their powers and attract them to profound recollection—may, I say, and even do well to consider Our Lord in some scene of His sufferings, not as formerly, by reasoning and discoursing upon the mystery, or by producing numerous acts or exciting sentiments of sorrow with more or less effort, but by quietly picturing to themselves the Son of God suffering for love of them, regarding Him with tender compassion, as a friend who witnesses the sufferings of a friend, as a bride who beholds the bridegroom treated with indignity.

It is not necessary, as I have said, to make any effort of the heart or the imagination; it is sufficient to cast a tender look of compassion upon Jesus Who is afflicted; for it is impossible to look upon the sufferings of one we love without being moved to compassion. Such was the sorrow of the Blessed Virgin when she beheld her divine Son dying on Calvary between two thieves. The terrible spectacle penetrated her inmost soul, and pierced it, as Simeon predicted, with a sword of grief. Yet she did not break forth into plaints and sighs; she did not reproach the Jews with their perfidy, their cruelty, their ingratitude. No; she stood silent at the foot of the cross, and gazed with tender compassion upon her dear Son everwhelmed with sufferings which she could not soothe.

In this manner may perfect souls contemplate the mysteries of the Passion of Our Saviour. They should not constrain their heart to sigh, nor endeavor to force tears from their eyes, but wait until the Spirit of God moves and inspires them, if He please, with tender and devout sentiments.

In truth, it is a grievous torment to suffer and make no moan. Devout souls who fain would sigh and relieve their overcharged hearts may do so without scruple by means of the following acts, but let them be made in a quiet, almost imperceptible manner.

The first is an act of thanksgiving to God the Son for having deigned to endure so much suffering and ignominy for love of them.

The second is an act of sorrow for having caused His sufferings and His death by the crimes they have committed since they came into the world.

The third is an humble prayer that He will deign to apply to them the fruit and the merit of the mystery they are contemplating: for example, if it is the suffering in the Garden of Olives, that He will console them in their afflictions and strengthen them in their combats; if it is the scene before Caiphas, when they struck His sacred face, that He will give them the grace to bear injuries with patience; if it is His appearance before Herod, that He will give them grace to despise the world and endure its contempt and neglect; if it is the pretorium of Pilate, that He will purify their flesh through the bleeding wounds which the scourges inflicted upon His own; if it is the carrying of His cross, that He will help them to bear their cross after Him; if it is His death on Calvary, that He will cause them to die to all their desires, to all their passions, and to all their vices. This, it seems to me, is the way pious souls may contemplate the Passion of Our Lord.

If it happen that they cannot fix their mind upon these sorrowful subjects, but desire to rest like a man overcome with sleep, then, as I have said, they must follow the attraction of the Holy Spirit, and close their eyes to all that is corporal and sensible, to let their soul be plunged in the Divinity, Which is the end and final term to which meditation on the truths and the example of Jesus Christ leads us; for He is the Way, the Truth, and the Life; the Way which leads to Truth, and the Truth which leads to Life.

These are the instructions which I have thought necessary to souls who desire to relish and practise the devotion of Calvary, whether they are still led by the way of ordinary meditation, or have attained the state of union and contemplation.

FIFTH TREATISE.

THE INTERIOR LIFE[1]

CHAPTER I.

ARTICLE I.

In what the Interior Life consists.

1.

THE interior life consists in two sorts of acts, viz., in thoughts and in affections. It is in this only that perfect souls differ from imperfect, and the blessed from those who are still living on earth. Our thoughts, says St. Bernard, ought to be "ever following after truth, and our affections ever abiding in the fervor of charity." In this manner, our mind and heart being closely applied to God, being fully possessed by God, in the very midst of exterior occupations we never lose sight of Him, and are always engaged in the exercise of His love.

[1] Father Lallemant.

II.

Good and bad religious differ from each other only in the nature of their thoughts, their judgments, and their affections. In this also consists the difference between angels and devils, and it is this that makes the former holy and blessed and the latter wicked and miserable. Accordingly we ought to watch with extreme care over our interior, and pay continual attention to regulate our judgments according to truth, and to keep our affections in subordination to charity.

III.

The essence of spiritual and interior life consists in two things: on the one hand, in the operations of God in the soul, in the lights that illumine the understanding, and in the inspirations that affect the will; on the other, in the co-operation of the soul with the lights and movements of grace. So that to hold communion with God, and to dispose ourselves to receive from Him larger and more frequent communications, we must possess great purity of heart, great strength of mind, and observe a constant and inviolable fidelity in co-operating with God and following the movement of His Spirit in whatever direction it may impel us.

IV.

One of the occupations of the interior life is the examining and ascertaining particularly three sorts of things in our interior; first, what comes from our nature—our sins, our evil habits, our passions, our inclinations, our affections, our desires, our thoughts, our judgments, our sentiments; secondly, what comes from the devil—his temptations, his suggestions, his artifices, the illusions, by which he tries to seduce us unless we are on our guard; thirdly, what comes from God—His lights, His inspirations, the movements of His grace, His designs in our regard, and the ways along which He desires to guide us. In all this we must examine and see how we conduct ourselves, and regulate our behavior by the Spirit of God.

We must carefully observe what it is that the Holy Spirit most leads us to, and in what we most resist Him; at the beginning of our actions ask grace to perform them well, and mark even the slightest movements of our heart.

We ought not to devote all our time of recollection to prayer and reading, but employ a portion in examining the disposition of our heart, in ascertaining what passes there, and discovering what is of God, what is of nature, what is of the devil; in conforming ourselves to the guidance of the Holy Spirit, and strengthening ourselves in the determination of doing everything and suffering everything for God.

ARTICLE II.

How we ought to imitate the Interior Life of God.

We ought to imitate the interior life of God in this, that He possesses within Himself an infinite life, as well by the operation of the understanding, by which He is the principle of the Person of the Word, as by that of the will, by which He is the principle of the Person of the Holy Spirit. Moreover, He acts externally to Himself, according to His good pleasure, by the production and government of the universe, without this exterior action causing any diminution or any change in His interior life, in such wise that in respect thereto He acts externally, as though He were not acting at all.

This is our model: in the first place, we ought to have within ourselves and for ourselves a most perfect life by a constant application of our understanding and will to God. Then we shall be able to go out of ourselves for the service of our neighbor without prejudice to our interior life, not giving ourselves up wholly to others, nor applying ourselves to exterior occupations, except by way of diversion, so to say; and thus our principal business will ever be the interior life. *Tuus esto ubique,* says St. Bernard to Pope Eugenius; *concha esto, non canalis.* Do not give thyself up to thy neighbor so as to be no longer thine own; possess thyself always; fill thyself with grace as a reservoir; then thou wilt be of use in communicating thereof to others. Be not like a canal, through which the water passes without staying therein.

This advice of St. Bernard ought to be the rule of evangelical laborers. But often they do the very reverse. They pour themselves forth entirely; they exhaust themselves for others, and remain themselves dry. All the marrow of their soul, if one may use the expression, all the vigor of their mind, spends itself in their exterior actions. There remains scarcely anything for the interior.

Hence it follows that, unless they take care, they have just ground to fear that, instead of being raised to heaven, according to the excellence of their vocation, they will be of the number of those who will be detained the longest time in purgatory and placed in the lowest ranks in glory.

Article III.

How it is that we make so Little Progress in the Interior Life.

This proceeds from three causes:

1. Exterior objects attract us to them by the appearance of some good which flatters our pride or our sensuality. This happens especially to those whose feelings are warm and who easily take fire.

2. The devil, exciting the phantoms of the imagination, awakening the recollection and the image of past things, corrupting and inflaming the humors of the body as occasions offer, produces in us anxieties, scruples, and a variety of passions. This he effects chiefly in those who, not having their heart as yet thoroughly purged, give him more hold upon them and are more in his power.

3. Our soul does not enter into itself except with pain, seeing there nothing but sins, miseries, and confusion; so that, to avoid this distressing and humiliating sight, it casts itself incontinently

into exterior things and seeks its consolation in creatures, unless we are careful to keep it to its duty.

CHAPTER II.

OF THE MOTIVES THAT LEAD US TO THE INTERIOR LIFE.

ARTICLE I.

We make No Progress in the Ways of Perfection unless we give ourselves to the Interior Life.

The exterior life of religious employed in the service of their neighbor is most imperfect, and even perilous, unless it be accompanied with the interior life ; and they who are engaged in these kinds of offices of charity and zeal, unless they join thereto exercises of interior recollection, will never make any notable progress in perfection.

1. And first, they will never attain the perfection of the purgative life. It is true they will have at times some of its sentiments. They will do things that appear great in the eyes of the world. They will preach; they will labor in missions; they will traverse seas and expose themselves to danger of death, and to the fatigue attendant on the longest journeys, for the salvation of their neighbor. But with all this they will never make much progress in the purgative life. The acts of virtue they perform will proceed partly from grace and partly from nature. They will never do such as are purely super-

natural, and under specious pretexts self-love will always make them follow their own inclinations and do their own will. They will fall continually into their ordinary faults and imperfections, and will be in great danger of being lost; for as they are occupied in anything but discovering the irregularities of their heart, they never think of purging it; so that it is continually filling with sins and miseries, which gradually enfeeble the strength of the soul, and end at last in entirely stifling devotion and the Spirit of God.

2. They will never attain to the perfection of the illuminative life, which consists in recognizing in all things the will of God; for it is only interior men who can discern it in everything. My superiors, my rules, the duties of my state, may indeed direct me in regard to the exterior, and indicate to me what God desires me to do at such a time and in such a place; but they cannot teach me the way in which God wills that I should do it. I know, for instance, that it is God's will that I should pray when I hear the clock strike which calls me to prayer according to my rule; but the rule does not tell me what my comportment ought to be during my prayer. My superior will tell me what God wills that I should apply myself to; but he cannot teach me how I ought to apply myself.

In order to do the will of God well, it is not sufficient to know that it is God's will; for example, that I should forthwith sweep my room. I must also know with what thought He would have me occupy myself while performing this exterior act of humility which my rule prescribes, for God desires to regulate the interior of my actions as well as the exterior. I must fulfil God's will as well in the manner as in the substance of the action. His providence extends to the direction of all my powers and all the movements of my heart. Without this there will be a void in my actions; they will not be full of the will of God; I shall do what He demands of me only in part and by halves; the best will be wanting, which is the interior. Thus I shall incur great losses of grace and glory, losses that are irreparable; and I shall be the cause of others, whose salvation and perfection I am bound to promote, incurring the same.

Where, then, shall I be able to learn the will of God in regard to the manner of performing well those things which He desires me to do? It must be in my own interior and in the depth of my own heart, where God gives the light of His grace, in order to enlighten me inwardly, that I may listen attentively to Him and converse familiarly with Him. I will walk in His light, which will enable me to see what He desires of me, and the means of performing it, and the interior perfection which it is His will I should practise therein.

3. It is clear they will never attain to the perfection of the unitive life, since it consists in the interior union of the soul with God.

For the rest, whoever is resolved to lead an interior life, and to be really spiritual and a man of prayer, must expect that when he has reached a certain point people will cry out against him; he will have adversaries and other contradictions; but in the end God will give him peace, and will make everything turn out to his profit and the advancement of his soul.

Article II.

Without Prayer we cannot acquit ourselves of the Duties of our Vocation, nor gather Fruit from our Ministrations.

I.

Without a solid devotion and a close familiarity with God, we cannot carry on our functions nor discharge them properly. The prophets, apostles, and other saints have wrought wonders because they were inspired by God and conversed familiarly with Him.

Saints succeed in everything because by their prayers they obtain a benediction and a virtue which render their labors efficacious. Although they be infirm and suffering from constant ill-health, like St. Gregory and St. Bernard, they effect wonders.

In vain we toil and form great projects for the glory of God and the service of souls: without prayer nothing can be hoped from our labor and undertakings; but with the gift of prayer we may do great things, even in matters of prudence and the management of affairs.

Let us season our exertions in behalf of our neighbor with recollection, prayer, and humility; God will make use of us for great ends, although we may not possess great talents.

We ought to undertake nothing, whatever the matter be, without having prepared ourselves for it by prayer.

II.

It is to God we ought to look for every success in our employments. We are His instruments, and we work under Him as under a master-architect, who, directing singly the whole design, allots to each one his task, according to the end he proposes, and the idea he has conceived. Thus we shall produce the more fruit the more united we are with God, and the more we yield ourselves to His guidance, always supposing we possess the talents and the capacity requisite for the active service of our neighbor. Now it is prayer that unites us to God. It is by this holy exercise that we dispose ourselves to receive the impression and movement of grace, as instruments to work out His designs.

III.

St. Gregory Thaumaturgus, explaining that saying of the Wise Man, "All is vanity," says that the devil displays before the eyes of men of the world honors, pleasures, riches, and all the creatures of the universe, like puppets which he sets in motion, shifting them, turning them, showing them in different aspects and different colors, decking them out with various ornaments and a false brilliancy; but in reality it is but a child's game, a vain amusement; there is nothing solid in it; it is but a pleasing illusion.

The devil employs the same artifice with those who compose the little world among religious; for in religion there is a little world, the elements of which are: the esteem of human talents; preference for employments, offices, and stations of importance; the love and the seeking for distinction and applause, or repose and an easy life. These are the things of which the devil makes, as it were, a puppet-show to amuse and deceive us. He sets it all moving before our eyes in such a way that we stop to gaze, and allow ourselves to be seduced by it, preferring vain appearances to true and solid goods.

IV.

Prayer alone can make us secure against this delusion. Prayer teaches us to judge soundly of things by looking at them in the light of truth, which dissipates their false splendor and fatuous charms.

Therefore it is that St. Ignatius desires that the professed and all those who have taken their last vows should give to prayer all the time they have remaining after fulfilling the duties of obedience. This ought to be the employment of those who in the colleges are not occupied with the office of regent, but only with hearing confessions, or some other duty which leaves them a good deal of leisure. They ought to be men of prayer, who by the help of their prayers sustain the whole house, the whole company—nay, the whole Church; and this is to be a Jesuit, this is to be the child of those great saints who desired more worlds to convert.

Behold how we may spend our days sweetly in the beauty of peace, in the security of a pure conscience and repose, rich with holy treasures: instead of wasting our time in trifles unworthy of an evangelical laborer, we ought to visit often the Blessed Sacrament, then apply ourselves to reading, then again return to our devotions, say the Rosary of the Blessed Virgin, and refer everything to prayer.

v.

As there are certain humors which, when they gain too much strength and are too abundant, cause the death of the body, so in the religious life, when action is carried to excess and is not moderated by prayer and recollection, it infallibly stifles the spirit.

And yet there will sometimes be found persons who, being occupied whole days and years in study and in the turmoil of exterior employments, will feel it difficult to devote a quarter of an hour a day to spiritual reading; and then how is it possible that they should become interior men? Hence it is that we gain no fruit, because our ministrations are not animated by the Spirit of God, without which, with all our talents, we cannot attain the end we are aiming at, and are but "as sounding brass and a tinkling cymbal."

An interior man will make more impression on

hearts by a single word animated by the Spirit of God than another by a whole discourse which has cost him much labor, and in which he has exhausted all his power of reasoning.

Article III.

Peace is not found except in the Interior Life, and our Dissatisfactions spring only from our not being Interior Men.

I.

Never shall we have peace until we are interior men and united with God. Repose of mind, joy, solid contentment, are found only in the interior world, in the kingdom of God which we possess within ourselves. The more deeply we enter therein, the more happy shall we be. Without this we shall always be in trouble and difficulty, always discontented and murmuring; and if any temptation, any rude trial, come upon us, we shall not overcome it.

II.

St. Augustine says that they who have an ill-regulated interior are like married men with peevish and ill-tempered wives. They leave home early in the morning and return as late as they can, because they dread a domestic persecution. In like manner, the former, having no peace in their interior, and finding there only remorse and reproaches of conscience, avoid as much as possible entering into themselves.

III.

If in our employments we practise the exterior of virtue without the interior, we are miserable, bearing the weight of exterior labor but never tasting interior unction and sweetness. This makes us fall often into notable faults; whereas, by means of recollection and prayer, we should effect more in our ministrations, with less difficulty, weariness, and danger, and with more perfection to ourselves, more advantage to our neighbor, and more glory to God. "This," adds Father Rigoleu in his collection, "is what our father director represented to us with much force, and it is one of the points he most urged upon us."

CHAPTER III.

THE OCCUPATIONS OF THE INTERIOR LIFE.

ARTICLE I.

Of Watchfulness over our Interior.

I.

Our principal study ought to be to watch over our interior, in order to ascertain its state and correct its disorders. To this the following considerations powerfully excite us:

1. We remain immersed, and, as it were, buried in a mass of faults and imperfections, which we never see till the hour of death, unless we exercise ourselves in observing the movements of our interior, wherein the devil and nature play strange parts while we are wholly absorbed in the hurry and excitement of exterior occupations.

2. The ruin of souls in the path of perfection proceeds from the multiplication of venial sins, whence follow a diminution of divine lights and inspirations, spiritual consolations, and other sources of grace; next, a great weakness in resisting the attacks of the enemy; and, finally, a fall into some grievous fault, which makes us open our eyes and perceive that, while we were thinking of something else, our heart was betraying us for want of watchfulness in guarding it, and from not entering into it to ascertain what was passing.

3. It is this living out of ourselves, and this carelessness in ordering our interior, which is the reason that the gifts of the Holy Spirit are almost without effect in us, and that the sacramental graces which are given us by virtue of the sacraments we have received, or are frequenting, remain without profit.

By sacramental grace is meant the right which each sacrament gives us, before God, of receiving from Him certain succors which preserve within us the effect that sacrament has wrought in our soul. Thus the sacramental grace of Baptism is a right which Baptism gives us to receive lights and inspirations to lead a supernatural life, as members of Jesus Christ, animated by His Spirit. The sacramental grace of Confirmation is a right to receive strength and constancy to combat against our enemies as soldiers of Jesus Christ and to win glorious victories over them. The sacramental grace of Confession is a right to receive an increase of purity of heart; that of Communion is a right to receive more abundant and efficacious succors to unite us to God by the fervor of His love. Each time we confess and communicate in a good state these sacramental graces and the gifts of the Holy Spirit increase in us; and yet we do not perceive their effects in our daily life. Whence comes this? From our unmortified passions, our attachments and disorderly affections, and our habitual faults. We allow these vicious principles to have more dominion over us than sacramental graces and the gifts of the Holy Spirit, so that the former keep the latter, as it were, bound and captive, without the power of producing their proper effects. And why do we let sin and the vicious principles of corrupt nature usurp this despotic empire over the divine principles of grace and the Spirit of God? It is for want of entering often into ourselves. If we did so, we should discover the state of our interior and correct its disorders.

II.

1. By watching over our interior we gradually acquire a great knowledge of ourselves, and attain at last to the direction of the Holy Spirit. And at times God brings before us in an instant the state

of our past life, just as we shall see it at the Judgment; He makes us see all our sins, all our past youth. At other times He discloses to us the whole economy of the government of the universe; and this produces in our soul a perfect subjection to God.

2. They who have applied themselves for three or four years to watch over their interior, and have made some progress in this holy exercise, know already how to treat a multitude of cases with address and absence of all rash judgment; they penetrate, as it were, naturally, the hearts of others, and discover almost all their movements by the knowledge they possess of their own interior, and of the natural movements of their own heart.

3. Without performing extraordinary mortifications, or any of those exterior actions which might be the occasion of vanity to us, by simple attention in watching our own interior we perform excellent acts of virtue and make prodigious advances in perfection; whereas, on the contrary, by neglecting our interior we incur incalculable losses.

4. These exercises may be practised at every age, at all times and in all places, in the midst of our exterior functions and in time of illness; and there is no business so embarrassing which does not allow us to enter into ourselves from time to time, to observe the movements of our hearts.

5. What exterior actions did St. Paul the Hermit perform, and so many other saints, and so many holy virgins? It is the merit of their interior life

which raised them to the highest ranks of the blessed.

But, alas! we are so little enlightened, or so bewitched with all the brilliancy of exterior employments, that we understand not the excellence, nor the necessity, nor the merit of that life which is hidden from the eyes of men and known to God alone.

III.

Nothing is so dangerous as to neglect the care of our interior, and to take no pains to know what is passing therein. This negligence and this ignorance give occasion to a multitude of venial sins, which dispose us insensibly to some mortal sin or great temptation, whence ensue fatal falls.

Such is often the end of the purely exterior life of those among us who are continually engaged in the tumult of action, abandoning the care of their interior under pretext of zeal and charity, because they labor for the service of their neighbor. But even should they not proceed to this extremity, it is still certain that by wasting themselves exteriorly, and giving scarcely any attention to the regulation of their interior in the exercise of their functions, they suffer incalculable losses of grace and merit. Their labors produce but very little fruit, not being animated by that strength and that vigor which come from the interior spirit, nor accompanied with the benedictions which God bestows on men of prayer and recollection. They do nothing purely for God; they seek themselves in everything, and always secretly mix up their own interest with the glory of God in their best undertakings.

Thus they pass their lives in this mixture of nature and grace, without once taking a single step forward towards perfection for ten or twenty years, the mind as distracted, the heart as hard, amid all the exercises of Christian piety and the religious life, as if they had never enjoyed all these aids.

At last death comes, and then they open their eyes; they perceive their illusion and blindness, and tremble at approaching the dread tribunal of God.

The means of avoiding all these woes is to regulate our interior so well, and to keep watch over our heart so carefully, as to have ground for desiring, rather than fearing, to appear before our sovereign Judge. It is this watchfulness that Our Lord so much recommends to us in the Gospel, when He says so often, *Vigilate*, "Watch." "Our father director," says Father Rigoleu, "requires nothing else from us but this constant attention to our interior."

ARTICLE II.

How Important it is that we should join the Interior Life with our Exterior Occupations.

I.

Our occupations are often indifferent in themselves, and yet may be most glorious to God, and more to His glory than others which in themselves are supernatural. Thus our studies and our office of regent conduce to the salvation of others, and promote the glory of God, more than would the assisting in choir and chanting the divine office, were such the practice of the society, as in other orders. But unless in this occupation of the classes and of study we act from the principle of the interior spirit, we are just like seculars, and often merit only chastisements in the next life.

II.

We ought to unite action and contemplation in such a way as not to give ourselves more to the former than to the latter, endeavoring to excel as much in one as in the other. Otherwise, if we throw ourselves altogether into the exterior life, and give ourselves wholly to action, we shall undoubtedly remain in the lowest degrees of contemplation; that is, we shall practise only ordinary prayer, and perform the other exercises of piety in an inferior and imperfect manner.

III.

We should unite action and the exterior life with contemplation in such wise as to give ourselves to the former in the same proportion as we practise the latter. If we make much mental prayer, we ought to give ourselves much to action; if we have made but moderate progress in the interior life, we ought to employ ourselves only moderately in the occupations of the exterior life; and if we are but little advanced in the ways of the interior, we ought to abstain altogether from what is exterior, unless obedience prescribes the contrary; otherwise we shall do no good to others and ruin ourselves.

IV.

We must be like the eagle, who soars into the air as soon as he has seized his prey. Thus we ought to retire for prayer after any active employment for our neighbor, and never intrude ourselves into such unless obedience enjoins it.

V.

Let us be thoroughly convinced that we shall gain fruit in our ministrations only in proportion to our union with God and detachment from all self-interest. A preacher when he is much followed; a missionary when he produces a great sensation; a confessor when he sees his confessional surrounded by a crowd of penitents; a director when he is the fashion; a person when he devotes himself entirely to good works—one and all flatter themselves they are gaining much fruit, and to judge from appearances we might believe it. The world praises them; applause confirms them in the good opinion they have of their success. But are they united to God by prayer? Are they perfectly detached from themselves? Do they act only from divine motives? Do not human views mix themselves up with their designs? Let them beware of deceiving themselves. Men are easily deceived in this matter. They seek God, it is true, but do they not also seek themselves? They intend the good of God and the good of souls, but do they forget their own glory and their own petty interests? They employ themselves in works of zeal and charity, but is it out of a pure motive of zeal and charity? Is it not because they find their own satisfaction in it, and love neither prayer nor study, and cannot live retired in their own room or endure recollection?

If we examine ourselves well, perhaps we shall find in our souls so little union with God, and in the service we render to our neighbor so much self-seeking, that we shall have just ground for doubting whether we do all the good to others that we imagine, and do not inflict more evil upon ourselves than we are aware.

To labor profitably for the salvation of others, we must have made great progress in our own perfection. Until we have acquired perfect virtue, we ought to practise very little exterior action. But if superiors lay too much upon us, we may trust that Providence will so dispose things that the burden will soon be diminished, and all will turn to the greater good of inferiors, if they are good men.

VI.

We must acquire virtues in a solid degree, and after that labor to promote the salvation of souls;

then exterior action will aid us in the interior life. But until we have acquired solid virtues and are closely united to God, exterior occupation will certainly be injurious to us.

Article III.

We ought not to engage in Exterior Occupations of our Own Accord.

It is not for us to choose our own employments. Of our own free will we ought to give our whole attention to ourselves, unless obedience imposes on us functions for the service of our neighbor. From obedience must come the movement which leads us to external action for the good of others. So long as it leaves us at rest, let us willingly remain so. God will know very well how to find us when He wishes to make use of us to His glory. It is great rashness to intrude ourselves into the government of souls—an office which the most perfect saints, the Ambroses and Gregories, fled from with fear. The blessed Louis Gonzaga had a scruple in having speculated for a moment as to what employment superiors would allot him.

CHAPTER IV.

ADVICE FOR THE INTERIOR LIFE.

Article I.

We ought to cultivate the Will more than the Understanding.

Application to study is befitting a religious, especially if he is called by his vocation to apostolic labors; but there are some who devote themselves thereto with more of passion and curiosity than zeal. We are sometimes bent only on filling the mind with such knowledge as serves rather to harden and chill it than to soften it by devotion and inflame it with fervor. It is the will we ought principally to cultivate. We have sufficient knowledge, but we are not sufficiently united to God. We ought to make it our chief study to acquire the spirit of prayer, and to become filled with a great love of God.

Cardinal du Perron, when dying, testified his repentance for having during life applied himself more to perfecting his understanding by the sciences than his will by the exercises of the interior life. Some of us will perhaps feel the same regret in the last passage. Woe to that knowledge which makes us neither humble nor better men!

ARTICLE II.

The Path of Faith is a Safer Way to Perfection than that of Sensible Graces.

God leads souls by two sorts of ways. Some He guides by interior lights, consolations, and sentiments of devotion. And this way is the most dangerous, because it gives occasion to self-love to luxuriate in favors of this kind, on account of the relish we find in them, and the high esteem we hence conceive of ourselves. Along this road lies the precipice of the bad angels, whose sin was pride, which puffed them up by the consideration of the spiritual goods they had received from God.

Others are led by reason and faith, assisted by the ordinary aids of actual graces, but without sensible consolations, except on rare occasions. And this road is the safest, and leads most directly to perfection, because therein we walk more in spiritual poverty and humility.

ARTICLE III.

The Best Mode of Practising the Virtues.

I.

We ought to tend continually towards God, without stopping short at His gifts and graces. Some are too much engrossed with the formal objects of virtues, which are merely natural. It would be far better to act on a principle which would raise us straight to God, as does the divine love. It is true that all the virtues lead us to Him by their own proper motives, but it is with greater slowness and with less perfection.

II.

There are some whose minds are intent upon discovering several motives of virtue with a view of performing their actions thereby, thinking by some such means to render them more agreeable to God. We ought merely to try to ascertain what virtue God desires we should practise in each action, and then simply perform that action in the presence of God, according to the intention with which He inspires us, and with the motive and purpose of imitating Our Lord.

It is to this end that the love of Our Lord is so strongly urged upon us, the motive of which is easy, suited to all the world, and full of sweetness. And the good that is done by the principle of this love—an act of temperance, for example, performed with the view of imitating Our Lord and pleasing Him, is far more excellent than when it is done simply to observe such moderation as temperance prescribes.

SIXTH TREATISE.

MEANS OF ACQUIRING PERFECTION.[1]

We must will to acquire it.—Spiritual books suggest a great many means of acquiring perfection, yet we may say that the only real means is a determined will. There is nothing difficult to a good will assisted by the grace of God. We cannot think that this assistance will be denied us, since the Son of God tells us we must be perfect even as His heavenly Father is perfect, and this we cannot be unless He help us.

They who will to acquire Perfection.—Inclination to good does not make a man righteous, any more than inclination to evil makes him wicked. To be good we must will what is good, and we are good in proportion as we will what is right. If you will to be perfect, you must avoid all that turns you from the practice of virtue, and embrace all that leads you thereto. If you do nothing it is because you do not will to accomplish anything. You may have a complacent admiration for perfection without any desire or will to be perfect.

Necessity of a Director.—A man who is wise will not attempt to go through a dangerous forest full

---

[1] P. Crasset, S.J.

of tortuous, winding paths without a guide; a prudent merchant will not go to sea without a good pilot. If you are without a good director you will miss your route and suffer shipwreck. God does not govern men by special revelations. The prudence so necessary in the spiritual life is a gratuitous gift bestowed upon us for the benefit of others and not for ourselves. "Woe to him that is alone!" says the Wise Man, "for when he falleth he has none to lift him up." If he wander from the right path there is none to bring him back. If he fall ill there is none to nurse him back to health. If enemies attack him there is none to defend him. Choose, therefore, a wise director and obey him faithfully.

We must recognize our Imperfection and Misery.—There are some souls who hope to become perfect in a day. As long as we have enemies we must combat them: as long as we have vices and faults we must resist them, and we are free from them only at the hour of death; so much so, that perfection almost consists in recognizing our misery and humbling ourselves for it before God. I fear much for those souls who imagine they have attained perfection and who complacently regard their virtues. I am of the opinion of St. Bernard, that "one who thinks he lacks nothing lacks everything." In the spiritual life a soul is ill indeed that believes itself in perfect health, and vicious indeed if it think itself devoid of any vice, for it is infested with pride, which brings all vices in its train.

We must be Faithful in Little Things.—Great things

depend upon little things, and little things lead to great. You will make great progress in virtue if you are faithful in little things. "He that is faithful in that which is least," says Our Lord, "is faithful also in that which is greater." What excuse may you offer for not being perfect, since God only asks of you what is easy and within your power? Do what you can, and what you are unable to do God will do for you. Do what is easy and God will do what is difficult. If you despise venial faults you will inevitably fall into grievous sins.

We must keep ourselves in the Presence of God.— "Walk before Me," said God to Abraham, "and be perfect." You will be perfect if you walk before God and always keep yourself in His presence. God is in the depth of your soul: you will find Him if you enter into yourself by recollection; you will lose Him if your thoughts are abroad and you are occupied with exterior things. He is pleased to dwell in solitude and silence. It is creatures that rob us of Him; fly them and you will possess Him in security. Where are you when you are not with God? What are you seeking when you possess God? Happy soul that carries its sovereign Good within its heart, that sees God in all things and all things in God!

We must avoid Dissipation.—To keep the soul in recollection and prevent it from wandering abroad we must close the doors of the senses, we must watch over our eyes and our ears. These are the windows through which the soul escapes; we are dissipated in proportion as we admit external matters into the citadel of our soul, or allow our thoughts to be engaged in them. Place guards at all the avenues which lead to your soul, and permit nothing to enter without knowing whence it comes and whither it tends.

We must be Faithful to Prayer.—If we are not men of prayer we shall never attain perfection. How can you be perfect if you do not love God? How can you love Him if you do not know Him? How are you to know Him if you do not consider and study Him? Now, it is in meditation that the soul learns the perfections of God, that it discovers His infinite beauty, that it recognizes His benefits, that it receives His caresses and is inflamed with His love.

We must mortify our Body and its Passions.—To pray well we have only to be faithful mortifying ourselves. The wood of the cross is needed to enkindle this fire in our hearts. The spirit gains in proportion to the weakness of the flesh, and the flesh in proportion to the weakness of the spirit. Observe moderation in your penances, and do nothing except by the order of your superiors.

We must keep the Thought of Death before us.— Only two things are necessary to become perfect in a short time: one is to believe that it is to-day that we are beginning to serve God; the other is that it is the last day we have to serve Him. If you were about to die, how would you perform this action? Perform all your actions in the same way, and you will soon become perfect.

Our Hearts must be attached to Nothing.—Consider as lost to you all that you can lose; do not be attached to anything the loss of which would grieve you. Let your heart be fixed upon nothing inferior to God; esteem nothing but what leads to God. The root of all our trouble in this life is that we esteem what we ought to despise, and despise what we ought to esteem.

Our Hearts must be detached from Everything.—Since a thing is perfect when it is united to its principle, man's perfection consists in being united to God. You will never be united to Him unless you are detached from all things. Take one step beyond creatures and you will find the Creator. Leave visible things and you will find the invisible. Pass beyond time and you will enter eternity. Detach yourself from all that is not God and you will find yourself united to God.

We must correct our Vices.—Perfection does not consist so much in filling as in emptying our hearts, in doing good as in avoiding evil. Open the doors of your heart and God will enter at once. Empty your heart of creatures and it will be filled with God. Correct your vices and God will sanctify you.

We must never choose for ourselves.—To hold to nothing, to be disposed for all that God wills, to have no choice or desire, indicate a perfect soul and one that is wholly abandoned to God. Preserve your freedom; let no creature enslave you. Do not be ruled by wicked masters. You could not have a more cruel master than your passions; when they no longer rule you in any way you have attained perfection.

We must conform ourselves in All Things to the Will of God.—Whatever path you choose in perfection, you will find none shorter, easier, or more secure than that of conformity in all things to the will of God. It is a devotion which is singularly free and unencumbered, and leads incontinently to union. Do all that God wishes and He will do all that you wish; be content with Him and He will be content with you; labor for Him and He will labor for you. A man who has no self-will does the will of God, for God's will takes the place of his own; and as the divine will is continually done, it is true to say that a man who is devoid of self-will does God's will without ceasing.

We must humble ourselves for our Faults.—To be righteous and appear so is a dangerous state. To appear righteous when we are not is a vicious state. To be righteous and appear the contrary is a state of perfection. God leaves us with faults to keep us humble and to protect us from vanity. There is nothing more dangerous than a reputation for great sanctity. Glory is the portion of the other life, humility of this. Bear your faults, holy soul, when you cannot get rid of them, and never cease to labor for your perfection. Our desire for perfection is, not unfrequently, the desire for our own excellence rather than our sanctification.

We must love Solitude.—To fly from the world, to seek solitude, to speak little to men and much to God; to do all that is required of us and yet recognize that we are unprofitable servants; to accomplish works worthy of praise and yet desire no praise—this is the summit rather than the path of perfection. You will never live safely among the throng until you have learned to appreciate solitude. Remain in your nest until your wings are fully fledged. Cast deep roots before you try to bear fruit; dig deep foundations before you attempt to raise your edifice. Your elevation will be in proportion to your former humility; your glory in heaven will be proportioned to your lowliness on earth.

We must die to our Desires.—Accustom yourself to do without creatures, to desire nothing outside yourself, and to be content with the enjoyment of God. Your desires are so many tyrants which make you the victim of ambition and self-love. Have but one desire, to do the will of God, or rather, do it unceasingly. Beginners should have a great desire for perfection, but they will never attain it until they die to all their own desires. What can a soul desire that possesses God? What may a soul seek that has found God? Keep yourself in peace whatever happens, and when your desires rebel, tell them that you know nothing comparable to peace of soul, and that you will not forfeit it for all the treasures of the world.

We must continually do Violence to ourselves.—If we would speedily become saints we must unceasingly do violence to ourselves. We reach life only through death, victory only through combat, repose only through labor, union only through detachment, perfection only through the cross and mortification. Give your flesh to God and He will give you His Spirit. Watch over your senses and He will watch over your heart. Guard the citadel without and He will guard it within.

Mortify yourself in little things and He will render you victorious in great.

We must love our Neighbor.—If we love our neighbor we are perfect, for the Apostle tells us it is the fulfilment of the law. It is also loving God, for it is keeping His commandments, which are almost all included in the precept of charity. Then love your neighbor and God will love you; assist him and God will assist you; excuse him and God will excuse you; bear with him and God will bear with you; pardon him and God will pardon you. If you were to work miracles and suffer martyrdom, yet had not charity, you would be nothing; and what will become of one who commits nothing but crimes and is a martyr only to the Evil One?

We must always think of God.—Let no week pass without Communion, no day without a cross, no hour without thinking of your soul, no moment without thinking of God. Is it not just that you should think of Him when He is lavishing benefits upon you—and are not His benefits unceasing? To do God's will is to think of Him. Offer Him the beginning of each action, and do not imagine that you have done nothing for Him if during the performance of the duty begun for Him you have not thought of Him: He knows your heart and your intentions. If you were asked for whom you were doing this action, would you not answer that you were doing it for God? Then have no fear: you have been laboring for Him even though some time has elapsed without your thinking of Him.

We must endure the Privation of Spiritual Consola-

tions.—Though we must not reject the consolations which God gives us in meditation, yet we must not be attached to them. A soul in the enjoyment of this sensible fervor receives gifts from God, but gives Him nothing; it enjoys much, but merits little. There is hardly any state in which a soul honors God and enriches itself more than in that of suffering. It honors God by the sacrifice of its mind, of its will, of its passions, and of all its powers. It enriches itself by the practice of all the most heroic virtues: faith, hope, charity, poverty, resignation, fidelity, humility, patience, and perseverance.

We must deny ourselves.—Live as one who passes beyond figures to truth, beyond death to immortality, beyond time to eternity. An eternity of happiness or an eternity of misery awaits you: you will attain the first by bearing your cross and denying yourself; you will reap the second by serving your passions and following your own will.

We must obey our Superiors.—You will know whether all is well with you by the obedience you render your superiors. "It is impossible," says Cassian, "for an obedient man to fall into delusions, and equally impossible for him to avoid them if he is not obedient." Your progress, your perfection, will be in proportion to your obedience. To the soul that sacrifices its spirit to God God gives His own; He does the will of one who does His will. If you will not renounce your own light you will lose that of faith and fall into error. Therefore obey all your superiors: obey in all that is not manifest sin; obey at all times, under all circumstances; obey in heart and mind.

We must be Master of our Hearts.—It is a pity to love and not know what we love; to have a heart and not be master of it. Watch over your affections ; love nothing too eagerly or in a manner to disquiet your heart. Keep always in mind this beautiful motto of St. Bernard: " Nothing short of God, nothing like God, nothing with God, nothing after God."

Abridgment of Perfection.—All the counsels that could be given concerning perfection might be almost reduced to four, which are like the four wheels of the chariot of sanctity, and the square of Christian justice: to abandon one's self to the providence of God ; to obey one's superiors in all things; to do harm to no one; to deny one's self by continual mortification. These constitute a sure road to perfection.

Part Third.

Union with God by Contemplation.

To have a proper understanding of the interior things of spirituality or mystical science, we must have recourse to desire and not to the understanding; to sighs and not to reading; to God and not to men; to Jesus, the Spouse, and not to the doctors; to mystical darkness and not to light; to the silently consuming fire and not to brilliant light. (St. Bonaventure.)

O spiritual souls, be not discouraged when you feel your forces weak, incapable, and, as it were, paralyzed. Rather believe that this is for you a happy condition, and that God comes to free you from all that is imperfect in your manner of treating with Him; that He takes you by the hand, that He guides you in the midst of this darkness. Let yourself be guided: walk confidently and safely: your eyes could never guide you so surely, your feet could never support you so firmly. (St. John of the Cross.)

CHAPTER I.

UNION OF THE SOUL WITH GOD THROUGH CONTEMPLATION.[1]

In what this Union consists.—The soul attains this divine union, is admitted to the nuptials of the Lamb, through three means: meditation, affection, and contemplation. Meditation instructs the mind; affection enkindles the heart; contemplation unites the soul with God.

Meditation purifies the soul of its vices and its errors; affection inflames it and impels it to practise good works; contemplation elevates it and causes it to enter into the chamber of the Bridegroom.

Meditation is for beginners; affection for those who are advancing; contemplation for the perfect.

In meditation the mind seeks; in affection the heart desires; in contemplation the soul finds what it sought and enjoys what it desired. The mind labors in meditation, the heart sighs in affection, and both mind and heart rest in contemplation. Thus the divine union is the enjoyment of God which the soul has sought in meditation,

---

[1] P. Crasset.

which it has acquired through affection, and which it has found through contemplation.

The word contemplation indicates an operation of the mind, an operation usually pertaining to scholars. But Christian contemplation has more to do with the heart than the mind. It is a repose, a peaceful enjoyment on the part of the soul which is not disturbed by any image of the mind or any emotion of the heart.

The soul that desires to be the spouse of Jesus Christ, and to receive the "kiss of His mouth," must first kiss His feet like Magdalen; must be purified by tears from its vices and evil habits; must kiss His hands by numerous good works. Then it must wait in silence and profound respect until Jesus Christ introduces it into the banquet-hall to receive that mystical kiss—that is, that divine Spirit—which St. Bernard says is a kiss of the Father and the Son. The soul is first a servant and fears its Lord; then it becomes a daughter and respects its Father; finally it becomes a spouse and loves only the Bridegroom. These are the degrees by which it ascends to contemplation and attains that mystical union.

St. Bernard, explaining these words of David describing the just man, "In his heart he hath disposed to ascend by steps," indicates four steps of this mystical ladder, which may be reduced to the three we have just mentioned. "The wise man," he says, "prepares in his soul the steps by which he may ascend to contemplation. The first step is towards the heart; the second is in the heart; the third is the heart itself. In the first the soul fears the Lord; in the second it listens to the Master; in the third it desires the Bridegroom; in the last it enjoys God."

Effects of Contemplation.—Who may explain the effects of this divine enjoyment? We may say of this marriage, or union of earth, what St. Paul says of that of heaven, that "eye has not seen, ear has not heard, neither has it entered into the heart of man to conceive what God has prepared for those who love Him." The soul suffering from the wound of love, which can be healed only by Him Who inflicted it, weeps disconsolately for the Bridegroom, and burns with desire to find Him and reveal its pain.

After a long quest it seems to fall into a death-like state; it is unable to speak, and knows not what it behooveth it to do or to say. A deep silence pervades the depth of its heart and dismays it, for it may not divine whence it comes. Then it enters into a night of darkness, which obscures all its natural light and powers. Its imagination is void of images, its mind speaks not, its heart is still, its memory is void, its passions are silent, its senses inert. It is during this silence, this night, that the Word descends from heaven, and that the soul becomes, in an ineffable manner, the spouse of Jesus Christ. Ask me not how this is effected; ask those who have experienced it. All I can tell you is, that the soul comes forth from these divine and ineffable operations so filled with God, so penetrated with His Spirit, that it no longer feels or is conscious of itself, and, like the rivers which flow into the sea, finds itself lost and swallowed up in God.

Then all creatures disappear before it, like shadows before the sun. It sees only the beauty of its divine Spouse, Who dwells in the depth of its heart; it hears only His voice, and enjoys naught but the sweetness of converse with Him and the ineffable joy of His presence. It cannot understand that any one may love or seek aught but Him.

God called Moses to the summit of Mount Sinai, and caused him to enter a secret place enveloped in clouds and darkness. Into like obscurity, appalling to nature, does God plunge the soul which aspires to this divine union. It fears to fall from this dizzy height into precipices which yawn below; but when the darkness and obscurity have completely enveloped it, it discerns Jesus transfigured, and contemplates God face to face, so to speak. It feels Him sometimes without seeing Him,—feels that He imprints Himself as a seal upon its heart, that His finger writes therein the law of love, which dissipates all its sadness and fears. In such moments the soul experiences consolation and joy so pure and so great that, like St. Paul, it knows not whether it is in heaven or upon earth. If this state were to continue nature would succumb to the violent efforts of love. When this union and these divine communications have ceased, the soul descends from the mount of contemplation, like Moses from Mount Sinai, resplendent with light, inflamed with the love of God, and giving forth heavenly odors which embalm the hearts of all with whom it speaks or who behold its prayer.

The Mystical State.—It is during the night, when the doors of the senses are closed, that the Bridegroom enters the heart of His spouse, while she wots not how or by what means He has entered; albeit her heart is buried in profound darkness, she knows that the wedding-feast is celebrating, and that the cold and insipid water of her devotion is changed into a delicious wine. At times she feels in the depth of her soul, if we may so speak, operations of the divinity so intense, so penetrating, so delicious, that she finds no human language adequate to express them.

Nuptials of the Soul.—The air then resounds with the sublime canticles which the chaste spouse chants to the glory of the Bridegroom. She quaffs, or rather she is inebriated with, the wine of consolations, so that she appears bereft of her senses to those who have not assisted at these divine nuptials.

Moses leads his flock and his powers into the desert, to be retired from all.

Philip, transported with joy, exclaims: "He hath shown me the Father; I desire nothing more."

Mary Magdalen says to the disciples, "I have seen the Lord;" and she affirms it though they treat her as a visionary.

The Spouse prepares a banquet in a cenacle closed to all creatures. The senses are sometimes invited; their pleasure then is so great that it penetrates to the very marrow of the bones, which, hard and insensible as they are, are constrained to exclaim, "O Lord, who is like unto Thee!"

As to the mind, it usually remains at the door of the heart where the nuptials are celebrated, and may not enter. It knows that the Spouse is within; but it cannot understand what is taking place until the doors are opened to it. O the ecstasy of the moment when this favor is granted! What must have been the rapture, the joy, of the sorrowful disciple of Jesus, at beholding his Lord, Whom he believed dead, living and gloriously risen from the dead! The soul then, transported with love, exclaims with St. Peter, not knowing what it says: "It is good for us to be here. O the happiness, the inebriating joy, of this presence! Let us make here three tabernacles: one for Faith, one for Hope, and one for Charity." But all this is of very brief duration: a heavenly cloud suddenly shuts out this glorious sun, which by a strange marvel is hidden from the mind, and enclosed, so to speak, in the heart, inflaming it with love. This is the couch upon which the Bridegroom is pleased to repose; it is here that He reveals to His spouse the most hidden secrets of the Divinity, lavishing upon her ineffable caresses incomprehensible to the human mind.

Happy the chaste souls called to these nuptials of the Lamb! Happy the dead who die in the Lord—who die to their light and their judgments; who die to their cares and their anxieties; who die to their desires and their fears. They will pass from fear to hope, from hope to love, from love to fruition, from fruition to union, and from union to transformation. Then God will wipe away their tears, and the Holy Spirit will bid them rest from their labors, for henceforth theirs will be a permanent peace, undisturbed by the accidents or vicissitudes of life.

O my heart! when wilt thou enter this mysterious silence? When wilt thou be plunged in these sacred obscurities? When wilt thou enter this kingdom of peace?

Come, holy souls, to this marriage-feast of Cana; Jesus awaits you and invites you. If the wine fails, Mary will supply it by causing her Son to work a miracle in your favor. Come, learned souls, come to learn in this school of love; abandon your brilliant reasoning, renounce your own lights. This science is not acquired by study, but by experience. It is the unction, and not the doctrine, which teaches. It is a science of the heart, and not of the mind. "Taste and see that the Lord is sweet." We recognize natural truths before we experience them; but we must experience these truths before we may know and comprehend them.

Dispositions for attaining this Union.—To attain this union, which creates a Paradise on earth, great mortification and recollection are necessary: mortification, to detach the heart from creatures; recollection, to unite it with God. We must abandon ourselves to His providence, without anxiety for the present or the future; we must allow ourselves to be governed by our superiors, without permitting nature to ask or refuse anything. We must renounce our own opinions, mortify our own will, resist our passions, and faithfully obey grace in all that it asks of us.

Detachment.—It is very difficult to converse with

God and with men. It is impossible to be recollected when our thoughts are constantly abroad; to be the slave of our heart and free in spirit; to be interested in everything and to think of nothing; to be filled with affections and void of distractions; to be spiritual, leading the life of the senses; to be a talkative man and a man of prayer. After Moses had conversed with God he veiled his face and conversed but little with men: this was to teach us that if we would enjoy the company of God we must fly that of men; at least, that to converse profitably with men we must be long practised in converse with God.

The Necessity of Meditation and Affection to attain this Union.—I fear much for those presumptuous souls who aspire to the rank of spouse before they have filled that of servant, who would rest before they have labored. Action must precede contemplation. Meditation must excite affection, must dispose the soul for union. It is through labor that we attain repose. Fear sustains love; penance supports hope; the Humanity of Jesus is the door through which we enter the palace of the Divinity. His infancy touches the heart, His Passion incites it to suffer, His beauty enraptures it, His goodness charms it, His benefits attract it, His love inflames, unites, and transforms it.

Have you been exercised in meditation, devout soul, before seeking contemplation? Have you labored before you have sought repose? Can you say that your peace is the fruit of your combats and your victories? Have you not entered into a pact with your passions? Have you not appeased and lulled them instead of putting them to death? Have you not made a truce with the enemies of God instead of conquering them and subjecting them to the empire of grace? Fear God in order to know Him, mortify yourself if you would enjoy Him, leave all to possess Him, renounce your own light and your own powers to behold and contemplate Him, for He has said, " Man shall not see Me and live." Then delay not, O Lord, to effect this death in me; let me die to all things that I may speedily behold Thee! Oh, when will this happy day be mine! When may I enter into the cabinet of the Bridegroom, or when will He come into the chamber of my heart, where, removed from all creatures, with closed doors, I may treat with Him as friend with friend?

Certain Graces are Lent, not Given us.—A passing grace does not constitute a state. Some graces, St. Bernard tells us, are lent us, others are given us; some, again, are attractions, and others are rewards. The graces of attraction precede merit: the graces of reward follow the attraction and crown merit. The graces of attraction last only for a time, the graces of reward always continue with faithful souls. We have no reason to feel assured of our state because we have been permitted to behold Jesus transfigured on Thabor. We may not believe that we have been elevated to the rank of spouse because we have been suffered to assist at the marriage-feast of Cana. A repentant sinner is sometimes permitted, in the beginning of his conversion, to enjoy God after the manner of the spouse, yet he has not for that reason attained the state of union. Because we have once or twice experienced the higher degrees of prayer is no reason for abandoning ordinary meditation. Fear, desire, sigh, labor, struggle, hope; but never presume on your merits.

Presumptuous Souls.—There are rash souls, says St. Bernard, who with overweening presumption dare to enter the chamber of the Spouse and to pray, 'Let Him kiss me with the kiss of His mouth!" They are without the wedding garment, yet they do not fear to present themselves at the marriage-feast. The Bridegroom, to punish them for their temerity, has them bound hand and foot and thrust into exterior darkness. A soul covered with wounds needs not the Bridegroom, but a physician. It should seek healing, not caresses. Only chaste lovers, pure, mortified souls, may aspire to such favors, and sing the canticle of the spouse, " Let Him kiss me with the kiss of His mouth." Only peaceful souls, victorious over their passions, may aspire to taste this ineffable union. Oh, who would dare to ask it! And yet, who could not but desire it!

Sighs of a Future Spouse.—Alas, Lord! by Thy grace I have long wept for my sins and washed them in the sacred waters of penance. I have long embraced Thy feet, and with the penitent Magdalen kissed them and watered them with my tears. Thou, in Thy goodness, hast presented me Thy hand to kiss, to excite me to good works. Then, may I hope to see Thy adorable face one day, and to receive—I say it with trembling—" the kiss of Thy mouth"?

Yes, thou mayest hope for this, devout soul, provided thou art humble and obedient, pure and mortified; provided thou seekest only to humble and not to exalt thyself; provided thou hast no will but that of God and thy superiors; provided thou dost abandon thyself to His providence, and desirest to be in time and eternity only what He wishes thee to be ; provided, finally, thou makest thyself worthy of this favor, and thinkest thyself eternally unworthy. For humility is the foundation of this tower of perfection; and we can rise only by first descending into the abyss of our miseries.

Humility necessary to become a Spouse.—Oh, how I admire a soul that rises to the contemplation of God by the contemplation of its own unworthiness! You will never attain this intimate union with God unless you are persuaded, not only theoretically, but practically, and by long experience of your miseries, that God is all and that you are nothing; that He is light and that you are darkness; that He is wisdom and that you are folly; that He is strength and that you are infirmity; that He is goodness and that you are malice. If you are not penetrated with these truths, and if you find yourself anything but an abyss of faults and imperfections, you are far from the goal you are seeking. If you believe honestly and unfeignedly that you are the weakest of men, the most ungrateful of Christians, and the greatest of sinners, you have already made great progress toward union. Oh, the folly of a soul that thinks itself possessed only of virtues and merits, and is at a loss to discover what it lacks !

He who believes he lacks nothing lacks everything. You will be in the disposition to attain contemplation when you are persuaded that your malice equals, in a measure, God's goodness; that as He is the fulness of all blessings, you, in your capacity, are the fulness of all evils. Oh, the beautiful union of all with nothing, of abundance with indigence, of fulness with emptiness! Until, like Jeremias, you recognize your poverty, God will not enrich you with His graces; and if you do not free your heart of all self-esteem, you never will be filled with the Spirit of God, which is the Father of union and the sacred tie which unites the soul to Jesus Christ in the shadows of faith, with which He overshadows it when it abandons itself completely to the will of God, and says with the Blessed Virgin, "Behold the handmaid of the Lord: may it be done to me according to His word"

CHAPTER II.

THE DOCTRINE OF ST. FRANCIS DE SALES IN REGARD TO CONTEMPLATION.[1]

DIVINE LOVE SEEKS SOLITUDE AND SILENCE.[2]

PRAYER may be called a manna, on account of the different flavors and divine sweets which love discovers to those who make use of it. But it is a hidden manna which falls in the desert before the dawn of day; that is to say, it is not the fruit of lights and science; its sweets can only be tasted in solitude. When we converse with God alone, then we may say of the soul, "Who is she, that goeth up by the desert, as a pillar of smoke of aromatical spices of myrrh, and frankincense, and of all the powders of the perfumer?" (Canticles iii. 6.) It is the spouse herself, who entreats her beloved to conduct her into solitude, that they may both converse in secret: "Come, my beloved, let us go forth into the field, let us abide in the villages" (Ibid. vii. 11).

The great attraction which persons of prayer experience is to converse with God in perfect solitude. The blessed Mother Teresa of Jesus relates

---

[1] "Treatise on the Love of God."
[2] Book VI., ch. i.

of herself that in the commencement of her spiritual career she had a singular devotion to those mysteries which represent only the person of Our Lord, as during His prayer in the Garden of Olives, or when He waited for the Samaritan woman near the well; she thought that when her divine Master was alone He would attract her more powerfully, and that she would be sooner united to Him.

Love seeks not for witnesses of its words; and even when those who love have nothing to communicate which requires secrecy, they take pleasure in conversing in private. The reason of this probably is, that they only speak for each other; and it would seem to them they did not speak for themselves alone if their interview could be overheard. Besides this, they make the most ordinary observations in a manner so peculiar as to mark the love from which their words proceed. There is nothing uncommon in the words they use; but the tone, the emphasis, and the manner which accompanies everything they say render their language so singular that they alone can understand it. The title of friend publicly conferred on an individual signifies but little; but when uttered in private it comprehends a great deal, and becomes more expressive in proportion to the secrecy with which it is spoken.

DIFFERENCE BETWEEN MEDITATION AND CONTEMPLATION.[1]

Contemplation is nothing more than a loving and simple attention of the mind to divine truths, continued for some time. By comparing it with meditation, you will easily comprehend in what it consists.

The young bees which have not begun to work are called nymphs, and when they commence to make honey they are named bees. So it is with prayer: it is called meditation in the beginning, and when it has produced the love of God it receives the name of contemplation. Bees fly through the fields about their hives to feed on the flowers and extract their juice; and after having laid up a sufficient provision, they continue to labor for the pleasure which the sweetness of the honey procures them. So we meditate to acquire the love of God; but after having obtained it, we contemplate—that is, we turn our attention to the divine goodness, being attracted by the ineffable sweetness which love discovers to us in this attention. A desire to obtain the love of God induces us to meditate; and love, when we have acquired it, leads us to contemplate.

THE KNOWLEDGE OF GOD IS LESS NECESSARY TO US THAN LOVE.[2]

The will, it is true, only tends to what is good through the medium of the understanding, which

---

[1] Book VI., ch. iii.
[2] Book VI., ch. iv.

proposes it to its view. But when it has once felt its attractions, it does not require the help of the understanding to attach itself thereto more and more closely, because the delight it takes in its object, and the pleasure it expects to derive from it by union, attract it to love and desire its enjoyment. Love resembles all other passions, of which knowledge is the principle and source, though not the rule and measure.

We are induced to love God by the knowledge which faith gives; but when we have begun to love His infinite goodness, love increases our natural tendency thereto, as this inclination reciprocally augments love.

HOW CONTEMPLATION REDUCES ALL THIS TO SIMPLE UNITY.[1]

We shall now consider how meditation is changed into contemplation. After the multiplied reflections which constitute meditation have excited devout and pious sentiments, we unite these different feelings and extract their essence and virtue. The peculiar qualities of each affection are thus mixed and united, and from this union proceeds an affection which may be called the substance and quintessence of all the others; it is in itself more lively and active than all the various affections from which it is derived, since it includes the virtues and various properties of each; it is termed the contemplative affection.

Water separates into numerous streams in pro-

[1] Book VI., ch. v.

portion as it runs farther from its source, and forms several channels, through which it flows, unless great care be taken to confine it to one. In the same manner, the perfections, which all emanate from God, divide in proportion as they are separated from this first principle; and according as they approach it they reunite, until they become totally engulfed in this one sovereign perfection, which is the one thing necessary, the better part chosen by Magdalen, which shall not be taken from her.

THE VARIOUS MEANS WHICH LEAD TO CONTEMPLATION.[1]

As great assiduity in hearing the word of God is usually necessary for attaining contemplation, also spiritual conferences and discourses with pious persons, according to the example of the ancient fathers of the desert, the reading of spiritual works, prayer, meditation, singing the divine praises, and great care to occupy the mind with holy thoughts, and as contemplation is the term to which all these means are directed, those who perform these spiritual exercises are called contemplatives and the manner in which they employ themselves is termed the contemplative life. This name is very applicable, because the principal part of this manner of life consists in the operation of the understanding, by which we consider the beauty and the amiability of the sovereign Being, with an amorous attention—that is, with

[1] Book VI., ch. vii.

love which animates the attention of the mind, or with attention which proceeds from and increases love.

LOVE COLLECTS THE POWERS OF THE SOUL.[1]

It is the natural property of infinite goodness to attract and unite to itself everything capable of feeling its impressions. Our soul, which possesses this capability, always tends to what is good, and inclines thereto as to its treasures or the object of its ardent love. When God infuses into the heart a certain indefinable sweetness, which proves that He is present in a particular manner, all the interior powers, and even the exterior senses, bend, as if by common assent, to this inmost part of the soul, to enjoy the company of the amiable and beloved Spouse, Who causes His presence to be so sensibly felt there.

A person who has just communicated may, by the certainty which faith gives him, experience this truth, revealed to him not by flesh and blood, but by the Eternal Father Himself, that, by the adorable Sacrament of the Eucharist, his body and soul enjoy the real presence of the body and soul of Jesus Christ. When the mother-pearls have received the infusion of the drops of the morning dew, they always carefully close their shells, not only to preserve what they have collected, and prevent the sea-water from mingling with the drops distilled from the heavens, but also because the freshness of the dew is analogous to their nature,

[1] Book VI., ch. vii.

and would afford them pleasure, were they capable of feeling it.

This is the case with many devout persons after they have participated in the Sacrament by excellence, which contains the mystical dew of all heavenly graces and benedictions; their soul then becomes consecrated in itself not only to adore its King, Who is present therein, but also to taste the inexpressible consolation and incredible heavenly sweetness, springing from the germ of immortality, which by the light of faith they discover to have been planted in their hearts.

We must not lose sight of what has been said at the commencement of this chapter, that the recollection of which we speak is the work of love, which, being first aware of the presence of God by the sweetness diffused in the heart, obliges the soul to unite its powers and attention, and direct them to its Beloved. All this is effected with ease and pleasure, love communicating to the soul an inclination to direct all its powers to God, Who attracts them with so much sweetness. The infinite goodness of the Almighty attracts and binds all hearts more powerfully than cords and chains can fasten and restrain the body.

RECOLLECTION IS FREQUENTLY PRODUCED AND INCREASED BY A GENTLE, REVERENT FEAR.[1]

We must also observe that this recollection is not always produced by the sweet conviction that God is present in the heart; other causes may

[1] Book VI., ch. vii.

produce a similar effect, provided they tend to place the soul in the divine presence. In attentively considering the sovereign majesty of God, Who beholds us, we are sometimes seized with so lively a feeling of respect and delicious fear that all our interior powers are immediately concentrated and recollected in themselves, just as the unexpected presence of a great prince recalls the wandering thoughts of the most distracted mind, and produces the exterior respect and reverence due to the dignity of the person present. It is said that there are certain flowers which close their leaves when the sun shines, and bloom again when his light is withdrawn. This is a figure of what occurs in the state of recollection of which we speak: at the remembrance of the presence of God, at the conviction that He looks on us from the height of His exalted throne in heaven, or from any part of the earth beyond ourselves, though we may not actually reflect on that ordinary presence by which He dwells within us, the powers of the soul, that they may be more undividedly directed to this divine object, immediately unite, animated with respect for the divine Majesty, and a holy fear, springing from love, which gives much glory to God.

OF THE REPOSE OF A SOUL RECOLLECTED IN GOD.[1]

The soul having entered into itself, for the purpose of being wholly recollected in God, or before God, is solely attentive to His sovereign good-

[1] Book VI., ch. viii.

ness; but this attention is so simple, so sweet, so easy, so imperceptible, that the soul is sometimes not aware of being occupied. The operation which takes place in it is so delicate that it can scarcely perceive it, and is liable to mistake it, as we are sometimes deceived respecting the nature of rivers which flow very smoothly and calmly. Persons who sail on these rivers, or who look at them, imagine that they have no motion; they think they can neither see nor feel any because there are no waves or billows to render the motion sensible. This is the sweet repose of the soul, which St. Teresa terms prayer of quiet; it does not differ in the least from what she styles the sleep of the powers of the soul. This repose may be more or less profound; it sometimes increases to so great a degree that the soul appears to be asleep, and all its powers, except the will, seem inactive and motionless. It does nothing but receive the impressions of the happiness and satisfaction which result from the presence of its Beloved.

What is still more admirable is that the will enjoys this content without perceiving it; because the soul is entirely occupied with Him Whose presence constitutes its bliss, and its thoughts are quite diverted from itself. In this situation it may be compared to a person who falls into a gentle sleep while surrounded by a large party: he partly sees what his friends are doing; he receives their caresses, but he does not notice them, because he is not reflecting on them and is not aware of feeling them.

However, the soul, which in this sweet repose enjoys God by a feeling sense of His presence, without perceiving that it enjoys it, still clearly proves that it highly prizes this happiness, and prefers it to all others, when any event is about to deprive it of it. It then complains loudly; it grieves, and even sheds tears like an infant which is awakened before it has slept sufficiently; it gives evidence of regret which plainly shows the satisfaction it derived from its slumber, since it weeps for its loss as for the privation of a great advantage. For this reason the divine Spouse, addressing the daughters of Jerusalem, conjures them by the roes and harts of the fields not to stir up nor make the beloved to awake till she please (Cant. ii. 7).

It appears that Magdalen was absorbed in this prayer of quiet when, seated at Our Redeemer's feet, she listened to His word. I pray you consider her attentively in this circumstance. She is seated, perfectly tranquil; she utters not a word; she sheds not a tear; no sob convulses her breast; no sigh escapes her heart; she is motionless; she does not pray; Martha passes from time to time through the room, but Mary is unconscious of her presence: what, then, is she doing? She is listening—that is all; she is in a state of total inaction. That is, she remains at Jesus' feet like a precious vase, receiving drop by drop into her heart the sweet myrrh distilled by the lips of her Beloved. Hence the divine Bridegroom, jealous of His sacred spouse's repose, will not have Martha awaken her: " Martha, Martha, He says, "thou art careful and art troubled about many things. But one thing is necessary. Mary has chosen the better part, which shall not be taken away from her." What was the part Mary had chosen? To remain recollected at the feet of Jesus, and to enjoy the peace and repose of this recollection.

Remember then, Theotime, that if God attract you by this simple and filial confidence, you must remain tranquilly near Him, without exerting yourself to make marked acts of the understanding or the will: for this loving confidence and repose of soul include excellently well all the exterior acts you could make to satisfy your inclination. It is better thus to sleep in the arms of Our Saviour than to watch elsewhere.

OF THE MANNER IN WHICH THE SOUL ENJOYS REPOSE IN GOD IN THE PRAYER OF QUIET.[1]

The soul in this state of holy recollection has no further need of the memory any more than of the understanding: when we are enjoying the presence of a friend we need not tax our imagination to represent him to us. It suffices that our will come forward and accept the sweetness of the divine presence: the other powers, without making any effort, have only to enjoy the repose which God's presence affords.

Wine mingled with honey is used, as we have already observed, to recall the fugitive bees to their hive. It is also employed to appease them when they mutiny and destroy one another. The

[1] Book VI., ch. ix.

person who superintends the hive throws some of the mixture into it, and the most seditious of the bees, attracted by the agreeable perfume, seem to forget their enmity, and are only occupied in tranquilly enjoying the sweets presented to them.

O my God! when by Thy amiable presence Thou infusest into our hearts Thy heavenly perfumes, far more fragrant than wine and honey, all our interior powers cease to act, and enter into delicious repose, which imparts so great a calm and such perfect content that not one of them attempts the slightest motion.

The will alone, which may be termed the spiritual sense of smell, is sweetly occupied in feeling without perceiving the inestimable advantage which results from the presence of God.

OF THE DIFFERENT DEGREES OF THE PRAYER OF QUIET, AND THE MEANS WHICH SHOULD BE EMPLOYED TO PRESERVE THE HOLY REPOSE OF THE SOUL.[1]

The minds of some persons are active, and abound in thoughts and arguments. Others find great facility in considering and accounting for what occurs within them; they wish to see and examine everything, to reflect continually on what passes in their interior, and to account to themselves for everything they do. In order to be assured of their advancement, they are incessantly considering their operations, and always occupied with themselves.

[1] Book VI., ch. x.

There are others who are not satisfied with being contented, unless by marked acts they feel their happiness. These last may be compared to persons who, being defended against the inclemency of the weather by warm clothing, cannot be persuaded that this is the case unless they know the quality and quantity of their clothes; or, who, finding their coffers replenished with riches, cannot believe themselves wealthy unless they know exactly the number of pieces of gold and silver which compose their treasure.

The minds of these different characters are liable to be disturbed and distracted during prayer. If the Almighty introduce them to the holy repose of recollection in His presence, they will voluntarily quit it, to consider how they acted while it lasted; and if their happiness be great, they will sacrifice the tranquillity they enjoy to examine the extent of their calm and peace. Instead of occupying their will in tasting the ineffable delights of the divine presence, they will invite their understanding to reason on the sweetness of these delights. In this they are like a spouse who, instead of being occupied with her bridegroom, amuses herself with examining the ring he gave her on the day of their marriage. Ah, what a difference, Theotime, there is between being occupied in God, Who constitutes our happiness, and occupying ourselves with the contentment which God gives us!

Therefore, a soul which God invites to rest lovingly in Him in the prayer of quiet should abstain as much as possible from reflections on itself and its state. The repose it enjoys is extremely delicate;

a look suffices to prove a disturbance thereto, or even to destroy it effectually; to preserve it, it should be careful not even to be aware of its existence. By being too much attached to this prayer it forfeits it; the real way to love its sweets is not to be anxious to know the extent of its enjoyment, that thereby it may not be tempted to attach its affections thereto.

If it happen, during the enjoyment of holy repose in prayer, that the soul is tempted by curiosity, and distracted by reflecting on what occurs within it, it should quickly oblige its heart to resume the sweet and peaceful attention to the presence of God from which its thoughts have strayed. However, we must not imagine that we are in danger of forfeiting this holy quiet on account of movements, either of mind or body, in which levity and indiscretion have no share; for, as St. Teresa observes, it is a species of superstition to be so jealous of our repose as to refrain from coughing, and almost from breathing, for fear of losing it.

God, Who is the Author of this peace, will not deprive us of it for such motions of the body as are unavoidable, or even for involuntary distractions and wanderings of the mind. Though the understanding and the memory may escape the bounds of restraint and wander on strange and useless thoughts, yet the will, when once attracted by the charms of the divine presence, will still continue to enjoy the same delights. It is true that the calm is not then so perfect as it would be if the understanding and the memory were in union with the will; yet a real spiritual tranquillity is certainly and effectually enjoyed, since it resides in the will, which governs all the other powers of the soul.

It is, however, certain that the soul would enjoy more calm and sweeter peace if no noise were made near it, and that it could refrain from all interior and exterior motion. It would willingly devote its attention solely to the divine presence, which imparts such ineffable delights; but it cannot always prevent some of its faculties from disturbing it; and then, not to incur the privation of its repose, it concentrates itself in its will, this being the power through which it enjoys the presence of its Spouse.

When the will is attracted and sweetly restrained by the happiness it derives from the presence of God, it should not endeavor to recall the other powers when they are diverted from this object; thus to separate from its divine Spouse would be to sacrifice its repose. Its efforts to recall the attention of these volatile powers would also prove vain and ineffectual. Besides, nothing is more efficacious in bringing them back to their duty than the tranquil perseverance of the will in holy quiet, because the heavenly sweetness diffused in the heart, as a perfume whose fragrance is gradually communicated to all the powers of the soul, invites them to return and unite themselves to the will, that they may share its happiness.

SELF-DENIAL IS THE SAFEST MEANS OF ESTABLISHING OURSELVES IN THE PRESENCE OF GOD.[1]

How excellent a method of preserving ourselves in the presence of God is it to abandon ourselves to His will forever! By this means we can always have God present, even in the most profound sleep, which deprives us of our will; therefore nothing can establish us more perfectly in that species of presence of which we treat. If we love God, we must be anxious never to lose sight of Him: we fall asleep not only under His eyes, but in the manner most pleasing to His divine majesty; not only to conform to His holy will, but through the pure and sole motive of conformity.

During sleep we are abandoned to the will of God; consequently we are in His presence; we could not be more so if God Himself were to lay us in our beds, as a sculptor places his statue in a niche. Those who live in a state of continual submission to the will of God never quit His divine presence: the couch on which they repose cannot interrupt it, as the nest in which the feathered songsters take their rest does not prevent their being under the unsleeping eye and untiring care of Providence. If we reflect on this truth on awakening, we should be easily convinced that God has been ever present to us, and that our slumbers have not separated us from Him. And why? Because we have slept, as it were, under the shadow and immediate protection of His holy will. We might then truly exclaim with Jacob,

[1] Book VI., ch. xi.

The Lord has indeed been with me; I have slept in His presence; I have been cradled in the arms of His paternal providence, and I knew it not.

PERFECT SUBMISSION TO THE WILL OF GOD KEEPS THE SOUL IN CONTINUAL PRAYER.[1]

This sort of quiet in which the will does nothing but simply acquiesce in the will of God, remaining in His presence without aiming at anything higher than to remain near Him, in conformity to His will, is a sovereignly excellent prayer, because self-interest has no share therein, the faculties of the soul derive no satisfaction from it, and even the will only enjoys it by soaring to the highest regions of the mind, which is called the most sublime spot, where it simply acquiesces in the will of God, and is satisfied at His leaving it destitute of happiness, in order to procure His own felicity. To pronounce, in a word, the eulogium of this species of prayer, the sovereign perfection of love, which is ecstatic by nature, consists in paying no attention whatever to our happiness, but solely to that of the Almighty, or, in other words, in desiring no other satisfaction than that which God derives from the accomplishment of His ever-adorable will.

[1] Book VI., ch. xi.

CHAPTER III.

LETTER OF ST. FRANCIS DE SALES TO ST. JANE FRANCES DE CHANTAL.[1]

THERE are three marks by which we may know when we may act interiorly, and whether it is God Who is attracting the soul to simple and tranquil attention in His presence. The first is when we can no longer meditate, when we cease to feel our former pleasure in it, but experience, on the contrary, great aridity in the holy exercise. The second is when the heart has no desire to fix the imagination or the senses on any special object, either exterior or interior. The third and more certain mark is when your soul takes pleasure in being alone with God in a state of loving attention, undisturbed by special consideration of any kind, in the enjoyment of an interior peace which is rest, producing no act or exercise of its powers, will, memory, and understanding, at least by reasoning, which is to go from one thing to another, but simply preserves a loving general attention. We must be able to discern these marks before abandoning meditation. Then, though the soul, in this state of attention, seem to do nothing, and to have no occupation, for the reason that

[1] Monastery of Turin.

it does not act through the senses, let it not think its time lost or uselessly employed; for, though the powers of the soul cease to act, the intelligence continues. And, finally, let it suffice you to know that, in the cases of which we are treating, it is sufficient if the understanding be withdrawn from special objects, whether spiritual or temporal, and that the will have no desire to think upon them; this applies too when the operation is confined to your intellect, my child, for, when the latter acts jointly with the will, which it nearly always does in a greater or less degree, the soul sees that it is occupied, inasmuch as it feels seized with love, without knowing or understanding what it loves. God, in this state, is the Agent preparing and teaching the soul; and the soul, on its part, receives the spiritual favors given it, which are attention and divine love combined.

The soul, therefore, should continue simply in loving attention to God, without making any special acts other than those to which God inclines it, remaining, as it were, pensive and passive within itself, as one in a state of sincere and loving attention, opening its eyes from time to time to cast an amorous glance upon the Beloved. For God is treating with the soul in giving it this simple and loving attention, and the soul is responding by accepting it with a sweet and tranquil consciousness, and thus love is united with love.

For if the soul, on its part, wish to act or bear itself otherwise than very simply and tranquilly, discarding all reasoning, it will hinder the blessings which God communicates to it in this state of loving attention.

Therefore your soul must be very tranquil, after the manner of God; and to this end it is necessary that the spirit be disengaged and dead to self, for any special thought, or reasoning, or taste, or self-reliance on the part of the soul would hinder and disquiet it, would break the silence which should reign in the senses and the mind in order that the soul may understand the profound and delicate word which God utters to the heart in this solitude, where, if it continue in peaceful and profound attention, it should hear God's voice as long as the silence lasts. When, therefore, the soul feels drawn to this silence, this attention, it should give itself up to it very simply, without any special effort or reflection, so that it may almost forget itself, and be free and disengaged to do whatever is required of it.

Take notice, my child, that when a soul begins to enter this simple, inactive state it should not, at any times or seasons, have recourse to meditation or expect spiritual revelations or favors. Let it, on the contrary, stand firm without support of any kind, the mind free and disengaged, that it may be able to say, after the manner of the prophet Habacuc, "I will stand watch over my senses, I will keep them in subjection; I will stand upon the fortress of my powers, permitting them, of themselves, to conceive no thought; I will watch and see what will be said to me, I will receive what will be communicated to me."

For this exalted wisdom, my child, can be received only by a mind that is withdrawn and detached from the senses and from special gratifications. Calmly and peacefully set your soul at liberty, free it from the yoke of its operations, and do not disturb it by any care or solicitude concerning either earthly or heavenly things; establish it in complete solitude. For the sooner it attains this tranquil inactivity, the more abundantly will the sweet, loving, solitary, peaceful spirit of divine wisdom be infused in it. The little that God effects in the soul in this holy leisure and solitude is a greater and more inestimable good than you can possibly imagine. God builds in each soul a spiritual edifice after the manner He pleases. Mortify nature, annihilate its operations in all that may be contrary to the designs of God, for this is your part, your duty; and God's part is to direct you to supernatural good, by means which you cannot know. In this leisure, affection is fittingly developed, and then we feel the darts of divine love much more keenly. Care clouds the spirit; rest develops it. It is necessary that all the human affections of souls melt of themselves, in an ineffable manner, and flow into the will of God; otherwise, how will God be all in all to the soul if there remain in it anything human?

As the wisdom of God, to which the understanding must be united, knows neither means nor measures, and falls not under limits of distinct or special intelligence, and as it is necessary for the perfect union of the soul with the divine wisdom that there be a certain similitude between them, it follows that the soul must be as pure and simple as possible, unmodified and unrestricted by any express or formal images, since God is not included in them. Thus the soul, to unite itself with God, must have neither form nor distinct intelligence.

The perfection of the memory consists in being so absorbed in God that the soul forgets everything in itself, and, removed from all the noise of thoughts and vain imaginings, peacefully reposes in God alone. The more the memory is freed from forms and notable objects not pertaining to the Divinity, or to the Humanity of God, the thought of which is always an aid in the end, He being the true Way, the Guide, and the Author of all good, the more it is plunged in God, and the more we shall be able to keep it void, awaiting God to fill it.

Therefore, what we have to do, to live in pure and absolute dependence upon God, is, not to stop at forms or images, but as often as they present themselves to turn the soul quickly to God, keeping it void of all things, in a state of loving attention; neither heeding nor thinking of these things, except as far as the memory of them may enable us to do and to understand what is of obligation for us: but this, again, must be done without relish or affection, lest they leave any hindrance or trouble in the soul.

Thus you may not cease to think and to remember what you have to do and what you should know, provided that in doing so you keep your heart free and detached from all things.

CHAPTER IV.

THE CONTINUAL PRAYER OF ST. FRANCIS DE SALES.[1]

God filled the centre of the soul of St. Francis de Sales, and the superior part of his mind, with a light so clear that he saw the truths of faith and appreciated their excellence at a single glance, while they excited great ardor, ecstasy, and rapture in his will; and he accepted the truths which were shown him with a simple acquiescent movement of the will. He was wont to call the place where this light shone the sanctuary of God, where nothing entered but the soul with its God; it was the place of his repose and his usual abode; for, notwithstanding his continual exterior occupations, he kept his mind in this interior solitude as much as possible.

Every aspiration and respiration of this blessed soul was a pure desire to live according to the truths of faith and the maxims of the Gospel. He used to say that the true way to serve God was to follow Him, and to walk after Him in the superior part of the soul, unsupported by consolation, devotion, or light other than that of pure,

[1] St. Jane de Chantal.

simple faith. For this reason he loved interior desolation. He told me once that it never mattered to him whether he was in consolation or desolation, and that when Our Lord gave him devotional sentiments he received them with simplicity; but that if it pleased God to withhold them, he never thought of them. But, as a fact, he usually enjoyed great interior consolation, as was evident in his countenance whenever he withdrew into himself, which he frequently did. He drew good thoughts from all things, turning them to the profit of his soul; but he received these great lights particularly when he was preparing his sermons, which he usually did in his walks. Study he told me, served him as meditation, and he usually left it much inflamed and enlightened.

Several years ago he told me that he no longer had any sensible devotion in prayer, and that God operated insensibly in him by means of sentiments and lights which He diffused in the superior part of his soul, and that the inferior part had no share in them. They were usually very simple views and sentiments of great unity, and divine emanations in which he was not absorbed, but received very simply, with great reverence and humility; for his method was to keep himself before God in a very humble, lowly attitude of singular reverence, albeit with the confidence of a favored child. On one occasion, speaking to me of his prayer, he compared it to oil poured upon a highly polished table, the stream of which spreads as it rolls; and he said that in the same manner a word or thought in meditation diffused a sweet affection through his soul which entertained him with great sweetness.

He frequently wrote me that I must remind him, when I saw him, to tell me what God had given him in prayer. But when I asked him he answered: "They are things so subtle, so simple, so delicate, that you cannot repeat them when they are over; only their effects remain in the soul."

For some years before his death he hardly took any time for meditation, for his duties were overwhelming. One day I asked him if he had made his meditation, and he answered: "No, but I am doing what is the same thing." That is, he always kept his heart united with God; he used to say that our prayer in this life must be one of work and action. But his life was truly a continual prayer.

From what has been said we can readily believe that he was not satisfied with merely enjoying this delightful union of his soul with God in prayer. By no means, for he loved God's will equally in all things. And I think that in his later years he had attained such purity that he desired, he loved, he beheld only God in everything; it was evident that he was absorbed in Him, and that nothing in this world, as he said, could afford him happiness but God. He could truly say, with St. Paul: "I live, now not I: but Christ liveth in me." This general love which he had for God's will was purer and more excellent because of the clear divine light which shone in his soul, protecting it from vacillation or deception by enabling it to recognize the rising impulses of self-love, which he faithfully resisted in order to unite himself more closely with God. Thus he told me sometimes, in the midst of his greatest suffering, that he experienced a fervor incomparably sweeter than that which he usually enjoyed; for by means of this union the bitterest things were made sweet to him.

He told me another time that he felt no restraint in the presence of kings or princes, but bore himself after his usual manner because he was interiorly occupied with the presence of God, which unceasingly inspired him with respect at all times and in all places.

To see him in prayer was to have your heart inspired with love for the holy exercise, as many persons experienced. Speaking of the prayer which contemplatives call the prayer of quiet, he said that to enjoy it for one single quarter of an hour he would accept two whole years of the fire of purgatory. Nevertheless, it was not for his own satisfaction that he said this, but to encourage the souls he addressed to give themselves to this holy exercise; for in all that he did he sought only the will of God. How often he repeated with rapture these words of David: "O Lord, what have I in heaven? and besides Thee what do I desire upon earth? Thou art the God of my heart, and the God that is my portion forever"!

CHAPTER V.

THE LIFE OF JESUS IN MARY.

Jesus Christ, having sacrificed His human life to God, His Father, has received from Him the privilege of being in the Church a source of divine life, the fulness of which He bears in Himself for all His children. This is why the Holy Spirit, in the Scriptures, tells all Christians, who are members of Jesus Christ, that they have received the grace of this first fulness, and that they have nothing in them of the life of God but what they have received from the life of Jesus Christ, and according to the measure in which He willed to impart it to them and make them participators therein. And the apostle St. Paul, always preaching the life of his Master and announcing what Jesus Christ is to the Church, says in several places that Jesus Christ is the fulness, not only of the law, but of the entire Church, whether on earth or in heaven; for He alone fills with His grace and His glory all the just and all the saints; He is all their life, their grace, and their virtue; He is in them all that they have in God, Who is in Jesus the sum of all things, perfecting in Himself all His creatures.

What Our Lord is to His Church He is *par excellence* to His blessed Mother. Thus He is her fulness, interior and divine; and as He sacrificed Himself more especially for her than for the entire Church, He imparts the life of God to her more abundantly than to the entire Church; and He gives it to her through very gratitude, and in thanksgiving for the life He received from her. As He has promised to return to all His members a hundredfold for the charity which He receives from them on earth, He would return to His Mother the hundredfold of the human life which He received from her love and piety; and this hundredfold is the divine life, inestimably precious and priceless; and, as she was both father and mother to Him, furnishing Him all the substance of His life, Jesus is now in her, giving her all the fulness and the superabundance of life suitable to so vast a subject of love and to one so capable of receiving the fulness of His dilection and His divine life.

Therefore, we must consider Jesus Christ our All, living in the Blessed Virgin in the plenitude of the life of God, of that life which He has received from His Father as well as that which He has acquired and merited for men through the ministry of the life of His Mother. It is in her that He manifests all the treasures of His riches, the splendor of His beauty, and the delights of His divine life. In her do we behold an epitome of the glory which His ignominy reflects upon the Church, and the happiness which He acquired for it by His sufferings, as well as all the riches which

He has merited for us by the misery and poverty of His cross.

Here, Jesus triumphs in His gifts, glories in the masterpiece which He has created, reposes in joy on the couch of delight which He acquired and prepared for Himself. O adorable sojourn of Jesus in Mary! O secret worthy of silence! O unfathomable mystery worthy of adoration! O incomprehensible communion! O union of Jesus and Mary inaccessible to the eyes of all creatures! If the angels, according to St. Paul, can neither see nor contemplate the abode, the communion, and the mystery of the spiritual intercourse of Jesus with His Church, if Jesus Himself tells His apostles that only in heaven will they understand how He abides in them and their reciprocal dwelling in Him, who may comprehend this dwelling, this heavenly and divine abiding, of Jesus in Mary and of Mary in Jesus? It is like to that of Jesus in His Father and the Father in Him. "I am in My Father, and you in Me, and I in you," says Our Lord. If He says this of faithful souls and of His intercourse with the universal Church, with how much greater reason may it be said of His blessed Mother, who is as superior to the rest of the Church as the light of the sun is to that of all other planets!

What can be more gratifying or more pleasing to Jesus than to see us go to this place of His delight, to this throne of grace, this adorable furnace of divine love, for the bond which unites all men? Where can we find a more abundant source of grace and of life than here where Jesus dwells, as in the source of the life of men—in the Foster-mother of His Church?

There is nothing more admirable than this life of Jesus in Mary, this holy life which He continually diffuses in her, this divine life with which He animates her, loving, adoring, and praising in her God, His Father, as a worthy supplement to her heart, in which He delights to dwell. All the life of Jesus, and all His love in the rest of His Church, even in His apostles and His dearest disciples, is nothing in comparison to what He is in the heart of Mary. There He dwells in all His fulness; He effects in her the work of the divine Spirit; He is but one heart, one soul, one life with her. There is nothing more admirable than this union, or this holy and mysterious unity, so to speak. It is a thing the consummation of which we may not grasp, and which has this consolation, that it is a masterpiece intended to endure forever.

Oh, how adorable is Jesus in His Mother! We cannot comprehend what He is in her, or in what manner God makes Himself so completely hers. It is a work of faith, and for this reason more holy and divine, and to be relished the more by interior souls. It is an abyss of love and of charity of which we cannot conceive; for we cannot know the extent of Jesus' love for Mary, nor the strength and purity of Mary's love for Jesus. Let us be wholly absorbed in Him, that we may be all that He is to God, His Father, and to His blessed Mother: a sacred holocaust to one and a victim of love to the other—for time and eternity. Let us bless this grand All for Whom Jesus and Mary are consumed, and let us renew our vows of fidelity to One and the Other, consecrating ourselves in them to God as holocausts of charity who desire only to be consumed.

Prayer.

O Jesus living in Mary, come and live in us in Thy spirit of sanctity, in the fulness of Thy power, in the perfection of Thy designs, in the truth of Thy virtues, in the communion of Thy divine mysteries; rule in us, conquer in us all the powers of the enemy, through the virtue of Thy Spirit, and for the glory of Thy Father. Amen.

Prayer of St. Ignatius.

Take, O Lord, my entire liberty. Accept my memory, my understanding, my whole will. All that I am, all that I have, Thou hast given me; I give it to Thee again, to be disposed of according to Thy good pleasure. Give me only Thy love and Thy grace; with these I am rich enough; I can desire nothing more.

BOOKS OF DOCTRINE, INSTRUCTION, DEVOTION, MEDITATION, BIOGRAPHY, NOVELS, JUVENILES, ETC.

PUBLISHED BY

BENZIGER BROTHERS

CINCINNATI: NEW YORK CHICAGO:
343 Main St. 36-38 Barclay St. 214-216 W. Monroe St.

Books not marked *net* will be sent postpaid on receipt of the advertised price. Books marked *net* are such where ten per cent must be added for postage. Thus a book advertised at *net* $1.00 will be sent postpaid on receipt of $1.10.

DOCTRINE, INSTRUCTION, ETC.

ABANDONMENT; or, Absolute Surrender of Self to Divine Providence. Caussade, S.J.	net, 0 60
ADORATION OF THE BLESSED SACRAMENT, THE. Tesniere.	net, 0 50
ANECDOTES AND EXAMPLES ILLUSTRATING THE CATHOLIC CATECHISM. Spirago.	net, 1 75
ANGELS OF THE SANCTUARY. Musser.	net, 0 20
APOSTLES' CREED. Müller, C.SS.R.	net, 1 10
ART OF PROFITING BY OUR FAULTS. St. Francis de Sales.	net, 0 60
AUTOBIOGRAPHY OF ST. IGNATIUS LOYOLA. O'Connor, S.J.	net, 1 25
BEGINNINGS OF CHRISTIANITY. Shahan.	net, 2 00
BLESSED SACRAMENT BOOK. Lasance.	1 50
BLOSSOMS OF THE CROSS. Giehrl. 12mo.	net, 1 25
BOOK OF THE PROFESSED. 3 volumes, each,	net, 0 90
BOY-SAVERS' GUIDE. Quin, S.J.	net, 1 75
BREAD OF LIFE. Willam.	net, 0 85
CAMILLUS DE LELLIS. By a Sister of Mercy.	net, 1 00
CASES OF CONSCIENCE. Slater, S.J. 2 vols.	net, 4 50
CATECHISM EXPLAINED, THE. Spirago-Clarke.	net, 3 00
CATHOLIC BELIEF. Faa di Bruno. 16mo, paper, *net*, 0.15; cloth,	net, 0 35
CATHOLIC CEREMONIES. Durand. Paper, 0.30; cloth,	0 60
CATHOLIC GIRL'S GUIDE. Lasance.	1 25
CATHOLIC HOME ANNUAL.	0 25
CATHOLIC PRACTICE AT CHURCH AND AT HOME. Klauder. Paper, 0.30; Cloth,	0 60
CATHOLIC'S READY ANSWER. Hill, S.J.	net, 2 00
CATHOLIC'S WORK IN THE WORLD. Husslein, S.J.	1 00
CEREMONIAL FOR ALTAR BOYS. Britt, O.S.B.	net, 0 40
CHARACTERISTICS AND RELIGION OF MODERN SOCIALISM. Ming, S.J.	net, 1 50
CHARACTERISTICS OF TRUE DEVOTION. Grou, S.J.	net, 0 75

CHARITY THE ORIGIN OF EVERY BLESSING.	net,	0 50
CHILD PREPARED FOR FIRST COMMUNION. ZULUETA, S.J. Paper,		0 05
CHRIST IN TYPE AND PROPHECY. MAAS, S.J. 2 vols.	net,	4 00
CHRISTIAN APOLOGETICS. DEVIVIER-MESSMER.	net,	2 25
CHRISTIAN EDUCATION. O'CONNELL.	net,	0 60
CHRISTIAN FATHER. CRAMER-LAMBERT.		0 50
CHRISTIAN MOTHER. CRAMER.		0 50
CHURCH AND HER ENEMIES. MÜLLER, C.SS.R.	net,	1 10
COMMENTARY ON THE PSALMS. (Ps. I-L.) BERRY.	net,	2 25
CORRECT THING FOR CATHOLICS. BUGG.		0 75
COUNSELS OF ST. ANGELA.	net,	0 25
DEVOTIONS AND PRAYERS BY ST. ALPHONSUS. WARD.	net,	1 25
DEVOTIONS AND PRAYERS FOR THE SICK-ROOM. KREBS, C.SS.R.	net,	0 50
DEVOTION TO THE SACRED HEART OF JESUS. NOLDIN-KENT.	net,	1 25
DEVOTIONS TO THE SACRED HEART. HUGUET.	net,	0 35
DIGNITY AND DUTIES OF THE PRIEST. ST. ALPHONSUS LIGUORI.	net,	1 50
DIVINE GRACE. WIRTH.	net,	0 50
DIVINE OFFICE. ST. ALPHONSUS LIGUORI.	net,	1 50
DOMINICAN MISSION BOOK. By a DOMINICAN FATHER.		0 75
ECCLESIASTICAL DICTIONARY. THEIN.	net,	6 00
EDUCATION OF OUR GIRLS. SHIELDS.	net,	1 00
EIGHT-MINUTE SERMONS. DEMOUY, D.D. 2 vols.	net,	3 50
EUCHARIST AND PENANCE. MÜLLER, C.SS.R.	net,	1 10
EUCHARISTIC CHRIST. TESNIERE.	net,	1 25
EUCHARISTIC LILIES. MAERY.	net,	1 00
ENCHARISTIC SOUL ELEVATIONS. STADELMAN, C.S.SP.	net,	0 50
EXPLANATION OF BIBLE HISTORY. NASH.	net,	1 75
EXPLANATION OF CATHOLIC MORALS. STAPLETON.	net,	0 50
EXPLANATION OF BALTIMORE CATECHISM. KINKEAD.	net,	1 00
EXPLANATION OF THE COMMANDMENTS. MÜLLER, C.SS.R.	net,	1 10
EXPLANATION OF THE COMMANDMENTS. ROLFUS.	net,	0 50
EXPLANATION OF THE CREED. ROLFUS.	net,	0 50
EXPLANATION OF GOSPELS AND OF CATHOLIC WORSHIP. LAMBERT-BRENNAN. Paper, 0.30; Cloth,		0 60
EXPLANATION OF THE HOLY SACRAMENTS. ROLFUS.	net,	0 50
EXPLANATION OF THE MASS. COCHEM.	net,	0 75
EXPLANATION OF THE PRAYERS AND CEREMONIES OF THE MASS. LANSLOTS, O.S.B.	net,	0 50
EXPLANATION OF THE SALVE REGINA. ST. ALPHONSUS LIGUORI.	net,	0 75
EXTREME UNCTION. PHILLIPS. Paper.		0 07
FIRST SPIRITUAL AID TO THE SICK. McGRATH.		0 60
FLOWERS OF THE PASSION. 32mo.		0 50
FOLLOWING OF CHRIST. THOMAS À KEMPIS. Leather,	net,	1 00
FOLLOWING OF CHRIST. THOMAS À KEMPIS. Plain Edition.		0 50
FOR FREQUENT COMMUNICANTS. ROCHE. Paper.		0 10
FOUR LAST THINGS. COCHEM.	net,	0 75

FUNDAMENTALS OF THE RELIGIOUS LIFE. Schleuter, S.J.	net,	0 60
FUTURE LIFE, THE. Sasia, S.J.	net,	2 50
GENERAL CONFESSION MADE EASY. Konings, C.SS.R.		0 15
GENERAL INTRODUCTION TO THE STUDY OF THE HOLY SCRIPTURES. Gigot.	net,	3 00
GENERAL INTRODUCTION TO THE STUDY OF THE HOLY SCRIPTURES. ABRIDGED EDITION. Gigot.	net,	1 75
GENERAL PRINCIPLES OF RELIGIOUS LIFE. Verheyen, O.S.B.	net,	0 50
GENTLEMAN, A. Egan.		0 75
GIFT OF THE KING. Religious H. C. J.	net,	0 40
GLORIES AND TRIUMPHS OF THE CATHOLIC CHURCH.		2 25
GLORIES OF MARY. St. Alphonsus Liguori. Net, 0.75. Edition in two volumes.	net,	3 00
GLORIES OF THE SACRED HEART. Hausherr, S.J.	net,	0 75
GOD, CHRIST, AND THE CHURCH. Hammer, O.F.M.		2 25
GOFFINE'S DEVOUT INSTRUCTIONS.		1 00
GREAT ENCYCLICAL LETTERS OF POPE LEO XIII.	net,	2 50
GREAT MEANS OF SALVATION. St. Alphonsus Liguori.	net,	1 50
GREETINGS TO THE CHRIST-CHILD.		0 75
GROWTH AND DEVELOPMENT OF THE CATHOLIC SCHOOL SYSTEM IN THE UNITED STATES. Burns, C.S.C.	net,	1 75
GUIDE FOR SACRISTANS.	net,	0 85
HANDBOOK OF THE CHRISTIAN RELIGION. Wilmers, S.J.	net,	1 50
HARMONY OF THE RELIGIOUS LIFE. Heuser.	net,	1 25
HEAVEN OPEN TO SOULS. Semple, S.J.	net,	2 00
HELP FOR THE POOR SOULS. Ackermann.		0 60
HELPS TO A SPIRITUAL LIFE. Schneider.	net,	0 50
HIDDEN TREASURE. St. Leonard.		0 50
HISTORY OF ECONOMICS. Dewe.	net,	1 50
HISTORY OF THE AMERICAN COLLEGE IN ROME. Brann.	net,	2 00
HISTORY OF THE CATHOLIC CHURCH. Alzog. 3 vols.	net,	10 00
HISTORY OF THE CATHOLIC CHURCH. Businger-Brennan.		2 25
HISTORY OF THE CATHOLIC CHURCH. Brueck. 2 vols.	net,	4 00
HISTORY OF THE MASS. O'Brien.	net,	1 50
HISTORY OF THE PROTESTANT REFORMATION. Gasquet.	net,	0 75
HOLINESS OF THE CHURCH IN THE NINETEENTH CENTURY. Kempf-Breymann.	net,	2 00
HOLY BIBLE, THE. Ordinary Edition. Cloth, 1.25 and in finer bindings up to 5.00. India Paper Edition, 3.50 to		5 75
HOLY EUCHARIST. St. Alphonsus Liguori.	net,	1 50
HOLY HOUR, THE. Keiley.		0 15
HOLY HOUR OF ADORATION. Stang.		0 60
HOLY MASS. St. Alphonsus Liguori.	net,	1 50
HOLY VIATICUM OF LIFE AS OF DEATH. Dever. Paper, 0.30; Cloth,		0 60
HOW TO COMFORT THE SICK. Krebs, C.SS.R.	net,	0 50

HOW TO MAKE THE MISSION. DOMINICAN FATHER. Paper,	0 10
IMITATION OF CHRIST. See "Following of Christ."	
IMITATION OF THE SACRED HEART. ARNOUDT.	net, 1 25
INCARNATION, BIRTH, AND INFANCY OF JESUS CHRIST. ST. ALPHONSUS LIGUORI.	net, 1 50
IN HEAVEN WE KNOW OUR OWN. BLOT, S.J.	net, 0 60
INDEX TO WORKS OF ST. ALPHONSUS LIGUORI. GEIERMANN, C.SS.R. Paper.	net, 0 10
INSTRUCTIONS ON THE COMMANDMENTS. ST. ALPHONSUS LIGUORI. Cloth,	0 50
INTERIOR OF JESUS AND MARY. GROU, S.J. 2 vols.	net, 2 00
INTRODUCTION TO A DEVOUT LIFE. ST. FRANCIS DE SALES.	net, 0 50
LADY, A. BUGG.	0 75
LAWS OF THE KING. RELIGIOUS H. C. J.	net, 0 40
LESSONS OF THE SAVIOUR. RELIGIOUS H. C. J.	net, 0 40
LETTERS OF ST. ALPHONSUS LIGUORI. GRIMM, C.SS.R. 5 vols., each	net, 1 50
LIFE OF MOTHER GUERIN.	net, 2 00
LIFE OF BLESSED MARGARET MARY ALACOQUE. BOUGAUD.	net, 0 75
LIFE OF THE BLESSED VIRGIN. ROHNER-BRENNAN.	net, 0 75
LIFE OF CHRIST. BUSINGER-BRENNAN.	net, 10 00
LIFE OF CHRIST. COCHEM-HAMMER.	net, 0 50
LIFE OF CHRIST. BUSINGER.	2 25
LIFE OF HIS HOLINESS POPE PIUS X.	2 25
LIFE OF MADEMOISELLE LE GRAS.	net, 0 75
LIFE OF MOTHER PAULINE VON MALLINCKRODT.	net, 1 50
LIFE OF ST. CATHARINE OF SIENNA. AYMÉ.	1 00
LIFE OF ST. IGNATIUS LOYOLA. GENELLI, S.J.	net, 0 75
LIFE OF SISTER ANNE KATHARINE EMMERICH. WEGENER-McGOWAN.	net, 1 75
LITTLE ALTAR BOY'S MANUAL.	0 20
LITTLE LIVES OF THE SAINTS. BERTHOLD.	0 75
LITTLE MANUAL OF ST. ANTHONY.	0 15
LITTLE MANUAL OF ST. JOSEPH. LINGS.	0 15
LITTLE MANUAL OF ST. RITA. McGRATH. Cloth, 0.50; Leather,	0 75
LITTLE MASS BOOK. LYNCH. Paper.	0 05
LITTLE MONTH OF MAY.	0 35
LITTLE MONTH OF THE SOULS IN PURGATORY.	0 35
LITTLE OFFICE OF THE BLESSED VIRGIN MARY. Edition in Latin and English. Cloth, net, 0.85, and in finer bindings up to net, 1.50. Edition in Latin only, Cloth, net, 0.70, and in finer bindings up to	net, 1 50
LITTLE OFFICE OF THE IMMACULATE CONCEPTION. Paper,	0 05
LITTLE PICTORIAL LIVES OF THE SAINTS.	1 50
LIVES OF THE SAINTS. BUTLER.	net, 0 50
LOURDES. CLARKE, S.J.	net, 0 50
MANNA OF THE SOUL. LASANCE. Vest Pocket Edition.	0 40
MANNA OF THE SOUL. LASANCE. Extra Large Type Edition.	1 25
MANUAL OF SELF-KNOWLEDGE AND CHRISTIAN PERFECTION, A. HENRY, C.SS.R.	0 50

MANUAL OF THEOLOGY FOR THE LAITY. Geiermann, C.SS.R. Paper, 0.30; Cloth,		0 60
MANUAL OF THE HOLY EUCHARIST. Lasance.		0 85
MANUAL OF THE HOLY NAME.		0 50
MANUAL OF THE SACRED HEART.		0 35
MARY HELP OF CHRISTIANS. Hammer, O.F.M.		2 25
MARY THE QUEEN. Religious H. C. J.	net,	0 40
MASS AND VESTMENTS OF THE CATHOLIC CHURCH. Walsh.	net,	2 00
MASS DEVOTIONS AND READINGS ON THE MASS. Lasance.		0 85
MASS-SERVER'S CARD. Per doz.	net,	0 35
MEANS OF GRACE. Brennan.		3 50
MEDITATIONS FOR ALL THE DAYS OF THE YEAR. Hamon, S.S. 5 vols.	net,	6 50
MEDITATIONS FOR EVERY DAY IN THE YEAR. Baxter, S.J.	net,	1 50
MEDITATIONS FOR EVERY DAY IN THE YEAR. Vercruysse, S.J. 2 vols.	net,	4 00
MEDITATIONS FOR EVERY DAY IN THE MONTH. Nepveu-Ryan.	net,	0 50
MEDITATIONS FOR MONTHLY RETREATS. Semple, S.J.	net,	0 60
MEDITATIONS FOR THE USE OF SEMINARIANS AND PRIESTS. Branchereau, S.S. 5 vols., each,	net,	1 00
MEDITATIONS FOR THE USE OF THE SECULAR CLERGY. Chaignon, S.J. 2 vols.	net,	5 50
MEDITATIONS ON THE LAST WORDS FROM THE CROSS. Perraud.	net,	0 50
MEDITATIONS ON THE LIFE, THE TEACHING, AND THE PASSION OF JESUS CHRIST. Ilg-Clarke. 2 vols.	net,	4 00
MEDITATIONS ON THE MYSTERIES OF OUR HOLY FAITH. Barraud, S.J. 2 vols.	net,	3 50
MEDITATIONS ON THE PASSION OF OUR LORD.		0 50
MEDITATIONS ON THE SUFFERINGS OF JESUS CHRIST. Perinaldo.	net,	0 50
MIDDLE AGES. Shahan.	net.	2 00
MISCELLANEOUS WRITINGS OF ST. ALPHONSUS LIGUORI.	net,	1 50
MISSION BOOK FOR THE MARRIED. Girardey, C.SS.R.		0 50
MISSION BOOK FOR THE SINGLE. Girardey, C.SS.R.		0 50
MISSION BOOK OF THE REDEMPTORIST FATHERS.		0 50
MISSION REMEMBRANCE OF THE REDEMPTORIST FATHERS. Geiermann, C.SS.R.		0 50
MOMENTS BEFORE THE TABERNACLE. Russell, S.J.	net,	0 50
MORAL PRINCIPLES AND MEDICAL PRACTICE. Coppens, S.J. 12mo.	net,	1 25
MORALITY OF MODERN SOCIALISM. Ming, S.J.	net,	1 50
MORE SHORT SPIRITUAL READINGS FOR MARY'S CHILDREN. Madame Cecilia.	net,	0 50
MY PRAYER-BOOK. Lasance. Imitation leather, 1.25; India paper, 2.00. With Epistles and Gospels, India paper,		2 25
NAMES THAT LIVE IN CATHOLIC HEARTS. Sadlier.	net,	0 50
NARROW WAY. Geiermann, C.SS.R.		0 60
NEW MANUAL OF ST. ANTHONY.		0 60
NEW MISSAL FOR EVERY DAY. Lasance. Imitation leather, 1.50. Gold edges, 1.75, and in finer bindings up to		5 00

NEW TESTAMENT. 12mo Edition. Large Type. Cloth. *net,* 0 50
16mo Edition. Illustrated. Cloth. *net,* 0 60
32mo Edition. Flexible cloth. *net,* 0 24
32mo Edition. Stiff cloth. *net,* 0 30
32mo Edition. American seal, red edges. *net,* 0 60
32mo Edition. American seal, gold edges. *net,* 0 75
NEW TESTAMENT AND CATHOLIC PRAYER-BOOK COMBINED. Khaki or black cloth, *net,* 0.35; Imitation leather, khaki or black, *net,* 0 75

OFFICE OF HOLY WEEK. Cut flush, *net,* 0.24; Silk cloth, *net,* 0 30
OUR FAVORITE DEVOTIONS. Lings. 0 85
OUR FAVORITE NOVENAS. Lings. 0 85
OUTLINES OF DOGMATIC THEOLOGY. Hunter, S.J. 3 vols. *net,* 6 00
OUTLINES OF JEWISH HISTORY, from Abraham to Our Lord. Gigot. 8vo. *net,* 1 75
OUTLINES OF NEW TESTAMENT HISTORY. Gigot. *net,* 1 75

PARADISE ON EARTH OPENED TO ALL. Natale, S.J. *net,* 0 50
PASSION AND THE DEATH OF JESUS CHRIST. St. Alphonsus Liguori. *net,* 1 50
PASTORAL LETTERS. McFaul. *net,* 2 00
PATRON SAINTS FOR CATHOLIC YOUTH. Mannix. Each vol. 0 75
PEARLS FROM FABER. Brunowe. 0 35
PICTORIAL LIVES OF THE SAINTS. 3 50
POLICEMEN'S AND FIREMEN'S COMPANION. McGrath. Cloth, 0.25; American Seal, 0 50
POLITICAL AND MORAL ESSAYS. Rickaby, S.J. *net,* 1 75
POPULAR LIFE OF ST. TERESA. Porter. *net,* 0 50
PRAYER-BOOK FOR RELIGIOUS. Lasance. Cloth, *net,* 1.50; American Seal, *net,* 2 50
PRAYERS FOR OUR DEAD. McGrath. Cloth, 0.35; Imitation leather, 0 60
PREACHING. St. Alphonsus Liguori. *net,* 1 50
PREPARATION FOR DEATH. St. Alphonsus Liguori. *net,* 1 50
PRINCIPLES, ORIGIN, AND ESTABLISHMENT OF THE CATHOLIC SCHOOL SYSTEM. Burns. *net,* 1 75
PRIVATE RETREAT FOR RELIGIOUS. Geiermann, C.SS.R. *net,* 1 75

QUEEN'S FESTIVALS, THE. Religious H. C. J. *net,* 0 40
QUESTIONS OF MORAL THEOLOGY. Slater, S.J. *net,* 2 25

RAMBLES IN CATHOLIC LANDS. Barrett, O.S.B. *net,* 2 50
REASONABLENESS OF CATHOLIC CEREMONIES AND PRACTICES. Burke. Paper, 0.15; Cloth, 0 35
RELIGIOUS STATE. St. Alphonsus Liguori. *net,* 0 50
ROMA. Pagan, Subterranean, and Modern Rome in Word and Picture. Kuhn. Cloth, *net,* 10.00; Full red morocco, *net,* 16 00
ROMAN CURIA AS IT NOW EXISTS. Martin, S.J. *net,* 1 50
ROMAN MISSAL. Embossed cloth, and in finer bindings, *net,* 1 85
ROSARY, THE CROWN OF MARY. Dominican Father. Paper, 0 10
RULES OF LIFE FOR THE PASTOR OF SOULS. Slater-Rauch. *net,* 1 25

SACRAMENTALS OF THE CHURCH. LAMBING. Paper, 0.30; Cloth,	0 60
SACRED HEART BOOK. LASANCE. Im. leather, 0.85; Am. Seal,	1 25
SACRED HEART STUDIED IN THE SACRED SCRIPTURES. SAINTRAIN, C SS.R.	net, 0 75
SACRIFICE OF THE MASS WORTHILY CELEBRATED. CHAIGNON-GOESBRIAND.	net, 2 00
ST ANTHONY KELLER.	net, 0 75
ST ANTHONY WARD	net, 0 50
ST CHANTAL AND THE FOUNDATION OF THE VISITATION. MSGR. BOUGAUD.	net, 3 00
SAINT FRANCIS OF ASSISI. DUBOIS, S.M.	net, 0 50
SAINTS AND PLACES AYSCOUGH.	net, 2 00
SANCTUARY BOYS' ILLUSTRATED MANUAL. McCALLEN.	net, 0 50
SCAPULAR MEDAL. GEIERMANN, C.SS.R. Paper,	0 05
SECRET OF SANCTITY. McMAHON.	net, 0 50
SERAPHIC GUIDE.	0 65
SHORT CONFERENCES ON THE SACRED HEART. BRINKMEYER.	net, 0 50
SHORT COURSE IN CATHOLIC DOCTRINE. Paper,	0 10
SHORT HISTORY OF MORAL THEOLOGY. SLATER.	net, 0 50
SHORT LIVES OF THE SAINTS. DONNELLY.	0 75
SHORT MEDITATIONS FOR EVERY DAY. LASAUSSE.	net, 0 50
SHORT STORIES ON CHRISTIAN DOCTRINE. McMAHON.	net, 1 00
SHORT VISITS TO THE BLESSED SACRAMENT. LASANCE. Cloth,	0 15
SOCIALISM AND CHRISTIANITY. STANG.	net, 1 25
SOCIALISM: ITS THEORETICAL BASIS AND PRACTICAL APPLICATION. CATHREIN-GETTELMANN.	net, 1 75
SODALIST'S VADE MECUM.	0 55
SOLDIERS' AND SAILORS' COMPANION. McGRATH. Cut flush, 0.15; Silk Cloth or Khaki, 0.25; Imitation leather,	0 50
SOUVENIR OF THE NOVITIATE. TAYLOR.	net, 0 60
SPECIAL INTRODUCTION TO THE STUDY OF THE OLD TESTAMENT. GIGOT. Part I, net, 1.75. Part II,	net, 2 25
SPIRAGO'S METHOD OF CHRISTIAN DOCTRINE. MESSMER.	net, 1 75
SPIRIT OF SACRIFICE, THE, AND THE LIFE OF SACRIFICE IN THE RELIGIOUS STATE. GIRAUD-THURSTON.	net, 2 25
SPIRITUAL CONSIDERATIONS. BUCKLER, O.P.	net, 0 50
SPIRITUAL DESPONDENCY AND TEMPTATIONS. MICHEL-GARESCHÉ.	net, 1 25
SPIRITUAL EXERCISES FOR A TEN DAYS' RETREAT. SMETANA, C.SS.R.	net, 0 90
SPIRITUAL PEPPER AND SALT. STANG. Paper, 0.30; Cloth,	0 60
SPOILING THE DIVINE FEAST. ZULUETA, S.J. Paper,	0 07
STORIES FOR FIRST COMMUNICANTS. KELLER.	net, 0 50
STORY OF JESUS SIMPLY TOLD FOR THE YOUNG. MULHOLLAND.	0 75
STORY OF THE ACTS OF THE APOSTLES. LYNCH, S.J.	net, 2 00
STORY OF THE DIVINE CHILD. LINGS.	net, 0 40
STORY OF THE FRIENDS OF JESUS. RELIGIOUS H. C. J.	net, 0 40

STORIES OF THE MIRACLES OF OUR LORD. Religious H. C. J. — net, 0 40
SUNDAY MISSAL, THE. Lasance. Imitation leather, 0.75; American seal, — 1 25
SUNDAY-SCHOOL DIRECTOR'S GUIDE. Sloan. — net, 1 00
SUNDAY-SCHOOL TEACHER'S GUIDE. Sloan. — net, 0 50
SURE WAY TO A HAPPY MARRIAGE. Taylor. — 0 50

TALKS WITH THE LITTLE ONES' ABOUT THE APOSTLES' CREED. Religious H. C. J. — net, 0 40
TEXTUAL CONCORDANCE OF THE HOLY SCRIPTURES. Williams. — net, 3 50
THOUGHTS AND AFFECTIONS ON THE PASSION OF JESUS CHRIST FOR EVERY DAY IN THE YEAR. Bergamo, O.M.Cap. — net, 2 25
THOUGHTS AND COUNSELS FOR THE CONSIDERATION OF CATHOLIC YOUNG MEN. Doss-Wirth. — net, 1 25
THOUGHTS ON THE RELIGIOUS LIFE. Lasance. — net, 1 50
TRAINING OF CHILDREN AND OF GIRLS IN THEIR TEENS. Madame Cecilia. Paper, 0.30; Cloth, — 0 60
TRUE POLITENESS. Demore. — net, 0 75
TRUE SPOUSE OF CHRIST. St. Alphonsus Liguori. 1 vol. edition, net, 0.75; 2 volume edition, — net, 3 00
TWO SPIRITUAL RETREATS FOR SISTERS. Zollner-Wirth. — net, 1 00

VENERATION OF THE BLESSED VIRGIN. Rohner-Brennan. — net, 0 50
VICTORIES OF THE MARTYRS. St. Alphonsus Liguori. — net, 1 50
VIGIL HOUR. Ryan, S.J. Paper. — 0 10
VISITS TO JESUS IN THE TABERNACLE. Lasance. — 1 25
VISITS TO THE MOST HOLY SACRAMENT. St. Alphonsus Liguori. — 0 50
VOCATION. Van Tricht-Conniff. Paper. — 0 07
VOCATIONS EXPLAINED. Cut flush, — 0 10

WAY OF INTERIOR PEACE. De Lehen, S.J. — net, 1 50
WAY OF SALVATION AND OF PERFECTION. St. Alphonsus Liguori. — net, 1 50
WAY OF THE CROSS. Illustrated. Paper, — 0 05
WAY OF THE CROSS, THE. Large-type edition. Method of St. Alphonsus Liguori. Illustrated. — 0 15
WAY OF THE CROSS. Illustrated. Eucharistic method. — 0 15
WAY OF THE CROSS. By a Jesuit Father. Illustrated. — 0 15
WAY OF THE CROSS. St. Francis of Assisi. Illustrated. — 0 15
WAY OF THE CROSS. Illustrated. St. Alphonsus Liguori. — 0 15
WHAT CATHOLICS HAVE DONE FOR SCIENCE. Brennan. — net, 1 25
WHAT THE CHURCH TEACHES. Drury. Paper, 0.30; Cloth, — 0 60
WHAT TIMES! WHAT MORALS! Semple, S.J. Paper, 0.20; Cloth, — 0 50
WITH CHRIST, MY FRIEND. Sloan. — net, 0 90
WITH GOD. Lasance. Imitation leather, 1.25; American Seal, — 2 00
WOMEN OF CATHOLICITY. Sadlier. — net, 0 50

YOUNG MAN'S GUIDE. Lasance. Imitation leather, — 0 75

NOVELS

AGATHA'S HARD SAYING. MULHOLLAND.	net, 1 00
BACK TO THE WORLD. CHAMPOL.	net, 1 35
BALLADS OF CHILDHOOD. EARLS, S.J.	net, 1 00
BLACK BROTHERHOOD, THE. GARROLD, S.J.	net, 1 35
BOND AND FREE. CONNOR.	net 0 50
"BUT THY LOVE AND THY GRACE." FINN, S.J.	1 00
BY THE BLUE RIVER. CLARKE.	net, 1 35
CARROLL DARE. WAGGAMAN.	net, 1 00
CATTLE TRAIL OF THE PRAIRIES.	net, 0 50
CIRCUS-RIDER'S DAUGHTER. BRACKEL.	net, 0 50
CLIMBING THE ALPS.	net, 0 50
CONNOR D'ARCY'S STRUGGLES. BERTHOLDS.	net, 0 50
CORINNE'S VOW. WAGGAMAN.	net, 1 00
DAUGHTER OF KINGS, A. HINKSON.	net, 1 25
DION AND THE SIBYLS. KEON.	net, 0 75
DOUBLE KNOT, A, AND OTHER STORIES.	net, 0 50
ELDER MISS AINSBOROUGH. TAGGART.	net, 1 25
ESQUIMAUX, THE.	net, 0 50
FABIOLA. WISEMAN.	net, 0 50
FABIOLA'S SISTERS. CLARKE.	net, 0 50
FATAL BEACON, THE. BRACKEL.	net, 1 00
FAUSTULA. AYSCOUGH.	net, 1 35
FINE CLAY. CLARKE.	net, 1 35
FLOWERS OF THE CLOISTER. LA MOTTE.	net, 1 25
FORGIVE AND FORGET. LINGEN.	net, 0 75
FRIENDLY LITTLE HOUSE, THE, AND OTHER STORIES.	net, 0 50
FURS AND FUR HUNTERS.	net, 0 50
GRAPES OF THORNS. WAGGAMAN.	net, 1 25
HANDLING MAIL FOR MILLIONS.	net, 0 50
HEART OF A MAN, THE. MAHER.	net, 1 35
HEARTS OF GOLD. EDHOR.	net, 1 00
HEIRESS OF CRONENSTEIN. HAHN-HAHN.	net, 0 50
HER BLIND FOLLY. HOLT.	net. 1 00
HER FATHER'S DAUGHTER. HINKSON.	net, 1 25
HER FATHER'S SHARE. POWER.	net, 1 25
HER JOURNEY'S END. COOKE.	net, 0 50
IDOLS; OR THE SECRET OF THE RUE CHAUSSEE D'ANTIN. NAVERY.	net, 0 50
IN GOD'S GOOD TIME. ROSS.	net, 0 50
IN THE DAYS OF KING HAL. TAGGART.	net, 1 25
IN SPITE OF ALL. STANIFORTH.	net, 1 25
IVY HEDGE, THE. EGAN.	net, 1 35
KIND HEARTS AND CORONETS. HARRISON.	net, 1 00
LADY OF THE TOWER, THE, AND OTHER STORIES.	net, 0 50
LIFE UNDERGROUND.	net, 0 50
LIGHT OF HIS COUNTENANCE. HARTE.	net, 0 50

"LIKE UNTO A MERCHANT." Gray.	net, 1 35
LINKED LIVES. Douglas.	net, 1 35
LITTLE CARDINAL, THE. Parr.	net, 1 25
MARCELLA GRACE. Mulholland.	net, 0 50
MARIAE COROLLA. (Poems.) Hill, C.P.	net, 1 25
MARIE OF THE HOUSE D'ANTERS. Earls, S.J.	net, 1 35
MELCHIOR OF BOSTON. Earls, S.J.	net, 1 00
MIGHTY FRIEND, THE. L'Ermite.	net, 1 35
MIRROR OF SHALOTT. Benson.	net, 1 35
MISS ERIN. Francis.	net, 0 50
MONK'S PARDON, THE. Navery.	net, 0 50
MR. BILLY BUTTONS. Lecky.	net, 1 25
MY LADY BEATRICE. Cooke.	net, 0 50
NOT A JUDGMENT. Keon.	net, 1 25
ON PATROL WITH A BOUNDARY RIDER.	net, 0 50
ONLY ANNE. Clarke.	net, 1 35
OTHER MISS LISLE, THE. Martin.	net, 0 50
OUT OF BONDAGE. Holt.	net, 1 00
OUTLAW OF CAMARGUE. Lamothe.	net, 0 50
PASSING SHADOWS. Yorke.	net, 1 25
PAT. Hinkson.	net, 1 35
PERE MONNIER'S WARD. Lecky.	net 1 25
PILKINGTON HEIR, THE. Sadlier.	net, 1 25
PRISONERS' YEARS. Clarke.	net, 1 35
PRODIGAL'S DAUGHTER, THE. Bugg.	net, 1 00
PROPHET'S WIFE, THE. Browne.	net, 1 25
RED INN OF ST. LYPHAR. Sadlier.	net, 1 00
REST HOUSE, THE. Clarke.	net, 1 35
ROAD BEYOND THE TOWN, AND OTHER POEMS. Earls, S.J.	net, 1 25
ROSE OF THE WORLD. Martin.	net, 0 50
ROUND TABLE OF AMERICAN CATHOLIC NOVELISTS.	net, 0 50
ROUND TABLE OF FRENCH CATHOLIC NOVELISTS.	net, 0 50
ROUND TABLE OF GERMAN CATHOLIC NOVELISTS.	net, 0 50
ROUND TABLE OF IRISH AND ENGLISH CATHOLIC NOVELISTS.	net, 0 50
RUBY CROSS, THE. Wallace.	net, 1 25
RULER OF THE KINGDOM, THE. Keon.	net, 1 25
SECRET CITADEL, THE. Clarke.	net, 1 35
SECRET OF THE GREEN VASE. Cooke.	net, 0 50
SENIOR LIEUTENANT'S WAGER, THE, AND OTHER STORIES.	net, 0 50
SHADOW OF EVERSLEIGH, THE. Lansdowne.	net, 0 50
SHIELD OF SILENCE, THE. Henry-Ruffin.	net, 1 35
SO AS BY FIRE. Connor.	net, 0 50
SOGGARTH AROON, THE. Guinan.	net, 1 25
SON OF SIRO. Copus, S.J.	net, 1 35
STORY OF CECILIA. Hinkson.	net, 1 25
STREET SCENES IN DIFFERENT LANDS.	net, 0 50
STUORE. (Stories.) Earls, S.J.	net, 1 00

TEMPEST OF THE HEART, THE. GRAY.	net	0 75
TEST OF COURAGE, THE. ROSS.	net,	0 50
THAT MAN'S DAUGHTER. ROSS.	net,	1 00
THEIR CHOICE. SKINNER.	net,	0 50
THROUGH THE DESERT. SIENKIEWICZ.	net,	1 35
TIDEWAY, THE. AYSCOUGH.	net,	1 50
TRAIL OF THE DRAGON, THE, AND OTHER STORIES.	net,	0 50
TRAINING OF SILAS. DEVINE.	net,	1 25
TRUE STORY OF MASTER GERARD. SADLIER.	net,	1 25
TURN OF THE TIDE. GRAY.	net,	0 75
UNBIDDEN GUEST, THE. COOKE.	net,	0 50
UNDER THE CEDARS AND THE STARS. SHEEHAN.	net,	1 50
UNRAVELLING OF A TANGLE. TAGGART.	net,	1 00
UP IN ARDMUIRLAND. BARRETT, O.S.B.	net,	1 25
VOCATION OF EDWARD CONWAY. EGAN.	net,	1 25
WARGRAVE TRUST, THE. REID.	net,	1 25
WAY THAT LED BEYOND, THE. HARRISON.	net,	1 00
WEDDING BELLS OF GLENDALOUGH. EARLS, S.J.	net,	1 35
WEST AND THE GREAT PETRIFIED FOREST, THE.	net,	0 50
WHEN LOVE IS STRONG. KEON.	net,	1 25
WINNING OF THE NEW WEST, THE.	net,	0 50
WOMAN OF FORTUNE. REID.	net,	1 25

JUVENILES

ADVENTURE WITH THE APACHES. FERRY.	net,	0 40
ALTHEA. NIRDLINGER.	net,	0 50
AS GOLD IN THE FURNACE. COPUS.		1 00
AS TRUE AS GOLD. MANNIX.	net,	0 40
AT THE FOOT OF THE SAND-HILLS. SPALDING.		1 00
BELL FOUNDRY. SCHACHING.	net,	0 40
BERKLEYS, THE. WIGHT.	net,	0 40
BEST FOOT FORWARD, THE. FINN.		1 00
BETWEEN FRIENDS. AUMERLE.	net,	0 50
BISTOURI. MELANDRI.	net,	0 40
BLISSYLVANIA POST-OFFICE, THE. TAGGART.	net,	0 40
BOB O'LINK. WAGGAMAN.	net,	0 40
BROWNIE AND I. AUMERLE.	net,	0 50
BUNT AND BILL. MULHOLLAND.	net,	0 40
BY BRANSCOME RIVER. TAGGART.	net,	0 40
CAMP BY COPPER RIVER. SPALDING.		1 00
CAPTAIN TED. WAGGAMAN.	net,	0 50
CAVE BY THE BEECH FORK. SPALDING.		1 00
CHARLIE CHITTIWICK. BEARNE.		1 00
CHILDREN OF CUPA. MANNIX.	net,	0 40
CHILDREN OF THE LOG CABIN. DELAMARE.	net,	0 50
CLARE LORAINE. "LEE."	net,	0 50
CLAUDE LIGHTFOOT. FINN.		1 00
COLLEGE BOY, A. YORKE.		1 00
CUPA REVISITED. MANNIX.	net,	0 40
CUPID OF CAMPION. FINN.		1 00
DADDY DAN. WAGGAMAN.	net,	0 40
DEAR FRIENDS. NIRDLINGER.	net,	0 50

DIMPLING'S SUCCESS. Mulholland.	net, 0 40
ETHELRED PRESTON. Finn.	1 00
EVERY-DAY GIRL, AN. Crowley.	net, 0 40
FAIRY OF THE SNOWS, THE. Finn.	1 00
FIVE BIRDS IN A NEST. Delamare.	net, 0 50
FIVE O'CLOCK STORIES.	net, 0 50
FLOWER OF THE FLOCK, THE. Egan.	1 00
FOR THE WHITE ROSE. Hinkson.	net, 0 40
FRED'S LITTLE DAUGHTER. Smith.	net, 0 40
FREDDY CARR'S ADVENTURES. Garrold.	net, 0 50
FREDDY CARR AND HIS FRIENDS. Garrold.	net, 0 50
GOLDEN LILY, THE. Hinkson.	net, 0 40
GREAT CAPTAIN, THE. Hinkson.	net, 0 40
GUILD BOYS' PLAY AT RIDINGDALE. Bearne.	1 00
HALDEMAN CHILDREN, THE. Mannix.	net, 0 40
HARMONY FLATS. Whitmire.	net, 0 50
HARRY DEE. Finn.	1 00
HARRY RUSSELL. Copus.	1 00
HEIR OF DREAMS, AN. O'Malley.	net, 0 40
HIS FIRST AND LAST APPEARANCE. Finn.	1 00
HOSTAGE OF WAR, A. Bonesteel.	net, 0 40
HOW THEY WORKED THEIR WAY. Egan.	net, 0 50
IN QUEST OF ADVENTURE. Mannix.	net, 0 40
IN QUEST OF THE GOLDEN CHEST. Barton.	net, 0 50
JACK. Religious H. C. J.	net, 0 40
JACK HILDRETH ON THE NILE. Taggart.	net, 0 50
JACK-O'LANTERN. Waggaman.	net, 0 40
JUNIORS OF ST. BEDE'S. Bryson.	net, 0 50
JUVENILE ROUND TABLE. First Series, Second Series, Third Series, each,	1 00
KLONDIKE PICNIC, A. Donnelly.	net, 0 50
LEGENDS AND STORIES OF THE HOLY CHILD JESUS. Lutz.	net, 0 50
LITTLE APOSTLE ON CRUTCHES. Delamare.	net, 0 40
LITTLE GIRL FROM BACK EAST. Roberts.	net, 0 40
LITTLE LADY OF THE HALL. Ryeman.	net, 0 40
LITTLE MARSHALLS AT THE LAKE. Nixon-Roulet.	net, 0 50
LITTLE MISSY. Waggaman.	net, 0 40
LOYAL BLUE AND ROYAL SCARLET. Taggart.	1 00
LUCKY BOB. Finn.	1 00
MAD KNIGHT, THE. Schaching.	net, 0 40
MADCAP SET AT ST. ANNE'S. Brunowe.	net, 0 40
MAKING OF MORTLAKE. Copus.	1 00
MAN FROM NOWHERE, THE. Sadlier.	1 00
MARKS OF THE BEAR CLAWS. Spalding.	1 00
MARY TRACY'S FORTUNE. Sadlier.	net, 0 40
MELOR OF THE SILVER HAND. Bearne.	1 00
MILLY AVELING. Smith.	net, 0 50
MIRALDA. Johnston.	net, 0 40
MORE FIVE O'CLOCK STORIES.	net, 0 50

MOSTLY BOYS. FINN.		1 00
MYSTERIOUS DOORWAY. SADLIER.	net,	0 40
MYSTERY OF CLEVERLY. BARTON.	net,	0 50
MYSTERY OF HORNBY HALL. SADLIER.	net,	0 50
NAN NOBODY. WAGGAMAN.	net,	0 40
NED RIEDER. WEHS.	net,	0 50
NEW BOYS AT RIDINGDALE. BEARNE.		1 00
NEW SCHOLAR AT ST. ANNE'S. BRUNOWE.	net,	0 50
OLD CHARLMONT'S SEED-BED. SMITH.	net,	0 40
OLD MILL ON THE WITHROSE. SPALDING.		1 00
ON THE OLD CAMPING GROUND. MANNIX.		1 00
OUR LADY'S LUTENIST. BEARNE.		1 00
PANCHO AND PANCHITA. MANNIX.	net,	0 40
PAULINE ARCHER. SADLIER.	net,	0 40
PERCY WYNN. FINN.		1 00
PERIL OF DIONYSIO, THE. MANNIX.	net,	0 40
PETRONILLA, AND OTHER STORIES. DONNELLY.	net,	0 50
PICKLE AND PEPPER. DORSEY.		1 00
PILGRIM FROM IRELAND. CARNOT.	net,	0 40
PLAYWATER PLOT, THE. WAGGAMAN.	net,	0 50
POLLY DAY'S ISLAND. ROBERTS.		1 00
POVERINA. BUCKENHAM.	net,	0 50
QUEEN'S PAGE, THE. HINKSON.	net,	0 40
QUEEN'S PROMISE, THE. WAGGAMAN.	net,	0 50
QUEST OF MARY SELWYN. CLEMENTIA.		1 00
RACE FOR COPPER ISLAND. SPALDING.		1 00
RECRUIT TOMMY COLLINS. BONESTEEL.	net,	0 40
RIDINGDALE FLOWER SHOW. BEARNE.		1 00
ROMANCE OF THE SILVER SHOON. BEARNE.		1 00
ST. CUTHBERT'S. COPUS.		1 00
SANDY JOE. WAGGAMAN.		1 00
SEA-GULL'S ROCK. SANDEAU.	net,	0 40
SEVEN LITTLE MARSHALLS. NIXON-ROULET.	net,	0 40
SHADOWS LIFTED. COPUS.		1 00
SHEER PLUCK. BEARNE.		1 00
SHERIFF OF THE BEECH FORK. SPALDING.		1 00
SHIPMATES. WAGGAMAN.	net,	0 50
STRONG-ARM OF AVALON. WAGGAMAN.		1 00
SUGAR CAMP AND AFTER. SPALDING.		1 00
SUMMER AT WOODVILLE, A. SADLIER.	net,	0 40
TALES AND LEGENDS OF THE MIDDLE AGES. CAPELLA.	net,	0 50
TALISMAN, THE. SADLIER.	net,	0 50
TAMING OF POLLY, THE. DORSEY.		1 00
THAT FOOTBALL GAME. FINN.		1 00
THAT OFFICE BOY. FINN.		1 00
THREE LITTLE GIRLS, AND ESPECIALLY ONE. TAGGART.	net,	0 40
TOLD IN THE TWILIGHT. SALOME.	net,	0 50
TOM LOSELY: BOY. COPUS.		1 00
TOM PLAYFAIR. FINN.		1 00
TOM'S LUCK-POT. WAGGAMAN.	net,	0 40
TOORALLADDY. WALSH.	net,	0 40

TRANSPLANTING OF TESSIE. Waggaman.	net, 0 50
TREASURE OF NUGGET MOUNTAIN. Taggart.	net, 0 50
TWO LITTLE GIRLS. Mack.	net, 0 40
UNCLE FRANK'S MARY. Clementia.	1 00
UPS AND DOWNS OF MARJORIE. Waggaman.	net, 0 40
VIOLIN MAKER, THE. Adapted by Sara Trainer Smith.	net, 0 40
WAYWARD WINIFRED. Sadlier.	1 00
WINNETOU, THE APACHE KNIGHT. Taggart.	net, 0 50
WITCH OF RIDINGDALE. Bearne.	1 00
YOUNG COLOR GUARD. Bonesteel.	net, 0 40

FATHER LASANCE'S PRAYER-BOOKS

MY PRAYER-BOOK. Imitation leather, red edges, $1.25, and in finer bindings.

THE YOUNG MAN'S GUIDE. Imitation leather, red edges, 75 cents, and in finer bindings.

THE CATHOLIC GIRL'S GUIDE. Imitation leather, red edges, $1.25, and in finer bindings.

THE NEW MISSAL FOR EVERY DAY. Imitation leather, red edges, $1.50, and in finer bindings.

THE SUNDAY MISSAL. Imitation leather, red edges, 75 cents, and in finer bindings.

MANNA OF THE SOUL. Vest-pocket Edition. Silk cloth, 40 cents, and in finer bindings.

MANNA OF THE SOUL. Extra-Large-Type Edition. Imitation leather, red edges, $1.25, and in finer bindings.

Complete list of Father Lasance's prayer-books sent on application.

BENZIGER'S MAGAZINE

To introduce Benziger's Magazine we are offering a three-months' trial subscription for 50 cents. Each subscription starts with the beginning of a long novel of about 100,000 words, which is finished in three numbers, so that each trial subscriber gets it complete. The price of this novel when afterward published in book form is $1.35 net, by mail $1.50.

Besides this long novel there are in the three numbers ten to twelve complete stories by the foremost Catholic writers. There are also six pages of "Question Box," devoted mostly to religious subjects and imparting a great deal of practical information.

www.ingramcontent.com/pod-product-compliance
Lightning Source LLC
Chambersburg PA
CBHW030739230426
43667CB00007B/766